DANIEL
REVISITED

DISCOVERING THE FOUR MIDEAST SIGNS
LEADING TO THE ANTICHRIST

MARK DAVIDSON

THOMAS NELSON
Since 1798

Published in Nashville, Tennessee, by WestBow Press, an imprint of Thomas Nelson. WestBow Press and Thomas Nelson are registered trademarks of HarperCollins Christian Publishing, Inc.

Thomas Nelson titles may be purchased in bulk for educational, business, fund-raising, or sales promotional use. For information, please e-mail SpecialMarkets@ ThomasNelson.com.

Any Internet addresses, phone numbers, or company or product information in this book are offered as a resource and are not intended in any way to be or to imply an endorsement by Thomas Nelson, nor does Thomas Nelson vouch for the existence, content, or services of these sites, phone numbers, companies, or products beyond the first printing of this book.

ISBN: 978-0-7180-8113-3 (sc)
ISBN: 978-0-7180-8115-7 (e)

Printed in the United States of America.

CONTENTS

List of Illustrations

Figures

TABLES

PREFACE

IN NOVEMBER 1997, AFTER YEARS OF ATTENDING CHURCH BUT not having surrendered everything to Him, the Lord showed me that He had to be my God, and He chose me as one of His. In relationship with Him, He revealed to me who He is and how He works. Following Him and obeying Him became all-important. I had been a student of end-time prophecy most of my life, but at that time did not care about it. But after September 11 I felt in my soul like I was missing something— that I was missing knowing God's plan for this world, and that what we thought was supposed to happen in the end times wasn't happening.

What started as a question in the days after September 11, 2001, became a prayer to God asking for wisdom. It was He who set me on a path for a major research project delving into history and Holy Scripture. My research led me to discovering the Four Signposts in 2003 and resulted in the self-publishing of *Daniel Revisited* with WestBow Press in January 2014.

The message of *Daniel Revisited* is a fresh and new look at Daniel 7 (the vision of the four beasts) and 8 (the vision of the ram and goat) that yields a series of four great events, which, if true, must occur in the Middle East prior to the Rapture and Tribulation. I call these four events the Four Signposts. In Matthew 24 our Lord called these events the beginning of birth pains.

This new interpretation of Daniel is a plain reading of Scripture illuminated by documented world, ancient, and medieval history. This simple reading of Scripture includes straightforward meanings of verses like Daniel 8:17, which says in the NIV, "understand that the vision concerns the time of the end." Such a reading forces us to disregard all the traditional meanings given us by commentaries over the last eighteen centuries. These commentaries tell us that Daniel 8 is about Alexander the Great and the ancient Persian Empire. But this cannot be so. Such a reading can be hard for some, but it is straightforward; and from what events in the Middle East are telling us, it is slowly showing itself to be the truth.

Since this message is so unlike any other end-time message, it must overcome many hurdles. Tradition and momentum must be reversed. Most of us have heard that the Rapture and Tribulation are all that remain between us and the glorious return of Jesus Christ. And most of us have heard this all our lives! What comes as a surprise to people is that four events must occur first over several years. So instead of waiting only for the Rapture, we must go through troubles as the Middle East descends into a chaos that will astound us all and deleteriously affect the economy of the world.

In other words, the idea that the Rapture is imminent is wrong—not because of the Rapture being before or after the Tribulation, but because there are four previously unrecognized events that must occur first: the Four Signposts.

Like any good theory, the Signpost interpretation yields predictions: events to happen in God's timeline in the end times. The first event—the First Signpost—was that Iraq's government would have to be changed. The Bible was not saying how it would be changed or from what form to what form—only that it would be changed. The imagery in Daniel 7 of changing a lion's mind to a man's mind suggested the change would be from a more savage form of government to a more civil form of government. I remember that at the time I discovered the Signposts, President George W. Bush announced that American forces were going into Iraq to remove Saddam Hussein from power and install a democratic form of government. I was astounded.

Incredible as all this was, it was the ominous Second Signpost that was the biggest motivator for me to write this book and get the message out. I realized the Lord was placing me in the position of watchman, and having discovered this terrible event to come, I had to tell the church.

Since discovering the Signposts in 2003, I have felt out of place and perhaps a bit like an alien in many churches. While churches talk about blessings and the Rapture, I see that the next event is Iran's terrible invasion of the Middle East. Most of the church is expecting an "end times" very different than the one I discovered and wrote about in this book. This next event is going to change the world.

Since the first publication of *Daniel Revisited* in early 2014, two major news events have appeared. They further prove that the Second Signpost is approaching like an unstoppable train. They are enablers for the Second Signpost. The first is the Iran Nuclear Deal. The second is the emergence of the Islamic State (IS).

The very presence of an agreed nuclear deal with Iran will result in silence from most of the international community as Iran completes its nuclear arsenal. The devil is in the details of the specific points of the Iran Nuclear Deal. These details include the fact that inspectors can only be from countries with diplomatic relations with Iran (read Russia and China but not the US), and that Iran has up to twenty-four days to hide whatever it wants to keep from any inspectors who might object. Also, the inspections are restricted to uranium enrichment facilities instead of weapons facilities. With the bomb in its possession, Daniel 8:4 will be fulfilled: the Persian ram gets to do all it wants.

And then there is the Islamic State (IS). IS has a twofold significance: it is both a preview of the Second Signpost and a catalyst for its arrival.

IS is a preview due to three conditions that exist within the territory of IS that will also exist across the entire Middle East during the Second Signpost. The first condition is the erasure of the old European-created boundary between Iraq and Syria. During the Second Signpost, most of the old boundaries in the Middle East will be erased. The second condition is the butchery that IS fighters exhibit. The way they kill is tortuous and bloody. The second horseman, who embodies and signals the start of the Second Signpost, is given power to allow men to *butcher* one another. That same Greek word (*sphazo*, Strong's #4969) used in Revelation 6:4 is used elsewhere in Revelation to describe the way Jesus, the Lamb of God died—a tortuous and bloody death. We will likely see Iran exhibit this same butchery across the Middle East. The third condition is that IS declared a caliphate in the Middle East. Starting with the Second Signpost and with each passing Signpost, the main leader involved in each Signpost will declare the caliphate, ending with the Antichrist himself in the Fourth Signpost.

IS also serves as a catalyst. Iran as the Persian ram of Daniel 8 will run north, south, and west. Until IS came along, there was no enemy for Iran to conquer to the west because Iran controlled all the nations in that direction. Now, however, Iran has a reason to charge to the west—and that is to destroy IS. Iran will do so quickly and handily.

IS is even a catalyst for Turkey and the Third Signpost. It creates an excuse for Turkey to invade Syria. While there, Turkey could remove Syrian President Assad from power. Assad needs to be removed from power to allow Turkey and Syria to join in the four-nation Confederacy during the Third Signpost. If this doesn't make sense to you now, rest assured: all will become clear as you read on.

Only now is the message of the Signposts reaching a wider audience. I give most of the credit for the relative success of the book to my readers, who spread the news of the book by simple word of mouth. This translated into getting the attention of WestBow's parent company, Thomas Nelson.

I thank our Lord that He has brought Thomas Nelson alongside to assist in the worldwide spread of this message to the church. I also thank Him for Thomas Nelson choosing *Daniel Revisited* to be part of their family of books that inspire the world.

All readers of *Daniel Revisited* can be encouraged that the message will become more widely known. Doors will be opened. Many readers have said that the Four Signposts should become widely known when the Second Signpost begins. I can see God plainly working to make this happen.

I pray that when the Second Signpost strikes, brothers and sisters will not despair but be armed with the knowledge that this is a definite sign given in His Word that Christ is indeed coming and is at the door. I pray that brothers and sisters take this one-time opportunity to witness to the lost that they too may know the Lord Jesus Christ as we can literally see His arrival coming closer day by day! Praise You, Lord Jesus! Amen.

Mark Davidson
September 3, 2015

ACKNOWLEDGMENTS

F IRST AND FOREMOST, I WANT TO THANK MY WIFE, THE WOMAN
whom I know God prepared to be at my side. Your support, patience,
and partnership with me in the urgency to get this message out to the
saints have been invaluable. Thanks for your persistence in helping me
to piece together the thoughts and craft the words. This book would have
taken much longer to write without you. And, lastly, thanks for putting
up with all the talk about such depressing topics. I love you so very much.

I would like to thank Joel Richardson who has opened my eyes, and
the eyes of untold multitudes of the saints, to the Muslim Antichrist. If
any one person might be responsible for getting the Islamic Antichrist
theory up and running in the Christian community in these end times,
it is Joel. Thanks, Joel, for your encouragement in our earlier blog and
e-mail exchanges, where you said my work could stand on its own and
should be published. Thanks for your tips and guidance. Blessings,
brother.

Thanks go to my lifelong friend and brother Mike who scrutinized
the historical aspects of the book. Thanks for holding me accountable to
a high standard for the presentation of arguments in this book. I believe
you have only added to the credibility of its content.

ACKNOWLEDGMENTS

Thanks to my dear friend Dave, my "mainstream Christian reader" reviewer, for his views and suggested improvements. I am grateful, Dave, for your encouragement over the years for me to persist in the labor of writing this book.

Thanks go to the professionals at Thomas Nelson who made publishing this book possible. Special thanks go to my editors. Your insights into the issues were just what this book's message needed. You were chosen for your talents, but your tireless work and servant hearts have been a blessing as well.

And, finally, I give thanks and glory to God for His goodness and might. If this message is true then it has become clear that He has chosen to let His saints know what He is doing and how His plan is unfolding. Not only is the message a clear and wonderful story of how the chaotic events of the Middle East all obey His order in big and small ways, but it is a wonderful example of how He weaves world history together. It is He who is almighty and in control.

INTRODUCTION

THIS BOOK PRESENTS AN ENTIRELY NEW LOOK AT END TIMES Bible prophecy as recorded in the book of Daniel. If you have ever read Bible prophecy books before, you may be looking at this book and thinking, *Oh, no. Not another book that just recycles old theology and tries to make sense of what is going on in the end times.* On the contrary; the message of this book is truly different in ways that are absolutely astonishing.

This new look yields a fresh and compelling interpretation of the visions given in Daniel 7 and 8, telling of a remarkable series of major prophetic events to occur in the Middle East during the end times *prior* to the Tribulation. Through these events we are specifically warned about the step-by-step emergence of the Antichrist, and of the approach of the Tribulation, and we are pointed to the glorious return of Christ Himself. This new interpretation also shows us that a number of leaders will arise in the Middle East one after the other, and identifies for us which one indeed is the Antichrist to come.

Equally remarkable is that developments in the Middle East conclusively show us that the events this new interpretation predicts *have already started.* Exact prophetic events from Daniel 7 and 8 are being fulfilled right now. Not only that, but they have already happened in the Middle East in the past three decades. Therefore, we have compelling and startling evidence that we in 2013 are well into the end times. Of course, this new interpretation also runs contrary to the popular idea that the visions in Daniel 7 and 8 were fulfilled fully or partially in ancient times.

What kind of news events are we talking about? One was the democratization of Iraq. Another was the rule of Saddam Hussein, including his coup, his wars, and the question of his weapons of mass destruction (WMD). Another is the ongoing struggle and conversion of the secular governments in Egypt, Turkey and Libya into more Islamist governments. Yet another that is not as well reported is the growing power of Iran's Revolutionary Guard. Its power is now exceeding the power of Iran's supreme leader in some ways. Still another is the rising tide of hostility between Sunni and Shia Muslims in the Middle East that will develop into a full-blown war revealed in prophecy. The civil war in Syria, first with the Syrian rebels and then with Islamic State, is a manifestation of this growing hostility. This new interpretation of the prophecies in Daniel requires all these things to specifically happen to fulfill Scripture. I know all of this may sound amazing—it did to me when I discovered it—but if you continue to the end of this book I believe your thinking on end times Bible prophecy will be forever changed.

Have you ever wondered why the predictions of the emergence of the Antichrist in Europe aren't happening? Have you ever puzzled over the significance of fundamentalist Islam and the violence going on in the Middle East, and how it might relate to the end times? Have you ever questioned where or when the detailed and dynamic unfolding of Bible prophecy will happen in these last days? By looking at Bible prophecy from a different perspective than that of the popular theology today, your eyes will be opened as never before.

Prior to 2002, I had no idea where we were on the prophetic timetable. I knew we were somewhere between the return of Israel and the Tribulation. I arrived at this new view of prophecy just after the invasion of Iraq and the ousting of Saddam Hussein in 2003. At that point, both recent and ongoing events in the Middle East took on new significance. I realized the events taking place were specific seasons—signs that Bible prophecy shows us are leading to the coming of the Antichrist. I saw right where we were in the unfolding of these events. At that moment of realization, the biblical significance of news events in the Middle East was no longer hidden.

BEWARE OF ASSUMPTIONS

To see this new interpretation requires a new, hard look at history, Scripture, and our assumptions. However, of these three, it is perhaps our assumptions that present us with the main hurdle to seeing these prophesied events when reading prophetic Scripture. The new interpretation presented in this book is the result of three stages of study.

The first is a serious study of ancient and medieval history that shines a light on Daniel. This enables the second stage, which is a change from old assumptions to new assumptions based on solid rationale. A study of real history demolishes the assumptions that have been built up over the centuries. Finally, with the new assumptions in mind based on real history, we undertake a careful reading, and pay attention to the exegesis of each and every verse in these chapters.

Now, one would think that a message presenting a more detailed study of history and Scripture pertaining to Daniel 7 and 8 should not be offensive to anyone. But, to arrive at this new interpretation, old assumptions must be challenged, and that is where offense may occur. These old assumptions create a mindset from which it is difficult to break free. But it is the cold, hard facts of documented history that allow us to think and see objectively. This allows us to read these passages in Daniel and plainly see what God is really trying to tell us. It may not seem intuitive, but is nevertheless true: we need to understand history to see what Daniel is telling us about the end times.

Like many Christians today, I was a staunch supporter of the idea of a Roman Antichrist before beginning this research. However, as I studied Roman and Islamic history, I could see that there was no good reason to hang on to these old assumptions. What assumptions am I talking about? There are two. The first, as I mentioned before, is that the Antichrist will be Roman or European. This assumption has been built upon for eighteen centuries going back to the writings of Hippolytus in AD 200. In this book I show compelling reasons, both historical and biblical, that the Antichrist is not only *not* European, but *cannot* be anything but a Muslim Arab.

The second assumption that needs to be changed is the idea that nothing more prophetically significant will happen until the Tribulation begins or the Rapture occurs. This idea has only been around for fifty years or so. Israel conquering Jerusalem and the Temple Mount in 1967 was hailed as a great fulfillment of prophecy, and it truly was. However, because people did not think that any other prophetic passage still needed to be fulfilled, except for the Tribulation or Rapture, this second assumption was born. But, if the interpretation given in this book is correct, then this assumption must fall by the wayside because it reveals a whole series of specific prophetic events leading right up to the Tribulation.

In other words, the next imminent prophetic event is not the Tribulation or the Rapture. This series of events that the Bible presents to us is essentially the changing of the seasons, as it were—the signs on the way to the Tribulation and the Antichrist.

Many Jews living in the time of Jesus had the wrong assumptions when reading prophecy. For example, some may have thought the Messiah came from Bethlehem only and could not also come from Galilee. The wrong assumption had a deleterious effect when the time came that this prophecy was relevant and being fulfilled. Likewise, we are coming into a time where our old assumptions will get in the way of our having a proper understanding of the times. Until thirty years ago, the rightness or wrongness of our assumptions didn't matter. Israel became a nation in

1948 and then conquered the Temple Mount in Jerusalem in 1967. That was a fulfillment of some of the end time prophecies regarding Israel. The times that were to reveal the Antichrist had not yet arrived.

In the years since 1967, we have been insisting on watching Europe—which will tell us nothing biblically significant—instead of watching the Middle East and understanding what events are telling us. In addition, the idea that nothing more must happen until the Tribulation or Rapture occurs actually programs us to not watch for any biblically significant event except for the Tribulation or Rapture. This could get us into serious trouble if our view does not change!

Just as some of the Jews of Jesus' time needed a change of perspective and assumptions to see that Jesus was Messiah, so we need a change in perspective and assumptions so we can see the ever-unfolding events of the coming of the Antichrist. Hopefully we do not become unteachable. If we do, we miss out on the comfort and strength given to us by our loving Father through Bible prophecy.

My Journey of Discovery

Discovery of this new interpretation was not my original intent. I didn't wake up one day and say, "I think I'll discover a whole new end-times interpretation of Daniel 7 and 8." Like most discoveries in human history, this was a complete surprise. It wasn't even on my radar. On the contrary; this discovery was merely the result of what started as a serendipitous quest for wisdom and an attempt to understand in some small measure what God was doing in these end times. Then the unexpected epiphany came when news events in the Middle East aligned with biblically significant events.

Many books have been written since the 1970s on the subject of Bible end-times prophecy. Probably one of the most popular of these books was Hal Lindsey's *The Late Great Planet Earth*, first published back in 1970. Its end-time timeline said the Antichrist would come from the area of the old Roman Empire and would rule over a revived Roman Empire formed from ten nations. It talked about the Soviet Union (which we will now refer to as Russia) leading an attack with a coalition of the Arab countries on Israel. This popular picture in prophecy really bloomed after the Six-Day War in which Israel won a stunning victory over her Arab enemies in 1967 and took possession of the Temple Mount in Jerusalem.

My mother gave me a copy of *The Late Great Planet Earth* when I was ten. I found the book fascinating, and from an early age I watched world events. I was watching for the second coming, just as millions of Christians have for the last two thousand years.

As I got older, I saw the European Common Market grow toward ten members. It included Italy and France and received Great Britain, Denmark and Ireland as its seventh, eighth and ninth members in 1973. Greece joined in 1981 as its tenth. It seemed that the revived Roman Empire was at our doorstep. Israel grew in population and strength. The Arab countries became more virulent and united in their hatred of Israel. The Soviet Union continued to gain strength and influence through the 1970s and 80s. By the time I was in college in 1980, the Soviet Union had even invaded Afghanistan, a Muslim country.

However, just as events in the 1980s were starting to look as if they were converging according to the popular view of prophecy, by 1990 the picture was falling apart. The world seemed to be diverging from the prophetic view of things that were *supposed* to happen. The European Union (EU) grew from ten to twenty-eight members. In addition, the socialist systems in many of the EU's member states left the European economy weak and governments in debt. The Soviet Union fell apart in 1991 and retreated from Afghanistan. Though Russia still had its nuclear weapons, it soon lost the conventional forces needed to lead an invasion of the Middle East. Not only that, but a major reason for Russia to invade the Middle East—for its oil—no longer existed, as Russia was now producing more oil than Saudi Arabia.

Then something not previously on the radar appeared. The

influence and threat of some Middle Eastern Muslim countries grew due to the funds provided by their petroleum resources. Terrorism loomed as a threat. Fundamentalist Islam began to rise, and the twin towers in New York City fell on September 11, 2001 as a result of a terrible terrorist attack.

In the months following September 11, it hit me how quiet it seemed in places like Europe in terms of incidents related to the prophecy picture. One could almost hear the crickets chirping there. Russia and Europe appeared to be out of the picture as the headlines were full of news about Iraq, suicide bombings, the ousting of Saddam Hussein, developments in Iran, and so on.

These thoughts nagged me. At that time it was thirty-five years after Israel took the Temple Mount, and we were even past the year 2000. Surely we were in the end times. Surely Jesus' return was now much closer. So wouldn't news events be of great significance relative to, or at least somewhat applicable to, prophetic scripture? When ecumenical meetings in Europe or developments with the euro were touted as prophetically significant, I had problems with the proposition. *Really?* I thought. *We are getting closer to Christ's return, and this is all anybody can come up with as significant events?*

On the other hand, in the Middle East there were suicide bombings, riots, revolutions, and even major wars; yet, I hadn't heard anything being specifically reported as prophetically significant there. These were all assigned to the "increasing wars and disasters" category. There seemed to be nothing in Scripture to connect ongoing Middle Eastern events to biblical end-times prophecy.

Something just didn't feel right. So I did what we as Christians are supposed to do; I sought the Lord's counsel and wisdom on the matter. Thankfully, the Lord saw fit to send me on a journey of discovery. Within days of beginning my quest for an answer, I found Joel Richardson's writings on Answering-Islam.org, a forum where Christians and Muslims discuss theology. His writings were later moved over to his own website at Joels-Trumpet.com. In his writings, he made arguments in support of a Muslim Antichrist. He later assembled his work into his landmark book, *Antichrist: Islam's Awaited Messiah* (republished by WND Books as *The Islamic Antichrist*), where he lays out his reasoning that the Antichrist and the false prophet are going to be Muslim. In his book he shows that the prophetic writings of the Bible (mostly from Revelation 13) and the eschatological writings of Islam talk about the same three figures. The three figures are (with biblical/Islamic names): the Antichrist/Mahdi, the false prophet/Isa, and Jesus Christ/Dajjal. It is incredible how parallel the two sets of writings are. The difference between the two, of course, is that Islam calls evil what the Bible calls good, and vice versa.

In essence, Richardson demonstrates that by having a proper and more complete knowledge of the religion of Islam and its writings, we need to watch for and anticipate a Muslim Antichrist. He proposed changing our expectation of a Roman Antichrist to that of a Muslim one.

The idea of a Muslim Antichrist was a big surprise to me, and it took a year or so to absorb and accept. I found myself somewhat offended by the idea; but I kept up the investigation because, as crazy or strange as this new concept seemed, it was a potential answer as to why Europe was quiet but the Middle East was chaotic.

As an ardent student of the Bible, I realized that I next had to reconcile the passages that argued for a Roman Antichrist. Passages like Daniel 2 and 9 support the argument for a particular Antichrist—a Roman one, or so I thought. I had to confront these arguments. No new concept can be accepted unless it is reconciled to Scripture.

Daniel 2, which contained the dream of the metal statue; and Daniel 9:26, which speaks of the prince to come from the people who destroyed the temple, both seemed to argue for a Roman Antichrist. I found that I needed an understanding of the documented ancient history and medieval history of both the Roman and Islamic empires in order to truly uncover what these passages are telling us. I discovered that these two passages were actually arguing for a Muslim Antichrist!

I then went back again to reread prophetic passages to see if the new assumption of an Islamic Antichrist changed the interpretation of prophetic scripture.

This is when I found the most astonishing thing: additional prophetic passages such as Daniel 7 and 8 were unlocked and unveiled. With Daniel 7 and 8 unveiled, I discovered also that the four horsemen of Revelation 6 were inextricably linked to those two chapters in Daniel. These three passages revealed an end-time fulfillment of events leading to the Tribulation and the emergence of the Antichrist. I didn't realize it at the time, but when I saw the awesome set of events in Daniel 7 and 8 being revealed with the horsemen of Revelation 6, I had discovered that the book of Daniel was beginning to be unsealed. The Lamb of God had already broken the first seal.

Now, if we expect the Antichrist to rise from a revived Roman Empire, no one *needs* to understand Islam or the history of Islam throughout the centuries. According to the mainstream picture of the end times, Islamists are just a bunch of religious zealots who get fooled by Mother Russia and are merely pawns. The popular belief is that the invasions of the Holy Land will be led by either Russian or European powers, with the Muslim countries surrounding Israel joining in at the last minute or even remaining bystanders. But, as we will see in this book, this couldn't be further from the truth. Islam is the major player in the end times. It is Europe that is the pawn or the bystander.

Our perceptions, limited education (particularly in the knowledge of Islam and history), and reliance on centuries-old commentaries that are really only suppositions and assumptions have kept us from seeing both where the Antichrist will arise and the events that warn us of his coming. These prophetic events are the end-times signs involving specific countries and developments in the Middle East. Don't worry, though, about the potential complexity of history, for in this book I take the reader by the hand and go through each concept one by one.

When I made these discoveries, it was 2003. Iraq had been invaded and Saddam Hussein had just been ousted and captured. For many who had the old assumptions of popular prophetic theology, this was just a side event in the Middle East. For me, it transformed in a flash to become the main event, front and center, in Bible prophecy. The blinders had fallen from my eyes!

It has been very comforting to see the Lord's plan in these end times unfolding like a script. Today, I don't wonder anymore about why something is happening in one country or the other in the Middle East. I don't bother worrying about what is going to happen next in a particular country. Mindful of God's Word and His plan as revealed in Daniel 7 and 8, I now wait expectantly for the next major prophetic event to occur involving a particular country, or for a major trend to converge with prophecy. Of course, I knew before that He is in control, but now I see plainly and tangibly Christ's coming through the events in the Middle East. I urge you to join me in this voyage of discovery.

At this point, you may be wondering how we could have missed all this until now. How could we as the church miss this new interpretation, and only now wake up to see what is truly happening both in Scripture and in the world? The only answer I keep coming back to is that Daniel was a sealed book—sealed, that is, until the end times.

Also, certain world events needed to occur before people could realize that events were fulfilling prophecy in any particular interpretation of Daniel. I believe the sealing of the book of Daniel is directly responsible for the initial and erroneous suppositions that started us down the wrong path over many centuries. The sealing of Daniel was also responsible for these suppositions becoming common knowledge, and then being raised to canonical status, so that today's theological culture blocks anything that would cross these popular assumptions.

In the next sections I explain the sealing of Daniel, and how wrong assumptions further contributed to that sealing. Today Daniel is being unsealed.

DANIEL SEALED

Twice in the book of Daniel (Dan. 8:26 and 12:4), Daniel was told to seal or shut up the words of visions and messages he had received from God. The first time Daniel was told to seal up the words was when he received the vision of the ram and goat in Daniel 8. At that time Gabriel also told Daniel, "*seal up* the vision, for it concerns the distant future" (Dan. 8:26, author emphasis). The second time Daniel was told to seal up words was after he had just received a long and important message as recorded in Daniel chapters 10 and 11. "But you, Daniel, *shut up* the words, and seal the book until the time of the end" (Dan. 12:4 NKJV, emphasis added).

The word that Daniel used for "seal up" pertaining to the vision in Daniel 8:26 and for "shut up" pertaining to the message in Daniel 12:4 was *catham* (Strong's #5640, pronounced *saw-tham*'). *Catham* means to stop up or to shut up a message, or to keep it a secret. The words themselves could be read, but they would have no meaning that man could discern correctly. It was as if the passage were written in code. He was also told in Daniel 8:17 that the vision of the ram and goat concerned the "time of the end." So how long were these words to be kept a mystery and shut up? We have our answer in Daniel 12:4.

In addition to keeping the meanings of Daniel 8, 10 and 11 secret, Gabriel also told Daniel to "seal the book until the time of the end" (Dan. 12:4 NKJV, author emphasis). The word recorded here for "seal" is *chatham* (Strong's #2856, pronounced *khaw-tham*'). Where *catham* (saw-tham') was used to convey the idea of keeping a message secret, *chatham* (khaw-tham') conveys the idea of physically sealing a book or scroll. Note that the book is to be sealed until the end times.

Now, if there is any doubt about the legibility of a sealed scroll or book, Isaiah 29:11 specifically teaches us that a scroll that is sealed cannot be read. It says, "For you this whole vision is nothing but words seal*ed* in a scroll. And if you give the scroll to someone who can read, and say to him, 'Read this, please,' he will answer, 'I can't; it is *sealed*' " (emphasis added).

God gave Judah a prophecy through Isaiah that was to be sealed. The word for *sealed*, used twice here in this verse, is the same used in Daniel 12:4: *chatham* (khaw-tham'). God was telling the people through Isaiah that if anyone tries to read a scroll that is sealed, the reader couldn't read it! Likewise, though the words in Daniel can be read, they cannot be understood. Not only that, but they cannot be understood until the end times.

Just as God shuts doors that no one can open, so too if the meaning of a vision is sealed until the end times, then why do we believe a sealed prophecy can be read and understood prior to the end times? Why do we give such weight to men's suppositions and assumptions that were made in centuries past? Great men of God, including the church fathers, have rightly interpreted God's Word except for that small portion that is sealed until the end times. Why should we be surprised at this? It is alright to guess and conjecture, as long as we the church recognize that this is what we are doing. But these guesses have received a status of being much more than what they are.

THE UNYIELDING VERSES OF DANIEL

Obviously, we can open a Bible and read from Daniel plainly, even the parts that are explicitly "sealed." However, the meaning has been hidden. How could the meaning of Daniel's visions be hidden? I believe God purposely used what I call the unyielding, or hard verses of Daniel. In my research I have come across a few verses in Daniel that are key to understanding the various visions and messages, but they have not yielded to pre-end-time attempts to properly interpret them. These verses are Daniel 2:40, 7:17, 8:17, 8:19 and 9:26. These verses will be thoroughly explained in this book.

To fully understand a passage in Scripture, every verse of that passage needs to be properly understood. If one verse is misunderstood, it can steer the interpretation of a whole passage away from truth. This concept seems straightforward enough.

These unyielding verses of Daniel in particular—as far as I can tell—have never been properly explained in any commentary over the centuries. This could be due to a number of reasons. One reason is the obvious meaning of a single verse ran counter to the popular interpretation of the whole chapter and so the verse was ignored (as is the case with 7:17 and 8:17, 19). Another is that a study of history is necessary to understand it correctly (as in the case of 2:40 and 9:26). Improper interpretation of these single verses has stood in the way of our truly arriving at a correct understanding of these visions.

This whole idea of some verses never being interpreted correctly may sound outrageous, but is true nonetheless. In this book I will attempt to prove to the reader that this is the case.

Probably the best way to understand an evolving consensus on the interpretation of a verse is to see the history of its commentaries.

As an example of what I am saying about these unyielding verses, we will look at one in particular, Daniel 2:40. This verse will be discussed thoroughly in chapter 1, but for now we will look at its commentary. Also, the purpose of this discussion of commentaries of a verse in Daniel is not to argue the proper interpretation itself—that is reserved for chapter 1. The purpose is to show how the commentaries themselves started the wrong assumptions, helped them evolve, and elevated them to the level of canon, and so actually contributed to cementing the sealing of Daniel.

We begin by looking at Daniel 2:40 itself. It says,

Finally, there will be a fourth kingdom, strong as iron—for iron breaks and smashes everything—and as iron breaks things to pieces, so it will crush and break all the others.

This verse is part of the text in Daniel 2 that gives us the interpretation of the dream of the metal statue. Daniel 2:40 tells us that the empire represented by the iron legs must crush and break into pieces "all the others," that is, all the preceding empires in the statue which were Babylon, Persia, and Greece—the gold head, silver chest, and bronze belly and thighs, respectively. This much is generally agreed.

Later in chapter 1 we will see the full explanation of how an empire can crush and break another empire, and which empire did so. Suffice it to say for now, at the very least, the empire that does the crushing must completely conquer the empire that is to be crushed. Conquest would include occupation of the enemy capital city; capture, exile, or death of the ruling dynasty of the conquered empire; and conquest of most of the enemy empire's land area and its population.

The identity of the iron-leg empire is the question. Depending on which empire it is, it completely changes the picture of end-times prophecy. It is generally agreed that the Antichrist to come will emerge from a revived version of whichever empire is represented by the iron legs. Almost all commentators say the empire is Rome and that it crushed all three preceding empires.

However, running counter to all the arguments of the popular view of a Roman Antichrist is the hard but ignored fact of ancient and medieval world history that Rome *never* conquered Persia. They were archenemies who were at war with each other on and off for six centuries, with neither empire able to conquer the other. Rome would conquer a few outlying provinces of Persia, and Persia of Rome, but that is as far as it went. Nevertheless, the popular view of theology says that the iron-leg empire is Rome. Past commentaries of Daniel 2:40 are probably the main single reason that this opinion has prevailed over the centuries.

In the next section we will look briefly at the major developments in the commentaries of Daniel 2:40 and draw some conclusions. For the sake of brevity in this introduction, some conclusions may seem unsubstantiated to the reader. This history is explained more thoroughly and the conclusions are substantiated in appendix A.

COMMENTARIES: FROM SUPPOSITION TO CANON

Before going down this path, please do not misunderstand what I am about to say here. Many great men of God have written commentaries on the entire Bible that are invaluable and have helped untold multitudes of the saints over the centuries. They have helped me immensely. These men were intelligent and God-fearing men who rightly interpreted the unsealed portion of Scripture. Therefore, I do not write lightly about this subject and these great men. But, we must open our eyes and realize that even the smartest and most saintly of men cannot properly read a passage if God has said it is to be sealed, until it is to be opened.

We will now see how this notion of Rome as the iron empire started as a supposition and in the end became canon. In this history, the first Christian commentary of Daniel 2:40 comes from Hippolytus, a bishop of Rome in about AD 200. He stated that the Empire of Iron had to be Rome.[1] He wrote elsewhere that Christ would return in AD 500 and that Rome would be the world power up until that time.[2] In addition, Roman historians from ninety years earlier faithfully recorded Trajan's exaggerated achievements that he had conquered Persia. Therefore, Hippolytus' position was a *supposition*; he arrived at a position based on his own presumptions on one hand, and false historical evidence on the other.

The next commentary comes from Jerome, the translator of the Bible into the Latin Vulgate. He wrote in AD 408 that the Empire of Iron was "clearly . . . the Romans."[3] A clue to his thinking behind this is found in a letter he wrote five years later, regarding the sacking of Rome in AD 410 where he wrote, "the city which had taken the whole world was itself taken."[4] If he thought Rome "had taken the whole world," it wouldn't be unreasonable to say he believed that additional historians' writings and Hippolytus' position were all correct. Jerome seemed to take for granted that Rome indeed did conquer all, including Persia. This was an *assumption*.

Going forward over eleven centuries we arrive at the time of the great and influential theologian John Calvin, during the Reformation. During those eleven centuries between Jerome and Calvin, Rome and Persia were at a standoff for over half that time until Islam came along and conquered Persia thoroughly. Over the remaining centuries Islam changed Persia's religion, culture, alphabet, and laws. Just a century before Calvin came along, Islam completed the conquest of the Eastern Roman Empire as well.

Like Jerome, Calvin also assumed Rome fulfilled the empire of the iron legs in Daniel 2:40. He argued that Rome's conquest of the four successors of Alexander, who all made up the bronze part of the statue in Daniel 2, counted as the conquest and crushing of the three preceding empires—Babylon the gold, Persia the silver, and Greece the bronze—when in fact it only covered the bronze.[5] The argument boils down to Rome's conquest of Syria and Babylon equaling a conquest of Persia.

In 1715, a century and a half after Calvin, Matthew Henry wrote in the great commentary that bears his name that Rome held "prevalency against all that contended against it."[6] The assumption continued with Henry, for Rome did not prevail against Persia, but only made some short-lived gains after which Persia could have been said to prevail right back against Rome.

Forty years after Henry, the theologian John Gill strengthened the assumption. He featured in his text a list of peoples that Rome had conquered which actually included the Persians by name.[7] This statement simply goes against historical fact. History shows us that such a statement would be equivalent to saying that a military power conquered the Americans by conquering Florida. At this point, the long-lived idea that Rome as the iron legs fulfilled Daniel 2:40 was becoming such a strong assumption that a statement was made that history plainly does not back up.

By the time Barnes came along with his commentary in the 1860s, the assumption had become *common knowledge*. Edward Gibbon, the famed historian who in the 1770s authored *The History of the Decline and Fall of the Roman Empire*, took the role of theologian when he wrote that iron Rome had conquered the other empires of gold, silver and bronze.[8] Barnes then wrote in his commentary that it was "scarcely necessary" to mention that the empire was Rome, and then he quoted Gibbon's aforementioned work.[9] The assumption became "common knowledge," for it was now in a respected work of history. Barnes quoted Gibbon regarding the gold, silver and bronze, but ignored what Gibbon wrote in a later chapter titled "Troubles in Persia."[10] In that chapter Gibbon mentions specifically that neither Rome nor Persia could conquer each other in all the centuries they contended with each other.[11] Gibbon unwittingly contradicted himself in his volume, and Barnes took the side of the contradiction that supported his assumption. Here we see that where "common knowledge" is involved, facts are not delved into too deeply.

A century after Barnes, this "common knowledge" found its way into canon. The translators of the Amplified Bible in 1962 added "Rome" in brackets directly to the scriptural text. Daniel 2:40 was then translated as, "And the fourth kingdom [Rome] shall be strong as iron, since iron breaks to pieces and subdues all things; and like iron which crushes, it shall break and crush all these" (AMP). The meaning of the verse itself was changed at this point. (Please do not take this as an attack against the Amplified Bible. I believe that almost all translations, including the Amplified, provide us with a saving knowledge of Jesus Christ. I am simply following a history here.)

Confirming this new canon, Hal Lindsey, the famous prophecy expert of the last four decades and staunch supporter of the centuries-old Roman Antichrist theory, quoted this very verse from the Amplified translation to argue his position in his 1970 book *The Late Great Planet Earth*.[12] The quote made his position more persuasive. Lindsey's book essentially provided the foundation for the popular prophetic theology of the day, since it was published just three years after Israel conquered all of Jerusalem and the Temple Mount.

So, across the span of eighteen centuries the first suppositions became assumptions, assumptions became common knowledge, and finally common knowledge became canon. This went on while, in fact, during those many centuries, Daniel was sealed until the end times.

The multi-century history of these commentaries stands as a witness to the fact that parts of Daniel are indeed sealed. Those who insist that Daniel 2:40 refers to Rome are merely repeating what has been repeated for centuries, without doing their homework in history. Unfortunately, since no one has really said anything different over the centuries, much momentum in church thought and culture must be overcome.

False histories, presumption, and misunderstandings all conspired to seal up the words of Daniel. God expressed His Word in such a way as to confound the wisdom of man, so man himself contributed to the sealing. If you doubt what I say about man contributing to the sealing of Daniel, just argue the point with others about the iron empire being Islam and see how many prophecy teachers vigorously defend the truly unfounded notion of Rome as the iron empire. There is your seal.

CANON BECOMES A RED HERRING

If indeed this book's new interpretation of Daniel 7 and 8 is correct— and the Antichrist will come out of the Islamic Realm (I will explain in chapter 1 why I refer to Islamic Realm with a capital "R") during the biblical events preceding the arrival of the Antichrist—then here in the end times the old assumption of the Roman Empire has become a red herring, a distraction. For those not familiar with this figure of speech, a red herring was a very strong-smelling smoked fish that was red in color. It was placed in the path of hunting dogs to purposely get them to veer off the path that would lead them to their prey. Today what we call a red herring is a logical fallacy that detracts from the real and important issue. This describes the situation perfectly.

The centuries-old assumption of a revived Roman Empire being the base of the Antichrist acts as a red herring, keeping untold millions of Christians from seeing what they truly need to see—the Antichrist emerging from the nations of the Middle East. Europe is under a microscope, while the Middle East is seen as an area of chaos until the Arabs form an alliance with Russia or Europe and they all attack Israel. The old assumption of a revived Roman Empire is keeping us from seeing that the chaos in the Middle East *is* the ongoing fulfillment of prophecy directly leading to the Antichrist. Until we shed this old notion, understand what history is telling us, and take a fresh look at Daniel, we will continue to look to Rome in vain for the Antichrist.

DANIEL IS NOW UNSEALING

How do we know that we are finally in the end times and that Daniel is unsealing? Two points to the argument come to mind. First, the chapters of this book will show the complete, step-by-step rationale of history shining a light on our understanding of Daniel 2 and 9. The arguments will show that the Antichrist cannot be European but must be Arab, and that the revived empire cannot be Rome but must be Islam.

Second, we will see in detail that events in the Middle East in the last thirty years, including those of today, are not just somewhat similar to what prophecy says, but are exactly fulfilling prophecy. Proof can be seen in actual news events. Therefore, history sheds light on Scripture to give us a new interpretation. Current events are fulfilling the prophecies displayed by this same new interpretation—to the letter. This has never happened before with the prophecies of Daniel 7 and 8. An integral part of this new interpretation stems from the four horsemen of Revelation 6. Four predicted events can be plainly seen from both Daniel 7 and 8 *and* Revelation 6.

Additionally, the actions recorded in Revelation 6 caused something to dawn on me. The only book or scroll to be sealed in the Bible was Daniel. In Isaiah 29:11 there was a scroll containing a single prophecy, but Daniel is the only whole book or scroll to be sealed. Might this suggest that somewhere in the Bible, a scroll would be *unsealed*? What is the most famous book or scroll in the Bible to be unsealed? That's right; it is the book (or scroll) handed to the Lamb of God in Revelation 5, the scroll which the Lamb unseals, seal by seal, starting in Revelation 6:1.

The four beasts of Daniel and the four horsemen of Revelation work in tandem. This is testimony to the fact that the breaking of the first four seals that releases the four horsemen is in reality the portion-by-portion unsealing of the book of Daniel, and involves the four beasts of Daniel 7. I suggest that the scroll held and unsealed by the Lamb is the book of Daniel.

As I show in this book, the first seal has already been broken, so the first horseman has been released—and so the first of the four events has already occurred. Incredibly, events in Iraq over the last thirty years have fulfilled the prophecy of the first horseman in exquisite and spine-chilling detail. Equally compelling is that all the signs are in place in Iran for the second seal to be broken, releasing the second horseman. Time is short.

CHAPTER OVERVIEW

The chapters in this book are laid out in a sequence that roughly parallels my journey of discovery.

As I mentioned before, the first step in my research was proving that Daniel 2 and 9 argue for a Muslim Arab Antichrist. In chapters 1 and 2 we will explore these passages of the Bible that provide two of the strongest arguments the popular theological community uses to "prove" a Roman Antichrist and a revived Roman Empire. By reviewing the history of both the Roman and Islamic empires we will see plainly that the Daniel passages actually overwhelmingly support a Muslim Antichrist with Islam as his kingdom. These two passages show us the real empire and the true people of the Antichrist.

After showing that indeed Daniel 2 and 9 *cannot* argue for a Roman

Antichrist but actually support a Muslim Antichrist, I wondered what made Islam unique. Why would Islam match so well with the Antichrist? In chapter 3 we will see a little of why Islam fits the profile for the Antichrist's religion. The Antichrist's religion contains elements of the themes in the Bible that display Satan's ongoing warfare with mankind.

Once I was able to accept the idea of a Muslim Antichrist with Islam as his empire, I was able to get beyond examining Scripture passages for "proof" of the nature of Antichrist, and I was able to study passages of Scripture simply for their content, using the new assumption that the Antichrist was to be an Arab Muslim. In chapters 4 through 7 of this book, we will see why our old and popular interpretations of these passages must change. Daniel 7 and 8 are popularly viewed as being fulfilled centuries ago. With our new paradigm of an Islamic rather than a Roman Empire, and by paying close attention to key verses in Daniel 7 and 8, these passages open up to show us the four sets of events to occur prior to the Tribulation.

Finally, in chapters 8 through 12 of this book I present the four events yielded from this new interpretation, in what I call the Four Signposts. In these chapters we will look at what happened in the Middle East to fulfill the First Signpost, the events going on now in preparation for the Second Signpost, and the trends and conditions leading to the Third and Fourth Signposts.

So, if you are ready, let us begin!

The Bible Shows Us the Antichrist Comes from Islam Rather Than Rome

ONE

THE ANTICHRIST'S ISLAMIC EMPIRE REVEALED

IN EXPLORING THE IDEA OF AN ISLAMIC ANTICHRIST IN THE Bible, I realized that the first step was to examine the prophetic passages that were used to argue for a Roman Antichrist. Two passages in particular are commonly used to "prove" a Roman Antichrist. The first is found in Daniel 2 and relates Nebuchadnezzar's dream of a giant metal statue, and Daniel's interpretation of that dream which tells us of the Antichrist's kingdom. The second passage is found in the last four verses of Daniel 9, which is known as the "Seventy Weeks" prophecy and tells us the Antichrist's ethnic background. Popular prophetic theology uses these two passages to show that the Antichrist comes from a revived Roman Empire and will be of Italian or at least European descent.

If the assertion that the Antichrist will be Muslim is true, then the first thing I needed to investigate was the historical evidence measured against these two passages of Scripture. The results would be able to tell me if a Roman Antichrist could be clearly proven or not, and hopefully show that a Muslim Antichrist is a better fit. If the idea presented in Joel Richardson's book about an Islamic Antichrist is indeed true, then these two passages would not only have to show that a Roman Antichrist is the wrong choice, but also verify that an Islamic Antichrist is the right choice.

It is interesting to note that knowledge of world history can actually affect our view of how a Bible prophecy was and is fulfilled. We will see in this chapter and the next that without an awareness of certain historical facts, we may think Rome fulfills the prophecies in these two passages. But having a better or more complete view of history allows us to see that Islam as the fulfillment is much more complete. That will in turn allow us to see the true interpretation of prophecy, and that it is being fulfilled these very days.

In Daniel 2, the Antichrist's end-time empire includes ten nations represented by the ten toes in the statue. There are parallels between this vision and other prophetic visions in the Bible that we will explore later in this book. As an example, in a parallel picture, Revelation 17:12 says ten kings will rule with the Antichrist. These ten nations will come from the historical Empire of Iron represented by the iron legs, which-ever empire it may be. In turn, whichever empire the legs represent also defines what end-time countries the feet and toes represent. The current popular thought, of course, is that the iron legs "clearly" represent Rome, and many arguments have been made in support of that. The question I had on my journey was, "How could the iron legs actually argue against Rome and argue for Islam instead?" The remainder of this chapter will answer this question.

We will also look at the second passage, Daniel 9:26, in chapter 2 of this book. This second passage mentions the "people" who burned down the temple in AD 70. Most scholars argue that these people are the Romans. After all, there were Roman soldiers in Jerusalem. Daniel 9:26 says that the people who burned down the temple were the people from whom the Antichrist will come. Does the fact that the soldiers were Roman soldiers make the case for Rome ironclad? Is there another way of looking at this passage? Indeed there is, and we will see how historical facts change one's perspective on this passage.

DANIEL 2: THE STATUE

King Nebuchadnezzar's mind wandered to thoughts of the things to come, so he was given a dream. He was troubled by the dream because he didn't understand it. Daniel asked the Lord for wisdom in this and was given the same dream and told the meaning of it. The dream started with a huge, splendid metal statue of a man composed of five parts; each part of this statue was made of different metals. The statue was struck in the feet by an uncut stone, and the metals of the statue turned into dust and blew away until nothing was left. The stone then became a mountain that filled the whole earth. The text for the dream is found in Daniel 2:31–35.

> You looked, O king, and there before you stood a large statue—an enormous, dazzling statue, awesome in appearance. The head of the statue was made of pure gold, its chest and arms of silver, its belly and thighs of bronze, its legs of iron, its feet partly of iron and partly of baked clay. While you were watching, a rock was cut out, but not by human hands. It struck the statue on its feet of iron and clay and smashed them. Then the iron, the clay, the bronze, the silver and the gold were broken to pieces at the same time and became like chaff on a threshing floor in the summer. The wind swept them away without leaving a trace. But the rock that struck the statue became a huge mountain and filled the whole earth.

The interpretation is given in Daniel 2:36–45. Daniel 2:45 tells us that this vision is a picture of future history from Daniel's perspective, "The great God has shown the king what will take place in the future. The dream is true and the interpretation is trustworthy."

We saw that the statue was made up of five parts, starting with the head and going down to the feet. The history starts in Daniel's time (about 600 BC) because in Daniel 2:38 Nebuchadnezzar was told, "You are that head of gold." Regarding the fifth and last part of the statue which is the iron and clay feet, we are told in Daniel 2:44, "In the time of those kings, the God of heaven will set up a kingdom that will never be destroyed, nor will it be left to another people."

So we can see that this dream covers all of the history of civilization from Daniel's time to the Second Coming of Christ. We know this because the head of gold, Nebuchadnezzar, was in Daniel's time, and the toes are in the time when God sets up a kingdom here on earth. This is when Christ returns, which is generally undisputed. So everything chronologically from the head to the feet is a summary of the history of the world after Daniel's time.

I agree with most Bible commentators who say the head of gold is the Babylonian Empire, the silver chest is the Persian Empire, and the bronze belly and thighs are the Greek Empire, which started under Alexander the Great. What I dispute here in this chapter is the popular view that the empire represented by the iron legs and feet is the Roman Empire. As we will see later in this book, the Bible has much to say to help the saints see what season we are in relative to the return of Christ. But, in order to see these things and to understand these prophecies, we must know the set of countries from which the Antichrist will come. If the iron legs represent the Roman Empire, then we need to watch countries like France, Italy, Spain, and perhaps other countries in Europe such as the UK and Greece. But if the iron legs represent the Islamic Realm, we need to watch countries such as Turkey, Iraq, Iran, Egypt, and other countries in the Middle East. They are two very different sets of countries. Bible prophecy can't inform us and comfort us if we insist on looking toward the wrong countries.

This vision in Daniel was given to the king of Babylon and is from the point of view of someone living in Babylon. The metals of the statue can be likened to conditions that the city of Babylon found itself in during the times of those empires. During the Babylonian Empire, the city of Babylon was like gold among metals—noble and first among all cities, the capital city. Being the center of the greatest empire at the time, it was also likely lavished with actual gold. During the time of the Persian Empire, Babylon was that empire's third capital, and of reduced importance, like silver. And during the Greek Empire, Babylon was not a capital at all, but an important center of trade and commerce. The metals become less valuable as time progresses and so does the status of the city of Babylon within the region. It is finally under the iron, as we will see, that Babylon is crushed.

The popular interpretation arguing for a Roman Antichrist is that the iron legs represent the Roman Empire. But let us carefully look at the interpretation of the vision of the statue, and in particular the iron legs. The Bible says about the legs in Daniel 2:40, "And the fourth kingdom shall be as strong as iron, inasmuch as iron breaks in pieces and shatters everything; and like iron that crushes, *that kingdom* will break in pieces and crush all the others" (NKJV, emphasis added). Daniel 2:40 is one of those verses mentioned in this book's introduction as being key to understanding the vision, and yet it has been unyielding in allowing a proper interpretation prior to the end times.

This verse says that the Empire of Iron would have to break, crush, and shatter all the other empires—Babylonian, Persian, and Greek. The phrase "breaks in pieces" is translated from the Aramaic word *deqaq* (Strong's #1855, pronounced dek-ak') meaning, to crumble or break into pieces. Another English word used by at least one translation is *pulverize*. The words *shatter* and *crush* are translated from the word *chashal* (Strong's #2827, pronounced khash-al') that means to subdue, to weaken, or to make feeble. The phrase "all the others" at the end of the verse refers to the three preceding empires—Babylonian, Persian, and Greek.

So how do we apply the idea of crushing and breaking into pieces the parts of a metal statue to affecting actual empires? The terms we have are *shatter* and *crush*, which mean to subdue and weaken, and *breaking in pieces*, which means to crumble or pulverize. These terms fit in a sequence of typical actions a conqueror may do to the conquered: first *subdue*, followed by *weaken*, and then *pulverize*.

So we begin with *subdue* which means "to conquer." By conquest one empire would occupy another and could weaken certain existing economic, social, or government infrastructures and institutions in the conquered empire. Enfeebling an institution of the conquered empire could include, for example, the disbanding of a native caste of priests that run a state religion.

Next, to understand the meaning of "to crumble" or "to pulverize" we must consider them in relation to the parts of a metal statue. The head of gold, the chest of silver, the belly and thighs of bronze must be so completely broken that all that is left of them are very small fragments. This would, of course, make their original form completely unrecognizable. What was once a gold nose or a gold ear is broken into so many small pieces that it is unrecognizable as a nose or an ear. Likewise, in the case of conquered lands and peoples, they would be completely unrecognizable when compared to their previous state.

For an idea of how a land can be so transformed that its end state is unrecognizable from its initial state, we need look no further than the history of the United States. In the 1600s when the Pilgrims first landed, the people living on the east coast of North America spoke a language other than English and practiced their own native religions. The people there hunted and wore the skins of animals. A few centuries later, we find the people living in North America speaking English, living in cities where there are skyscrapers and automobiles, and practicing a religion other than the one practiced by the indigenous people. The people there farm or work in factories and wear sewn or tailored cloth such as cotton or wool. We could say that area has undergone a tremendous transformation. A change in language, culture, and religion of a given people would qualify as transforming any area or empire so that it is unrecognizable.

So, in summary, for the Empire of Iron to fulfill Daniel 2:40, it would have to conquer the former three empires, enfeeble the various established institutions, and so change or transform those empires that they become unrecognizable from their earlier preconquered states. This transformation would include a loss of native language, religion, and other cultural identities. That really is a lot for the Empire of Iron—or any empire—to accomplish.

As one surveys history, an immediate problem arises with the iron legs being the Roman Empire. The popular prophetic picture clashes with real history, because Rome would have had to conquer Babylon, Persia, and Greece. But the Roman Empire never conquered the core part of the Persian Empire located east of the Euphrates River, and so certainly never crushed it!

Popular theology gives its own arguments as to why Rome is the Empire of Iron. One argument is the idea that Rome used iron weapons in their warfare—but so did other empires, which weakens this argument.

A second argument is that there are two iron legs, which they say represent the western and eastern empires of Rome. However, the bronze part of the statue that represents the Greek Empire includes the two thighs. No one arguing for the iron being Roman bothers with this detail. In fact, just as a single belly becomes two thighs, so Alexander's empire broke up into four pieces, but two dominated. They are known in Daniel 11 as the king of the North and the king of the South—Syria and Egypt (two political kingdoms as part of the Greek realm set up by Alexander the Great). And just as each thigh turns into a leg, and each bronze column becomes iron, so the Empire of Iron would have to conquer both the northern and southern kingdoms. If anything, using this logic, the two legs would need to be the Roman continuation of the parts of the Greek Empire. But this would require the Greek legs of the north and south to become the Roman legs of the north and south. However, Rome had an east and west, so the argument for Roman legs fails here also.

The third argument, which seems strongest to me but still ineffective, is that Rome has a reputation in the Christian community as being a crusher and breaker because of the way the Roman Empire treated the Christians and Jews. Christians are somewhat familiar with this since

Rome did crush a Jewish revolt in AD 70 by burning the temple and city of Jerusalem and enslaving its inhabitants. Rome did try for three hundred years to stamp out the Christian faith. However, we all know Christianity went on to take over the Roman Empire in the early fourth century AD and became its state religion. So Rome did successfully crush one province but at the same time it failed to crush a faith.

Generally, Rome did not end the language, religion, and culture of a conquered province unless there was rebellion, as was the case in Judea where the Jews lived. One could speak Latin and his or her own language. One could pay homage to the Caesars and practice his own religion, unless of course it clashed, as was the case with Judaism and Christianity. But Rome never trampled the language, religions, and culture of Spain, Gaul (France), Britain, North Africa, Egypt, Greece, Thrace, Asia Minor, and Syria. They were all allowed to continue their ways.

But that key passage of Daniel 2:40 which reveals "crushing and breaking" is not talking about doing that to individual provinces like Judea. To be the Empire of Iron, Rome had to conquer, subdue, crush, and enfeeble not *little* provinces, but the empires of Babylon, Persia, and Greece!

ROME DID NOT BREAK BABYLON INTO PIECES

Under Emperor Trajan, Rome managed to conquer Babylon in AD 116. He then formed the Roman province of Mesopotamia, having carved it out of the western edge of the territory of the Parthian (Persian) Empire.[1] Most of the province's territory was limited to the land between the Euphrates and the Tigris Rivers. However, Trajan died the very next year and his successor, Emperor Hadrian, reversed Trajan's strategy of expansion. Hadrian even abandoned the province of Mesopotamia containing Babylon.

The province was quickly abandoned for two reasons. First, the native people around Babylon started to revolt.[2] Second, a Mesopotamian province formed along the Euphrates River geographically projected out eastward from the normally north-south boundary with the Parthian Empire, so the Roman frontier in the east would become much longer and harder to defend. It would have been a serious drain on Rome's treasury.[3]

Over the next century, Babylon was taken and retaken by the empires of Rome and Parthia. Babylon was a border area between the Roman and Persian Empires, so in the end, Rome barely even occupied Babylon. Rome did not break into pieces the local Babylonian people or their Aramaic language.

One last note to make here regarding Rome and Babylon is that the dream of the metal statue was from Babylon's perspective. The Empire of Iron is viewed by many in western civilization as Rome simply because Rome also covered a large area for many centuries. But to Babylon, it barely registered as a historical blip, for Roman armies held it for only months at a time representing a capital city that was 1,700 miles away.

ROME DID NOT BREAK PERSIA INTO PIECES

The most glaring disagreement between real history and popular prophetic theology in interpreting Daniel 2:40 involves the fact that Rome never even conquered Persia. When Emperor Trajan conquered Mesopotamia and Armenia, Rome held them for barely one year. That was as far as Rome ever got in conquering and holding Parthian territory. History speaks with such a loud and clear voice here that any attempt at prophetic interpretation needs to take notice.

When expanded to its fullest extent at the beginning of the second century AD, Rome only bordered barbarian tribes to the north in Europe, the Sahara in the south, and the Atlantic Ocean in the west. Only in the east did Rome have a border with another great empire.

The Roman Empire had expanded east from Italy to Greece and to Asia Minor. Expanding farther east, it then conquered and formed the province of Syria in 64 BC. That province overlaps the western half of the present-day nation of Syria. Only starting at this time in Rome's history, it finally bordered an organized empire similar to itself in size and strength.

The empire to the east of Syria that covered the entire region of Persia was the Parthian Empire. The Parthian Empire was founded in a region known as Parthia, located to the south and east of the Caspian Sea. The native Parthians, an Iranian people, had been subjects of the Persian kings of the Old Testament era. The region of Parthia bordered the Seleucid Empire founded by Seleucus, one of Alexander the Great's generals. When Parthia expanded to cover all of Persia by conquering the entire Seleucid Empire it became a new Persian empire, known as the Parthian Empire.

There was almost constant warfare between the Roman and Parthian Empires. Will Durant wrote in his landmark work of history, *Caesar and Christ*, about the state of war between the Roman Empire and the Parthian Empire.

> Three centuries of war between the empires ended in a modified victory for Parthia; on the Mesopotamian plains the Roman legions were at a disadvantage against the Parthian cavalry.[4]

During the three centuries during which the Roman Empire and the Parthian Empire bordered each other, neither conquered the other. The Roman province of Syria was at times the frontier with Parthia—sometimes Syria was deep in Roman territory, and other times was a border province depending on the outcome of each war. Parthia also maintained the upper hand. Durant makes the distinction of limiting the length of times of war to three centuries, because after that time the Parthians were overthrown internally by the Sassanids. The three centuries of war started in 64 BC when Syria became a Roman province and ended in AD 227 when Parthia had an internal revolution. In AD 227 the Parthian Empire became the Sassanid Empire. The Sassanids were a priestly class who took over rule of the empire and restored the Zoroastrian religion to its old glory as it existed in the times of Darius and Xerxes.[5] Greek culture and language, planted five hundred years earlier by Alexander's conquests, began to quickly disappear from Persia under the rule of the Sassanids.[6] In other words, the culture of Persia began to reassert itself over the culture of Greece.

A century after the Sassanids took over the Persian Empire, the Roman Empire also changed. It was divided among Emperor Constantine's sons upon his death in AD 337 into east and west. Warfare continued between the Eastern Roman Empire and the Sassanid Empire. Emperor Julian of the Eastern Roman Empire, who ruled in his capital at Constantinople from AD 361–363, yearned to conquer the Sassanid Empire. Durant writes further of Julian:

> His last great dream was . . . to plant the Roman standards in the Persian capitals, and end once and for all the Persian threat to the security of the Roman Empire.[7]

Julian was killed in battle with the Persians, and his successor, Jovian, made peace with Persia by surrendering lands Rome had conquered seventy years before. So there was still no conquest by Rome. Through most of the fifth and sixth centuries AD, hostilities and wars continued between the Eastern Roman Empire and the Sassanid (Persian) Empire. A long and costly stretch of warfare ended in AD 629 with Emperor Heraclius of the Eastern Roman Empire defeating on the battlefield an army of the Sassanid Empire.[8] Rome accepted the Sassanids' surrender by taking back the Holy Land and Syria, which the Sassanid Empire had taken from Rome.

The state of war did finally come to an end between the two empires, but not in the way I'm sure that either empire desired: Islam conquered the Sassanid Empire first, then parts of the Roman Empire, followed by complete conquest of the Roman Empire centuries later.

In the few years after AD 629 when the last battle between the Romans and Sassanids ended, the great Muslim general Khalid ibn al-Walid began leading a small Arab Muslim army on raids in what is now Syria and Iraq, on the frontiers of both of these empires. Syria belonged to Rome and Iraq belonged to the Persian Sassanids. In AD 634, Khalid led a small Muslim army against a larger Roman army at the Battle of Yarmuk sixty miles southwest of Damascus.[9] It was probably the first time in history that the skill of the Arab horseman went up against the Roman cavalry in a major battle, and the Arab horseman proved superior.[10] Khalid won a decisive victory when the Roman army was annihilated. This left the Syrian province open for conquest: Damascus fell in AD 635, Antioch in AD 636, and all of Syria was conquered by AD 641.[11]

Meanwhile, as Syria was being conquered, a Muslim army went south from Syria and took Jerusalem in AD 638, and the entire Roman province of Egypt by AD 641.[12] These territorial losses reduced the Eastern Roman Empire to only the Balkan Peninsula in Europe and Asia Minor.

During the same period, another Muslim army won a series of battles against the Persians along the Euphrates River starting at the Persian Gulf. The last of these series of battles saw a Muslim army of 30,000 defeat a Persian army of 120,000 at the Battle of Kadisiya (also spelled al-Qadisiyyah) in AD 636. The Muslims won the battle when a sandstorm came up on the fourth day and blew sand into the faces of the Persians. The Muslim Arabs marched into the Persian capital city at Ctesiphon, which is only thirty miles downstream on the Tigris River from present-day Baghdad. The Muslims then thrust deep into the remainder of Persian territory and by AD 641 had neutralized the power of the Sassanid armies. The last emperor of the Sassanids was killed in AD 652, ending that empire.[13, 14]

The Islamic armies, rather than the Romans, had conquered Persia. What Rome could not do in seven centuries (64 BC to AD 629), the armies of Islam did in five years (AD 636 to AD 641). The Islamic Realm never let go of Persia, and has ruled it for the last thirteen centuries. After having lost Syria, Palestine, and Egypt by AD 641, the Eastern Roman Empire (known as the Byzantine Empire only after the empire ended in AD 1453) had to fight for its very survival against this new Islamic Empire that had just conquered its longtime archenemy.

So, in the end, the Roman Empire did not conquer or crush Persia (or Parthia or the Sassanids). The lands between the two empires (Armenia, Syria, and Mesopotamia) changed hands back and forth for seven centuries. Rome never had an opportunity to break Persia into pieces.

ROME DID NOT BREAK GREECE INTO PIECES

The Roman Empire did conquer Greece, and unlike either Babylon or Persia, it held on to it for most of Rome's existence. Greece was integrated into the empire by AD 146 as a formal province. However, Rome never "broke into pieces" or caused the Greek culture, language, or religion to crumble. In fact the Greek language and culture were so universal in the eastern Mediterranean basin that Roman government only took on the role of administrator and tax collector.

The Roman Empire was divided in the fourth century AD. The capital of the Eastern Roman Empire was Constantinople, which was geographically close to the center of the Greek seat of culture, Athens. When Islam finally conquered Constantinople and put the Eastern Roman Empire to an end in AD 1453, the Greek culture had still been preserved. The longstanding survival of the Eastern Roman Empire had allowed Greek classical literature and philosophy to be passed on to academic circles in Western Europe. Greek language, philosophy, and culture were never lost or transformed. So Rome did not crush or weaken Greece either.

ROME CANNOT BE THE EMPIRE OF IRON

The Roman Empire plainly does not qualify as the Empire of Iron in Nebuchadnezzar's dream because it did not successfully conquer and crush Babylon, Persia, and Greece. It left Babylon untouched, could not conquer Persia, and its own culture was subservient to Greek culture and language. Rome did not crush *any* of the other three empires.

THE TRUE EMPIRE OF IRON

To complete our discussion, we need to positively identify the Empire of Iron. This Empire of Iron had to conquer the lands and peoples of the Babylonian, Persian, and Greek Empires. And it had to do this after the time of the Greek Empire of Alexander the Great, since the iron legs are further down the statue from the Greek belly and thighs. The Empire of Iron would have had to conquer, subdue, and enfeeble the institutions of the three empires of Babylon, Persia, and Greece. It would have to break into pieces the religion, language, and culture of these people so that little was left compared to the time before any conquest.

So what empire would be the one that subdued and crushed the other empires if it wasn't Rome? History tells us there is only one possible candidate: the Islamic Empires. Before I move on to explain why Islam qualifies as the only candidate to be the Empire of Iron, let me explain why I use the plural, "empires." We must start the explanation by going back to the text of the vision in Daniel 2. In our English Bibles the word *kingdom* appears several times in that passage. Daniel 2:39–40 says of the kingdoms to come after Babylon, "After you, another kingdom will rise, inferior to yours. Next, a third kingdom, one of bronze, will rule over the whole earth. Finally, there will be a fourth kingdom."

The word behind "kingdom" is *malkuw* (Strong's #4437, pronounced mal-koo') and it is translated in the Bible as kingdom, reign, and realm. The meaning "realm" is more accurate than "kingdom" in this prophecy. History calls the second kingdom in Daniel 2:39 the Persian Empire. The third kingdom is widely known as the Hellenized or Hellenistic (meaning Greek) realm. The only time it was a single empire was during Alexander the Great's lifetime. For that brief time, it was the Empire of Alexander or the Macedonian Empire. But after Alexander died his empire was divided. The territory of his empire became Hellenized, that is, affected by Greek culture and language. This was due in large part to a massive flow of immigrants from Greece out across the Middle East.[15] But within the Hellenized realm there were several separate empires.

The empire of the iron legs conquered the territory of Alexander's empire, otherwise known as the Hellenized realm. All the empires and political entities that followed Alexander's empire shared the same Greek language and culture, within this realm. So there was only one Babylonian Empire in the Babylonian realm and one Persian Empire within the Persian realm. But there were several empires within the Greek realm. Likewise for Islam, there were several empires within the Islamic Realm. Also like Greece, Islam started as a unified empire that lasted for the first 120 years or so. After that it broke up into several empires within the realm. Islam was and is a political and religious entity that has birthed a culture of its own. So that is why I referred to the Empire of Iron as the Islamic Empires.

The Islamic community, the body of believers called the Umma, is its own realm. And at various times, it has been administered or conquered by various empires that not only could be said to have Islam as their state religion, but they would speak for Islam and enforce for Islam. Throughout Islamic history until 1924, the strongest and most widespread empire within the Islamic Realm usually claimed the caliphate—the office of the caliph, the leader of all of Islam.

The first politically organized Islamic empire, which started in AD 661, was called the Umayyad Caliphate. Prior to that the Islamic Realm expanded under the leadership of four leaders in a series called the "Four Righteously Guided Ones" (or the "Four Caliphs") who took over one after the other following the death of the founder, Muhammad. It was under these Four Caliphs that the Islamic Realm was responsible for completing the conquests of Babylon and Persia in AD 641. However, the Eastern Roman Empire remained and was the home and guardian of Greek culture. The Islamic empire responsible for completing the conquest of the Eastern Roman Empire much later in AD 1453 was the Islamic Ottoman Empire. When Constantinople fell, the conquest of Greece was complete.

The political empire with the most control within the realm, and which dominated the major periods in Islamic history, and also had the caliphate. The caliphate is the office of the caliph, the recognized leader of Islam. The periods of Islamic history are generally recognized as:

(1) The Four Caliphs ruling from Medina in Arabia (AD 632–661)
(2) Umayyad Caliphate ruling from Damascus (AD 661–750)
(3) Abbasid Caliphate ruling from Baghdad (AD 750–1258)
(4) Mamluk Empire/Caliphate ruling from Cairo (AD 1258–1519)
(5) Ottoman Empire/Caliphate ruling from Istanbul (AD 1519–1924)

In summary, Babylon, the Empire of Gold, was swallowed up by Persia, the Empire of Silver. In turn, Babylon and Persia were both swallowed up by Greece (actually called the Macedonian Empire or the Hellenized Realm), the Empire of Bronze. Then Islam initially swallowed up Babylon and Persia in AD 641. Islam at that time was a single political empire stretching from Spain in the west to Pakistan in the east. For centuries Islam was at war with the Eastern Roman Empire and slowly chipped away at it and weakened it. Finally in AD 1453, Islam, represented by the Ottoman Empire, swallowed up Greece (which by then was the Eastern Roman Empire). Islam, as the Empire of the Iron Legs, conquered all the other empires that preceded it in the statue of Daniel 2 and subdued them.

However, as I said before, conquest of the empires was merely the first step to subduing and breaking the other empires. In addition, the Empire of Iron, Islam, would have had to weaken, enfeeble, and crumble the various cultural institutions into bits so that each region was no longer recognizable compared to the way it was in pre-Islamic times.

Unlike the lack of evidence with Rome, the history of Islam has an abundance of proof. The challenge here was that there was much evidence to sift through and organize regarding Islam's methods and the results of its occupation of various lands. To fully expound on what Islam did to the lands it has occupied is beyond the scope of this book. I was able to boil the material down to a few key points. We will look at the basics of Islam to see how it was capable of "crushing and breaking" the other empires. We will then look at some of the evidence as to how the entire region's religion and language changed.

ISLAM IS NOT JUST A RELIGION

Islam is very different from any other religion and from any other realm. First of all, we Christians and Americans must realize that Islam *is* not *just a religion.* It is first and foremost a political system that has religious laws at its core.[16] These religious laws are employed to run an entire society. Islam presents a plan in its writings for building a religious and political world community. This community is known as the Umma in Islam. In this book hereafter when I refer to the area of Islam, the Umma, and the empire of the iron legs, I will call it the Islamic Realm.

The Qur'an was dictated by Muhammad, Islam's founder, and is the central holy book for Muslims. Second is the Hadith, a collection of books recording the sayings of Muhammad. Third is the Sira, a collection recording the various biographies of Muhammad. These three writings form the foundation of Islam's religion and society. Muslims view everything in the Qur'an as coming directly from Allah; and to a Muslim, Allah is God. Therefore anything written in it is considered divine and therefore sets the framework for the Islamic society's morals and religious duties.

Islam only covered the Arabian Peninsula at the death of its founder Muhammad in AD 632. Islam conquered lands from Spain to Pakistan and from the Sahara to Central Asia in less than one hundred years after Muhammad's death. Raiding and invasion of unbelievers' lands were coded in Islam's writings. The men in the ranks of the Muslim armies believed themselves not just mere soldiers; rather, they were on a divine mission carrying God's faith to the world. As an example, one of the Four Caliphs following Muhammad, Abu Bekr, wrote to his generals a reminder of who they were on the eve of the conquest of Syria in AD 635:

> Praise be to God and Mohammed his Prophet! This is to inform you that I intend to send an army of the faithful into Syria to deliver that country from the infidels, and I remind you that to fight for the true faith is to obey God.[17]

Additionally, General Khalid wrote a letter from his headquarters in newly conquered Babylonia to his adversary the Sassanid king, to entreat him to join the new faith and avoid war:

> Profess the faith of Allah and his Prophet or pay tribute to their servants. If you refuse both, I will come upon you with a host who love death as much as you love life.[18]

I remember as a child in school being taught that it was "Islam or the sword." But my historical research has shown that this was not the case. It was "Islam, or the tax (jizya), or the sword," as General Khalid's letter exemplified.[19]

The Islamic code said that after killing the soldiers of an opposing army, the Muslim fighters could take their goods as booty and take their women as wives or slaves.[20] They believed it was all ordained by God. Such are the "morals" or code of ethics instituted by Islam. The individual Muslim also believes he is forgiven of his words and actions just because he follows the laws and words of Islam.

Islam Broke Into Pieces the Original Religion of the Empires

Once an Islamic local government was set up in a given province or country, the typical population that was Muslim was 5 to 10 percent.[21] After conquest, the waiting phase or "siege" would begin. There was usually no direct compulsion to join Islam, but there were many incentives to join. Muslims were treated as first-class citizens, and all non-Muslims were treated as second-class citizens. Non-Muslims could not advance high in government. Non-Muslim adult males had to pay the annual jizya—a tax paid to the Islamic government just because they were not Muslim.[22] So "all" a non-believer had to do to stay a non-believer was put up with a tax, limited careers, and in addition wear certain colors, and accept that his or her witness in court was not as good as a Muslim's.[23] All political entities within the Islamic Realm have had these laws (because these political entities spoke for Islam) and these laws were enforced at varying degrees over the centuries. In many territories that were once part of the Eastern Roman Empire, many of the local inhabitants welcomed Muslim rule. This was the case because the jizya was usually much lower than the Roman Empire's taxes, and Islam did not persecute them for their various denominational Christian beliefs as the old Empire had done.[24, 25, 26]

To become a Muslim and enjoy all the rights of a full citizen, all one had to do was convert to Islam. Switching to Islam from whatever religion one practiced was relatively easy. To convert, a person would say publicly that Allah was God and that Muhammad was his messenger.[27] Then the new convert would pray five times a day, give alms to the poor, fast during the day in the month of Ramadan, and make one lifetime pilgrimage to Mecca if he were able. These four things, along with the initial confession are known as the Five Pillars of Islam.[28] The Five Pillars mark the activities of all Muslims around the world.

Once people were practicing the Muslim faith, fear was the force that kept people in the religion. The penalty was death for anyone who left Islam.[29] Another intimidating force of Islam for someone renouncing the religion was he would become a second-class citizen, should he somehow manage to evade death. Typically after three hundred to four hundred years of occupation, a nation or area might be half Muslim.[30] Depending on the region, the conquered population became almost completely Muslim by the twelfth to sixteenth centuries AD.[31]

Egypt and North Africa were also less than 10 percent Muslim around the time of the Muslim conquest prior to AD 700. The most striking change in this area was the complete emptying of the Christian church except for isolated areas. Will Durant wrote, "In Egypt a Coptic minority held out bravely, built their churches like fortresses, maintained their worship in secret, and survive to this day. But the once crowded churches of Alexandria, Cyrene, Carthage, and Hippo were emptied and decayed."[32]

Only those individuals or ethnic groups or nations that had resolve and a strong religious or cultural identity could resist a changeover to Islam. North Africa had a populous Christian community and presence in AD 750 that was almost completely gone in five hundred years. The Coptic Christian community of Egypt never did convert, however, and even today comprise 10 percent of the population in Egypt. They stand alone in that part of the Islamic Realm. Paul wrote that prior to the appearance of the Antichrist, "that Day will not come unless the falling away comes first, and the man of sin is revealed, the son of perdition" (2 Thess. 2:3 NKJV). Though I believe there will still be a great falling away in our day, those several medieval centuries witnessed a great falling away as well.

It was great: approximately half of the known world in the Middle Ages fell away from Christendom and into Islam. Today the nations within the Islamic Realm: Algeria, Iraq, Iran, Turkey, Saudi Arabia, Pakistan, Libya, and others are all 90 percent to 100 percent Muslim. Babylon and Egypt gave up their native religions as well as Christianity (except for the Coptic community). Iran lost its Zoroastrian religion.

With the majority of the population becoming Muslim over the centuries, much of the North African and Middle Eastern religious and political landscape would change in cities and towns. Churches and synagogues were either directly changed into mosques, or they were allowed to stand but could not be repaired or replaced. Either way the number of places of worship as an alternative to Islam dwindled greatly over the centuries. The most famous example of a church being changed to a mosque is the Hagia Sophia church in Constantinople built by Emperor Justinian in the sixth century AD. It was considered for centuries to be the grandest church building in all of Christendom. It was turned into a mosque after the Ottomans conquered Constantinople in AD 1453.

BREAKING INTO PIECES THE ORIGINAL LANGUAGE OF THE EMPIRES

Once Islam took over as the religion, the language had to change as well. Islam has its own language, which is Arabic. Islam's writings and traditions say that the Qur'an can only be studied and understood in Arabic, and if it is translated into any other language it is not really the Qur'an. To Muslims, the written or spoken Qur'an is God's presence.[33] So, for Muslims to study the Qur'an, the Hadith, and all the other important works, knowing Arabic is compulsory. Three major ethnic groups ruled Islam over the centuries, one after the other within Islam, and Arabic penetrated each to differing degrees.

The first ruling group was the Arabs themselves. Every Semitic and North African area wholly absorbed Arabic, and it became their only language. In Babylon, Syria, and the land of Israel, Arabic replaced Aramaic. Aramaic is only spoken now in small Christian communities in eastern Syria or western Iraq. Arabic spread from Egypt across North Africa to Morocco, and from Arabia up into Iraq and Syria.

The second ruling ethnic group was the Persians—an Indo-European group. They were converted to Islam, but also took over Islam. Persia fought to maintain its distinct culture for a few centuries, even though its religion was changing to Islam. There was a split within Islam, after Muhammad's death, over whom the successor should be. The majority of Islam—the Sunni sect—believed it should be the family of Muhammad. The minority—the Shia sect—believed it should be someone who had unique spiritual qualities from God, as Muhammad was believed to have had. Persia, resenting Arab administration, was sympathetic to the Shias who also resented the bulk of the Arabs who were Sunni. Persia adopted the Shia beliefs in the sixteenth century AD and so today Iran is the major Shia nation among the Muslim nations. In this way, Persia completely accepted and absorbed Islam.[34] This belief in Shia Islam has major ramifications today and for Bible prophecy, which we will revisit in chapter 10.

Farsi is the Persians' native language. However, Arabic was the language of Islam and so Arabic took over as the language of religion and academia. Farsi remained the tongue of administration and everyday life. However, Persia was forced to change the way Farsi was written. Its written form was changed to an Arabic alphabet, so today Farsi is written in Arabic letters.

The third ethnic group to rule Islam was the Turks. Islam had spread to central Asia by the ninth century AD and the nomadic Turkic people of central Asia accepted it readily. When they migrated south and west into present-day Iran and Turkey, the Turks took over. Their first major empire was the Seljuk Turk Empire and their second was the more familiar Ottoman Empire. Like the Persian people the Turks kept their native tongue for everyday life, but Arabic was the language of religion and academia. Like the Farsi language, the Turkish language was forced to use the Arabic alphabet as well. Only recently in this last century, with the reforms of Ataturk, was Turkish allowed to use Roman letters for its alphabet. We will see more of Ataturk and what he did in chapter 11.

Even the names of places on maps changed when Islam took over. As empires in the Islamic Realm came and went, cities changed in name or importance or were even abandoned. Initially, the Umayyad Empire had its capital in Damascus. However the empire to follow, the Abbasid

Empire, let Babylon go to ruin and built Baghdad. Baghdad, not Babylon, was the greatest city in the world in the tenth to twelfth centuries AD. The Fatimid Empire was centered in Egypt, built Cairo, and moved its capital there. Alexandria was bypassed. The ancient cities of Susa and Persepolis and Ctephison in Persia were replaced in importance by Isfahan. Cities in Asia Minor with Greek names were renamed using Turkish names. The famous city of Nicaea (of Nicene Creed fame) was changed to Iznik, for example.

So in comparing how the Middle East looked in AD 600 in pre-Islamic times, to how it looked one thousand years later in AD 1600, native religions had changed to Islam. Most churches, temples, and synagogues had changed to mosques. Native languages had changed to Arabic, or native alphabets changed to Arabic alphabets. Laws of various nations had changed to Sharia law. In this way Islam, the Empire of Iron, crushed the former Empires of Babylon, Persia, and the Hellenized Realm (the Greek Empire). Even though the modern nation of Greece has maintained its language and religion, the Hellenized Realm extending to India lost it language, culture, and religion to Islam.

THE ARABIZED PEOPLES OF THE TEN TOES

The vision of the metal statue in Daniel 2 mentions ten nations represented by the toes of the statue. Identifying the part of the world where these nations are located, since they will rule with the Antichrist (Rev. 17:12), will tell us where the Antichrist will rule. Since it seems we must reject Rome as the Empire of Iron, we must reject France, Spain, Italy, Greece and/or the UK as the nations that will rule with the Antichrist. Therefore the European Union, or any permutation of it, cannot be the formation of the Antichrist's kingdom. Instead, since the Empire of Iron is more likely Islam, we must consider and watch nations like Iran, Iraq, Turkey, Algeria, Egypt, and Saudi Arabia.

To consider and watch these nations instead of the European nations is a major step forward in our understanding of what is to come, and what Bible prophecy says about these nations in the end times. It frees us to ignore developments in the European Union, and to instead focus our attention on developments in Iraq, Iran, and Turkey.

The Islamic Realm's history matches well with the description of the feet in the statue in Daniel.

> Just as you saw that the feet and toes were partly of baked clay and partly of iron, so this will be a divided kingdom; yet it will have some of the strength of iron in it, even as you saw iron mixed with clay. As the toes were partly iron and partly clay, so this kingdom will be partly strong and partly brittle. And just as you saw the iron mixed with baked clay, so the people will be a mixture and will not remain united, any more than iron mixes with clay. (Dan. 2:41–43)

The native peoples living in the united Islamic Realm in the eighth century AD did not remain united. The Islamic Realm fractured from within in AD 750. Various factions in Islam claiming inheritorship from Muhammad (known as the office of the caliphate) took control over various parts of the Islamic Empires. The realm of Islam never fully reunited. Various empires controlled much if not most of the Islamic Realm, such as the Ottoman Empire. Starting in the 1830s and continuing to the 1930s, the Islamic Realm was carved up by the European powers, except for Turkey and parts of the Arabian Peninsula. Various political states such as Algeria, Egypt, and Iran were then given independence during the twentieth century.

The splintering of the Islamic Realm into many states is a fulfillment of the words "will not remain united" in Daniel 2:43. Additionally, there seems to be a play on words in the original Aramaic text of Daniel 2:43. It involves the Aramaic word *arab* (Strong's #6151, pronounced ar-ab'). Our English word *arab* comes from the Hebrew/Aramaic word *arab*—which is a person of Semitic origin living in or near Arabia. But the Hebrew/ Aramaic word *arab* also means to comingle, to mix. So our currently translated phrase "the people will be a mixture" can also be rendered as "the people will be *arab*." This is probably not what is directly intended in the translation, but the play on words is interesting to me.

It is a known fact that following the conquests of the lands from Morocco to Pakistan by the Arab Islamic invaders, Arabs by the millions migrated from the Arabian Peninsula and settled in all the major cities throughout the Islamic Realm.[35] They held all the important posts in administering the empire, and intermarried with the local population. For this reason, the people of Algeria, Egypt, Iraq, Jordan, Libya, Morocco, and Syria are all considered Arabs—both by the West, as well as by Muslims themselves. Many of these nations even formed the Arab League, which began its charter with:

His Excellency the President of the Syrian Republic,
   His Royal Highness the Emir of Transjordan,
   His Majesty the King of Iraq,
   His Majesty the King of Saudi-Arabia,
   His Excellency the President of the Lebanese Republic,
   His Majesty the King of Egypt, the King of Yemen,
   With a view to strengthen[ing] the close relations and numerous
ties which bind the Arab States . . ."[36]

Since the nations from Morocco in the west to Kuwait in the east, along with Iraq and Syria in the north are all considered Arab, and because non-Arab states like Iran and Turkey use Arabic as part of their being in the Islamic Realm, then all these peoples and cultures can be said to be "Arabized." Today the Islamic Realm contains many people who did not remain united, and who are all "Arabized," and are both intermarried with Arab people and use the Arabic language.

SUMMARY

The world community within Islam—set up by its founder and early leaders with morals and laws allowing it to conquer, occupy, bully and not relent nor apologize—has utterly changed each society that it has ruled. As Wafa Sultan wrote in her book, *A God Who Hates*, "Islam subjugated the cultures of all the peoples it afflicted."[37]

Will Durant wrote of the people who continued to live in the countries that Islam had conquered and now rules:

> Gradually the non-Muslim populations adopted the Arabic language and dress, the laws and faith of the Koran. Where Hellenism, after a thousand years of mastery, had failed to take root, and Roman arms had left the native gods unconquered, and Byzantine orthodoxy had raised rebellious heresies, Muhammadanism had secured, almost without proselytism, not only belief and worship, but a tenacious fidelity that quite forgot the superseded gods.[38]

Durant explained the situation well. Where Rome utterly failed to conquer and crush, Islam did so completely and seemingly effortlessly over several centuries. So Islam, by its very nature and steady occupation of many lands over centuries, has done a very thorough job of crushing, enfeebling, and breaking into pieces the former empires of Babylon, Persia, and Greece. These societies have been completely transformed so that their pre-Islamic form is no longer recognizable.

Therefore, my conclusion is that Rome never even came close to doing what Islam did, and Islam did it all. Therefore, the empire of the iron legs is Islam. No other entity conquered and broke into pieces the other three empires of the statue. The Islamic Realm fulfills Daniel 2:40 perfectly. Rome didn't fulfill Daniel 2:40 at all.

In the next chapter we will move on in our discussion to the second Bible passage that has been used in the past to argue for a Roman Antichrist.

TWO

THE ANTICHRIST'S ETHNIC BACKGROUND REVEALED

WE SAW IN THE LAST CHAPTER HOW THE FIRST PASSAGE OF Bible prophecy in Daniel 2, which many believe supports a revived Roman Empire for origination of the Antichrist, actually supports an Islamic Realm. We will now examine the second passage in Daniel 9:26, which is used in popular theology to prove that the Antichrist will be a Roman. Daniel 9:26 is one of the five unyielding verses of Daniel I mentioned in the introduction to this book. We will look at this passage and see if a study of history will change our view of this verse.

> After the sixty-two "sevens," the Anointed One will be cut off and will have nothing. *The people* of the ruler who will come *will destroy* the city and the sanctuary. The end will come like a flood: War will continue until the end, and desolations have been decreed. (Dan. 9:26, emphasis added)

This verse is part of the monumental "Seventy Weeks" passage. God gives Daniel an outline of the future history of his people, the Jews. Though a "seven" is typically translated "week" (as in seven days) in the Old Testament, in this passage ,"seven" is understood to be seven years. The "Anointed One" in the verse means "Messiah" (Hebrew), or "the

Christ" (Greek). The passage says Messiah arrives after seven "sevens" and sixty-two "sevens" ([7+62] x 7 years = 483 years).

After He, "the Anointed One," is killed and does not become king (which is what happened at the end of Christ's ministry on earth), "the people of the ruler" will come to destroy the temple and Jerusalem. These "people" are "of," or related to, the ruler who is understood to be the Antichrist. The Antichrist's actions are then mentioned in Daniel 9:27, which is a summary of the Tribulation where it says the Antichrist will make a covenant and then cause desolation of the temple, which continues until the end.

THE PEOPLE OF THE RULER WHO WILL COME

Daniel 9:26 says the "people" are "of" the "ruler who will come." The people who destroyed the city and sanctuary were four legions of Roman soldiers in AD 70. The Roman soldiers were in Roman uniform under a Roman banner and fighting for Rome. The Aramaic word in Daniel 9:26 translated "people" is *am* (Strong's #5971, pronounced ahm) and is defined as (1) a group of individuals, (2) a nation (such as countrymen), or (3) a tribe, kindred or ethnicity.

The word *people* as simply a "group of individuals" in this verse would make no sense. Why tie a generic group of individuals with no affiliation in AD 70 to the Antichrist almost two millennia later? The word *people* meaning "nation" makes more sense. In that case Daniel 9:26 would be telling us that the nation they represent politically, Rome, is also the political nation of the Antichrist. This is the idea behind popular theology saying that the Romans destroyed the temple and the city, and therefore will produce the Antichrist. And if the overall argument presented in this book contends that the Antichrist is Muslim, that argument might have to be stopped here. But we saw in the last chapter that the iron legs could not represent anything but Islam. How can the Antichrist have Islamic roots but come from the Roman Empire? I believe the answer is with the third meaning of *am,* which is how Daniel 9:26 can support a Muslim Antichrist.

The third meaning of *am* in Daniel 9:26 is a tribe, kindred, or ethnicity. Using this definition, the identity of *the people* from the quote of Daniel 9:26 above will tell us the ethnic background of the Antichrist. That is, if indeed we *can* identify the ethnic background of the soldiers. Remarkably, historical records do tell us parts of the answer.

THE ROMAN LEGIONS

Legions of Rome surrounded and destroyed Jerusalem and the temple. Popular theology tells us that it was plainly the Romans, because it was the Roman armies that came and destroyed the temple. But just as popular theology ignores history by saying that the iron legs are Rome, so too popular theology ignores history here.

Admittedly, one might think at first glance that a Roman army was composed of Roman men, presumably Italians. But this ignores history that tells us who the people were in that Roman army that destroyed the Jewish temple in AD 70; they were not Italians. Who were the individual soldiers—the people—in the Roman army that destroyed the temple? What was their ethnicity?

Around the time of the birth of Christ, emperors Augustus Caesar and Tiberius Caesar began a tradition of only recruiting for the legions north of the Po River in northern Italy, which meant no recruiting in the province of Italia that covered the entire Italian Peninsula.[1] This fact alone tells us that the soldiers of the legion that actually destroyed the temple were not Italians.

Recruits were drawn either from the surrounding province in which the legion was currently based, or from the region of the province from which the legion originated.[2] Soldiers in the legions were typically Roman citizens, but if they were not they were granted immediate Roman citizenship upon entering service.

Recruiting and enlistment was achieved by completely discharging the men in the legion, and refreshing the ranks of a legion all at once. Some soldiers would remain for a second term and these would become the new officers. An enlistment would happen every sixteen or twenty years.[3] Typically, over the course of the years between enlistments, a legion would shrink in size and not be refreshed until the periodic recruitment time.

Historical sources tell us that at the start of the siege of Jerusalem in AD 70, four Roman legions surrounded Jerusalem. Three legions, Legio V Macedonica, Legio XII Fulminata, and Legio XV Apollinaris were all camped to the west and northwest. One legion, Legio X, was camped to the east on the Mount of Olives.[4, 5]

All legions had a number, and almost all legions had an official title. The title typically came either from the area of the legion's origin or for a famous battle that it had won.

The first legion mentioned above, Legio V Macedonica, was named for its victories in Macedonia. It was based in the Roman province of Moesia in AD 62 when it discharged its soldiers and brought in new recruits. The recruits were from Moesia, which is present day Bulgaria.[6] Over the years it was deployed further east. It marched from Egypt to take part in the invasion of Judea.

The second legion, Legio XII Fulminata, was named "thunder." It started in Gaul in the western part of the Roman Empire at the time of Julius Caesar around 58 BC, and was used in various campaigns taking it east. Octavius moved it east and so the Twelfth's base was at Raphanaea in Syria in the years prior to the siege at Jerusalem. It had just completed a new recruitment in time for the siege at Jerusalem in AD 70.[7] Its recruits were presumably from Syria.

The third legion, Legio XV Apollinaris, was possibly named for Apollo, which was Augustus Caesar's personal deity. Legio XV was based in Egypt just before the siege of Jerusalem and its recruits would have been from Gaul (its original recruitment ground), or would have been Egyptians.[8] It marched out of Egypt with Legio V Macedonica, to Jerusalem.

The fourth legion, Legio X, was different from other legions in general. Legio X was legendary among the legions of Rome for the many great battles it fought. Its recruitments are also more complicated than those of the three previously mentioned legions.

Fortunately, many records are left behind of the histories of Legio X. Julius Caesar himself founded and recruited Legio X in 61 BC. The first recruits for Legio X were from southern Spain, in the province of Baetica. Legio X accompanied Caesar during his military campaigns, and was instrumental in his conquest of Gaul.[9]

If one digs into the history or identity of this legion, one will discover that Legio X was occasionally called Legio X Fretensis. There is debate based on relatively new information that "Fretensis" was a nickname, and that the proper name of the legion was Legio X. "Fretensis" is said to not make sense because it means "of the straits," which would have been off of Sicily, and Legio X never went there. Legio X had no official title. It was simply referred to as "the tenth" or "the famous tenth." It stood alone as the legendary legion. It took part in the conquests of Gaul and Britain. It fought on the Parthian and Armenian frontier, and it conquered Judea twice—in AD 70 and AD 135.[10]

Table 2-1 presents information on the recruitments of soldiers in Legio X over the years. The soldiers that made up Legio X during the destruction of the temple in AD 70 would have been from the eighth recruitment in AD 64. There are records to show that Spaniards made up the ranks from 61 BC to AD 24. Legio X operated in the western part of the Roman Empire up until about 30 BC. Octavian moved the base of Legio X to a town called Cyrrhus, near Antioch in Syria. For the three following recruitments (in 29 BC, 14 BC, and AD 4) records show new recruits were then marched to the new base all the way from Spain in the west to Syria in the east. There are no known recruitment records for the four recruitments from AD 24 to 84. We do know recruits came from the province of Pontus in present-day Turkey in AD 104. Pontus was located in north-central Turkey, on the shore of the Black Sea. The recruitment we are interested in, which took place in AD 64, is bolded in table 2-1.

Table 2-1. Recruitment data compiled for Legio X

RECRUITMENT	YEAR	RECRUITMENT LOCATION	LEGION BASE	ACTIVITY
1st[11]	61 BC	South Spain	Spain	Conquests of Britain/Gaul
2nd[12]	44 BC	South Spain	Spain	Civil War
3rd[13]	29 BC	South Spain	Syria	
4th[14]	14 BC	South Spain	Syria	Judea, census
5th[15]	AD 4	South Spain	Syria	
6th	AD 24	No record found	Syria	
7th	AD 44	No record found	Syria	Parthian wars
8th[16]	**AD 64**	**No record found**	**Syria**	**Jewish revolt**
9th	AD 84	No record found	Judea	
10th[17]	AD 104	Pontus	Judea	

It is highly probable that after three recruitments where troops were marched across the breadth of the empire (in 29 BC, 14 BC, AD 4), that recruits would have been drawn from the new home province of Syria and not Spain. Wherever possible, recruits came from the nearest sources of manpower. Citizens were found in communities nearer to a legion's base.[18] For many decades, legions like Legio X had dedicated recruitment grounds, but for the sake of expediency, recruiting grounds shifted. This happened particularly in the second half of the first century AD.[19] So it is highly likely that Legio X got its new recruits in AD 44 and AD 64 from communities surrounding its base in the province of Syria. Also, the very fact that records are missing for three or four recruitments following AD 4 may be a witness to the recruitment area being shifted away from Spain.

The People of the Legions

From this discussion of Roman legions we can now summarize the ethnic composition of the four legions surrounding Jerusalem. They are Moesians (same areas as Bulgaria and Serbia), Celts (area of France), Egyptians, and Syrians. The Egyptians and Syrians could have been in two legions each. At this point then, Daniel 9:26 can no longer be used to prove that the Antichrist must exclusively be Roman. The field is now opened up to Moesians, Celts, Egyptians, and Syrians. Italians are specifically excluded. We see now that if the Antichrist is to be a Muslim, he could be Syrian or Egyptian.

We also have an additional source of history. Josephus, in his account of the War of the Jews in AD 70, wrote that there were soldiers in the ranks of the Roman armies who were Arabian and Syrian. In addition to the legions themselves, every legion typically had some auxiliary soldiers from its local province. They would have been Syrian and Arabian. The lead Roman general, Titus, admonished the commanders of the troops for their barbarous acts:

> Moreover, do the Arabians and Syrians now first of all begin to govern themselves as they please, and to indulge their appetites in a foreign war, and then, out of their barbarity in murdering men, and out of their hatred to the Jews, get it ascribed to the Romans?[20]

Auxiliaries—additional armies—accompanied the legions and were almost always made up of "foreigners." These were people in a conquered province like Syria who did not yet have Roman citizenship but would receive it after twenty-five years of service.[21] So in addition to the Syrians within Legio X, and probably within the ranks of Legio XII Fulminata, there were Syrians most likely in the auxiliary ranks as well. Note from Titus' admonishment above that he specifically knew that some of his troops in the ranks were of Arabian and Syrian background. Titus also knew they had a hatred of the Jews. These troops were of ethnic groups that surrounded Judea, and who had a centuries-long history of antagonism with the Jewish people.

On a side note, in the quote above, I find it interesting that Titus was worried about the barbarity of the troops being "ascribed to the Romans." As it turned out his concern was justified, since popular theology has indeed ascribed the destruction of the temple to the Romans.

After the walls of Jerusalem were breached, the soldiers of the legions came into the temple grounds. Josephus wrote further that it was unidentified soldiers, wearing the uniform of the Roman legions that started the fire that ultimately consumed the temple in Jerusalem. He wrote:

> At which time *one of the soldiers*, without staying for any orders, and without any concern or dread upon him at so great an undertaking, and being hurried on by a certain divine fury, snatched somewhat out of the materials that were on fire, and *being lifted up by another soldier*, he *set fire to a golden window*, through which there was a passage to the rooms that were round about the holy house, on the north side of it.[22] (emphasis added)

Josephus wrote that Titus didn't want the temple damaged. Titus was awed by the grandeur of the temple and saw that stories about it were no exaggeration. Titus tried to stop the burning.

And now a certain person came running to Titus, and told him of this fire, as he was resting himself in his tent after the last battle; whereupon he rose up in great haste, and, as he was, ran to the holy house, in order to have a stop put to the fire; after him followed all his commanders, and after them followed the several legions, in great astonishment; so there was a great clamor and tumult raised, as was natural upon the disorderly motion of so great an army. Then did Caesar, both by calling to the soldiers that were fighting, with a loud voice, and by giving a signal to them with his right hand, order them to quench the fire. But they did not hear what he said, though he spake so loud, having their ears already dimmed by a greater noise another way; nor did they attend to the signal he made with his hand neither, as still some of them were distracted with fighting, and others with passion.[23]

PUTTING THE PIECES TOGETHER

We know from historical records that there were Egyptian and Syrian soldiers in at least two and perhaps three of the legions. We know there were Syrians and Arabians also in the ranks of the auxiliaries. Titus knew the Arabian and Syrian soldiers in his army had a hatred for the Jews. Two soldiers who were not identified started a fire in the temple, disobeying the wishes of their general, Titus. Before Titus could establish order, the soldiers under his command—Syrian, Egyptian, and Arabian soldiers wearing the Roman uniform—had already begun to destroy and burn the temple in a frenzy. What would drive supposedly disciplined soldiers to disobey the orders of their commander? It would have had to be an agenda, driven by greed or hatred or some other underlying factor. I would say those soldiers who had an agenda were more likely Syrian, Egyptian, and/or Arabian. There were Moesian and Celtic men in Roman uniform also, but before the siege at Jerusalem they presumably had no contact with the Jews.

These were Roman legions, with Roman leadership. But the soldiers in the legions—Syrian, Egyptian, and Arabian—were the ones who actually destroyed the temple. All the legions took part.[24] Daniel 9:26 plainly says, "The people . . . will destroy the city and the sanctuary." God's Word is being very exact here. I believe the word used in the original Aramaic text of Daniel for the English word *people* is used to refer to a tribe of people or kindred of people. In other words, it refers to the ethnic background of a people. Popular theology says that the people were Romans. But to say that is to ignore the history of the Roman legions, and to ignore the written chronicle of the destruction of the temple. The people were Syrians of the Roman province of Syria, and Egyptians of the Roman province of Egypt, and Arabians from the Roman province of Arabia. They were Roman citizens and Roman soldiers, but ethnically they were Syrians, Egyptians, and Arabians.

On a side note, Paul the apostle was in this same situation. In Acts 22:3 he declared he was a Jew, born in Tarsus and raised in Jerusalem. This was his ethnicity. But in Acts 22:25–29 Paul reveals to the authorities that he is a Roman ("Roman" in NKJV, "Roman citizen" in NIV, which are equivalent). So Paul also could have been called a Roman, though ethnically he was a Jew.

In AD 70 the people were Syrians, Egyptians, and Arabians. But we saw in chapter 1 that the Arabs migrated in large numbers out of the Arabian Peninsula when Islam conquered the Middle East in the seventh century AD. They intermarried with the local populations. Native Syrians and Egyptians would have become Arab over the centuries. Today, they call themselves "Arab," as we saw in the original charter of the Arab League.

Summary

Since the people in the Roman armies included Syrians, Egyptians, and Arabians, Daniel 9:26 can no longer be used to support the argument for a

Roman or European Antichrist. We saw in chapter 1 how the Antichrist's empire will be based in Islam, not Rome. Now we see from Daniel 9:26 that the "ruler who will come" will be an Arab. This conclusion would be consistent with a Muslim Antichrist, since the great majority of Arabs are Muslim.

THREE

WHAT'S SO SPECIAL ABOUT ISLAM?

A T THIS POINT IN MY JOURNEY OF DISCOVERY, I HAD ACCEPTED that a Muslim Antichrist was a given. The two major biblical arguments for a Roman Antichrist had been completely turned around and now argued for a Muslim Antichrist. But on further reflection I wondered why Islam would be the religious system chosen by God in the end times as the religion of the Antichrist. In other words, what made Islam so special?

Our Father, Jehovah God, is in control and His will is unfolding in the affairs of this world every day as time marches on to the return of His Son, our Savior Jesus Christ. So, of all the world's institutions, why choose Islam to be the power and religious base of the Antichrist?

We already saw in chapter 1 some of the factors within Islam that might contribute to it advancing across the world just before Christ's return. This would include the idea that the more zealous Muslims would be encouraged that Allah was behind them and that they could not be defeated, possibly resulting in great military victories.

But what might the Bible say that would make Islam unique in fulfilling its role in the end times? In daily reading of the Bible various themes caught my attention, and I realized that Islam was involved with these themes as well.

WHAT'S IN A NAME?

Let us start with the name of Islam's deity. The proper name of Islam's one and only God is Allah.

The word *Allah* actually has etymological roots in pre-Islamic times as the contraction of the older Arabic *Al-Ilah* which literally means "the God." In pre-Islamic Arabia, the name Allah was well established and referred to whatever god was one's god.[1] We know that the use of the term *Allah* predates Islam because people like those in Muhammad's Quraysh tribe sometimes used it in their names. Muhammad's own father was named Abdallah, which literally means "servant of Allah."

The Quraysh tribe, as well as all those living around Mecca, worshipped Hubal as their supreme god.[2] Since the Quraysh tribe's god was Hubal, then to the Quraysh and to Muhammad, Hubal *was* their Allah. So if they were to talk about Allah (before the time of Islam) they would be referring to Hubal. To other Arabs who did not think Hubal was the chief god, Allah would be some other god. There were 360 idols representing the pantheon of gods that the pre-Islamic Arabs worshipped and kept in the Kaabah (literally, "cube") in Mecca. The idol Hubal was one of the 360, but he was considered by the Quraysh to be the chief god of that "temple."[3] Hubal was also said to have been in the shape of a man.[4]

Muhammad started to claim to have heavenly visitations around his fortieth year in AD 610. In AD 630, after twenty years of building a new faith and filling the role of its Prophet, he conquered Mecca. He then destroyed the idols in and around the Kaabah, except Hubal. He proclaimed that Hubal wasn't just Allah for the Quraysh, but was Allah for everyone—for the universe. It sank in with everyone who followed Muhammad in the twenty years prior to AD 630 that Muhammad's Allah wasn't just a supreme god but was *the* God, the only God. The name of the one God wasn't to be Hubal—it was to be Allah. The name Hubal fell from use from then on. Muhammad named the Kaabah the holiest place on earth. Mecca was named the holiest city and it was decreed that no unbeliever was to ever set foot there.

To a person who speaks Arabic, but who is not Muslim (such as an Arab from pre-Islamic times or an Arabic-speaking Christian today), Allah is the equivalent of our word and name God. To that person Allah can be anything he or she believes Allah to be, just as in the English-speaking world a person who uses the name God may believe God to be just about anything. So anyone speaking Arabic can use the word *Allah* to refer to whatever god that person believes in to be god.

In Arabic-translated Bibles, the word used for the Arabic name of God is *Allah*. If a Christ-following Christian from a Muslim country like Yemen says his God is Allah, then you can be reasonably sure that his Allah and your Jehovah are the same God.

But to a Muslim, Allah is more than just the name of *the* God; it is the proper name of their only God. This is equivalent in language usage to our English proper name Jehovah. In America when someone mentions God they can mean any supreme being. But when someone, especially a Christian, mentions Jehovah, we know he or she usually means Father God, the God of Abraham, Isaac, and Jacob, the One who sent His Son Jesus Christ into the world.

So an Arabic-speaking non-Muslim talking about Allah may mean the same God we Christians believe in. But when a Muslim talks about Allah, we can know that it is an entirely different deity from our God, Jehovah. This can be confusing. The reason most people think of Allah as referring to the one God of Islam is that the vast majority of Arabic speakers who live in Arab countries are Muslim.

At the time of Muhammad's death in AD 632, regardless of what one may think of his religion or morals, he had converted the people throughout the Arabian Peninsula from being polytheists to monotheists. This would be a huge accomplishment for any single person in one lifetime. Muhammad had taken his tribe's god, Hubal, who was their Allah, and made it everyone's only God.

To those who are not believers of Islam—called *infidels* by Muslims—the god behind Allah is Hubal. It is a tradition that the idol Hubal was brought from Moab, and there is evidence that it came from somewhere north of Arabia.[5] Hubal would have been brought to Mecca centuries before Christ.

So what does this have to do with God's Word and the religion of the Antichrist? There is a very interesting possible connection.

In Old Testament times, the various nations surrounding Israel worshipped various false gods. In 1 Kings 11:33 and 2 Kings 23:13 we see which nations worshipped what gods as their chief gods. Ammon's chief god was Molech, which in Hebrew basically means "king." Moab's chief god was Chemosh, which in Hebrew means "to subdue" or "the powerful." Phoenicia's (Sidon's notably) chief goddess was Ashtoreth, who like Ishtar in Babylon, means "evening star." However, Baal worship seemed to be nearly universal; many nations in the Old Testament worshipped Baal.

Of all the false gods Israel got entangled with, Baal was primary. The name of Baal is mentioned in the Bible many more times than that of any other false god. Baal worship entangled Israel from the time of Moses to the time after the captivity of the Jews. God pronounced the most judgments on Israel because of their worship of that particular false god. It seems the one false god that the God of Israel was most against was Baal.

During the Israelites' forty years in the wilderness, God told Moses that those who worship Baal must be killed (Num. 25). In the time of the Judges, whenever the children of Israel would fall away from God, it was Baal they would follow. Judges 6:26–32 records how Gideon destroyed his family's own altar to Baal. In 1 Kings 18:16–46 Elijah had a contest on Mount Carmel against 450 prophets of Baal. In 2 Chronicles 24:7 we read that the wicked queen Athaliah, who sought to destroy the royal line of David, used the holy temple's gold implements for Baal worship.

In 2 Chronicles 33:3 the wicked king Manasseh took Baal worship to new heights.

The Hebrew word for our English word Baal is actually *H'Bal* which literally means "the Lord." So everywhere in our English Bible that the word Baal appears as a god or idol, the Hebrew word behind it actually means, "the Baal," meaning "the Lord."

Demons may pose as false gods such as "the powerful" (Chemosh) or "king" (Molech) or even the "evening star" (Ashtoreth). It is God Almighty who is all powerful, and it is His Son who reigns as King of kings. But only one entity and only one false god has the audacity to falsely call himself "the Lord." A prophecy regarding Satan shows some of his thoughts:

> You said in your heart, "I will ascend to heaven; I will raise my throne above the stars of God; I will sit enthroned on the mount of assembly, on the utmost heights of the sacred mountain. I will ascend above the tops of the clouds; I will make myself like the Most High." (Isa. 14:13–14)

From this passage it seems as if Satan wants to replace the Lord God and be "the Lord." I would think one reason God may be most against a false god calling himself "the Lord" is that it transgresses the very first commandment.

> "*I am the* Lord *your God*, who brought you out of Egypt, out of the land of slavery. You shall have no other gods before me." (Ex. 20:2–3, emphasis added)

God is trying to tell us that He is God and no one else. Only He is the Lord—no one else. In addition, God also warns us through Jeremiah about one major danger of Baal worship.

They think the dreams they tell one another will make my people forget my name, just as their ancestors *forgot my name through Baal worship.* (Jer. 23:27, emphasis added)

In response to His people possibly forgetting His name because of Baal worship, God tells us through Hosea about His people in the time following the return of Christ, "I will remove the names of the Baals from her lips; no longer will their names be invoked" (Hos. 2:17). God intends to purge the use of the words "the Lord" so that they are used only for Him.

Satan's intention of replacing the real Lord is consistent with his intention to replace the real Christ with his Antichrist. It would be consistent and not surprising that the Antichrist's religion would espouse a deity named "the Lord."

Now here is the connection I mentioned earlier: Baal in our English Bibles is actually translated from the Hebrew phrase "H'Bal," or "the Lord." As was discussed before, we know that Hubal was the god of the Kaabah and the god behind Allah. Just as Allah is the proper name of God in Islam, so Hubal was the proper name of that god in the Kaabah. We also know from tradition that Hubal came from the north, centuries before Muhammad.

What is not known for sure and only theorized is that what the Hebrews call "H'Bal" could be what the Arabs called Hubal. If the Arabs who imported this god from the north knew that H'Bal was translated in the local tongues as "the Bal" and not a proper name, they probably would have called it "al-Bal" (Arabic for "the Bal"). But the Arabs called it Hubal, making it a proper name in Arabic.

If this is all true, and Hubal is an import of H'Bal into Arab culture, then the entire religion of Islam could be said to be a modern repackaging of Baal worship. Again, no one really knows if H'Bal and Hubal are the same god. There is evidence supporting either position. But I found another prophecy that might support the idea that the two are the same.

On that last day when Christ returns, Jerusalem will be surrounded by the armies of the Antichrist. These Muslim armies will most likely be praying and bowing in worship toward the Kaabah containing Hubal, five times per day. God gives His Word through the prophet Zephaniah, prophesying about the end times and the return of Christ.

> "I will sweep away everything from the face of the earth," declares the LORD. "I will sweep away both men and animals; I will sweep away the birds of the air and the fish of the sea. The wicked will only have heaps of rubble when I cut off man from the face of the earth," declares the LORD. "I will stretch out my hand against Judah and against all who live in Jerusalem. I will cut off from this place *every remnant of Baal*." (Zeph. 1:2–4, emphasis added)

When I look at the modern state of Israel today, I don't literally see or hear of Baal worship occurring there. Of course the Bible could be referring to a spiritual Baal worship in the form of idols of the heart that people put ahead of God. On the other hand, if Islam is modern Baal worship, and the armies overrun Jerusalem, then this verse takes on a literal meaning.

If Islam is a repackaging of Baal worship, and Jehovah God was most angry at Israel when it worshipped Baal, then perhaps we can better understand why our God might be angry with and judge Islam upon the return of Christ. We will see more of God's future dealing with Islam in chapter 5. In that chapter we will see what God does to the fourth beast of Daniel 7.

ANTICHRIST—DENIAL OF THE SONSHIP OF CHRIST

If Islam is to be the religion of the Antichrist, one should expect doctrines of that religion to foster the very spirit of Antichrist.

> Who is the liar? It is the man who denies that Jesus is the Christ. Such a man is the antichrist—he denies the Father and the Son. No one who

denies the Son has the Father; whoever acknowledges the Son has the Father also. (1 John 2:22–23)

What does it mean to deny that Jesus is the Christ? It is to deny the very person and work of Jesus—the Messiah who came to die for us on the cross to save us from our sins so that whoever accepts His gift and then follows Him will have eternal life.

Of Himself Jesus said, "I told you that you would die in your sins; if you do not believe that I am the one I claim to be, you will indeed die in your sins" (John 8:24).

To deny who Jesus claims to be is to deny that He is the Messiah and the very Son of God, being of the same substance as the Father, and being in fact, God. John wrote at the beginning of his gospel about who Jesus was: "the Word was with God and the Word was God" (John 1:1).

To deny Jesus' work is to deny that Jesus died on the cross and physically rose from the dead. As Paul wrote, if Jesus didn't physically rise then He didn't conquer death and we are all still lost: "And if Christ has not been raised, your faith is futile; you are still in your sins" (1 Cor. 15:17).

So to deny who Jesus is—God, Son of God, Messiah—and what Jesus did—His death on the cross and His physical resurrection—is to be "an antichrist." Antichrist is anyone who is against God. This is the spirit of Antichrist of which John wrote.

This is how you can recognize the Spirit of God: Every spirit that acknowledges that Jesus Christ has come in the flesh is from God, but every spirit that does not acknowledge Jesus is not from God. This is the spirit of the antichrist, which you have heard is coming and even now is already in the world. (1 John 4:2–3)

Some people would believe that the Roman Catholic Church headquartered in Rome is the source of the Antichrist. Over the last many centuries the Roman Catholic Church has at times not been the best example of a Christian church on earth, to say the least. But one of its core doctrines, the Nicene Creed, which is recited by Catholics every Sunday in Mass, says of Jesus:

> We believe in one Lord, Jesus Christ,
> the *only Son of God*,
> eternally begotten of the Father,
> *God from God*, light from light,
> true God from true God,
> begotten, not made,
> of *one Being with the Father*;
> through him all things were made.
> For us men and for our salvation
> he came down from heaven:
> by the power of the Holy Spirit he was born of the Virgin Mary
> and became man.
> For our sake *he was crucified* under Pontius Pilate;
> *he suffered*, *died*, and was buried.
> On the third day *he rose again*
> in accordance with the Scriptures;
> *he ascended into heaven*
> and is seated at the right hand of the Father.
> He will come again in glory to judge the living and the dead,
> and his kingdom will have no end. (emphasis added)

Notice the italics. This creed says in so many ways who Jesus is and what He did. Now compare the Nicene Creed above to what Islam says. According to Islam, Jesus was created, not eternal.

> The likeness of Jesus with Allah is truly as the likeness of Adam. He created him from dust, then said to him, Be, and he was. (Qur'an 3:59)

According to Islam, Jesus is not the Son of God. To a Muslim that means Jesus is not the son of Allah.

> And say: Praise be to Allah! Who has not taken to Himself a son, and Who has not a partner in the kingdom . . . (Qur'an 17:111)

> And to warn to those who say: Allah has taken to Himself a son. (Qur'an 18:4)

> And they say: The Beneficient has taken to Himself a son. Certainly you make an abominable assertion! The heavens may almost be rent threat, and the earth cleave asunder, and the mountains fall down in pieces, that they ascribe a son to the Beneficient! (Qur'an 19:88–91)

> Allah has not taken to Himself a son, nor is there with Him any (other) god. (Qur'an 23:91)

It seems that the Qur'an goes to great lengths to deny the sonship of Jesus Christ. The language in the passage from the Qur'an chapter 19 about what would happen if it were believed that God has a Son sounds like divine judgment on earth. But it also reminds me of the language used in the Bible to describe the scene on earth on the day that the very Son of God returns!

Denying the sonship of Christ and denying His eternal nature is to deny everything Jesus is, and what Jesus has done for mankind to save us. This is the denial that John wrote about. To deny the Son is to be an antichrist. Any Muslim who knows his or her faith will tell you that Allah has no son. I certainly agree with that, because Islam's Allah, and Jehovah God are two totally different beings. It isn't Allah who has a son; it is Jehovah God the Father who has a Son, and His name is Jesus.

Islam denies who Jesus Christ really is, and that leaves the position of Messiah open for the Antichrist to fill, in the eyes of the world.

ISHMAEL AND ENMITY WITH THE HUMAN RACE

The story of the conception and birth of Ishmael is given in Genesis 16. God promised Abraham and Sarah that they would have a son. Sarah (or Sarai at the time) did not wait for the fulfilling of God's promise of a son and had her husband take Hagar, her Egyptian slave, as another wife. But when Hagar became pregnant, Sarah began mistreating her so Hagar ran away. An angel of the Lord told Hagar to go back to Sarah and gave her a prophecy about her son.

> You are now with child and you will have a son. You shall name him Ishmael for the LORD has heard of your misery. He will be a wild donkey of a man; his hand will be against everyone and everyone's hand against him, and he will live in hostility toward all his brothers. (Gen. 16:11–12)

Ishmael lived a life of conflict. He founded a nation (Gen. 25:12-18) and it is possible the culture he founded was one of conflict as well. The word *brothers* at the end of the Genesis 16 passage above comes from the Hebrew word *akh* (Strong's #251, pronounced awkh) and can mean "brothers" in the familial sense or the widest sense—kindred or tribe.

The Quraysh tribe from which Muhammad came had for centuries claimed to be descended from Ishmael, and they were raiders. When Islam came along, it was realized that Muslim would not raid against Muslim anymore, but that Muslims would raid against everyone else. Just before his death, Muhammad said:

> [K]now that every Muslim is a Muslim's brother, and that the Muslims are brethren; fighting between them should be avoided, and the blood shed in pagan times should not be avenged; Muslims should fight all men until they say, "There is no god but God."[6]

So you can see that Muhammad himself, a proclaimed descendent of Ishmael, carried on his ancestor's tradition of being against everyone by making it a basic tenet of Islam.

Wafa Sultan, in her book, *A God Who Hates*, notes that Islam itself, which was founded among Arabic nomadic tribesmen, reflects the culture of fear in which it was founded.[7] In pre-Islamic times, the relationship between the nomad and his environment was based on mistrust and fear. There was always a fear of being raided—of being killed or being pillaged. The only time they weren't fearful is when they themselves were the raiders raiding someone else.

In essence Islam codified and legalized raiding against unbelievers, the infidels (*kuffar*). Islam, like its founder, and like its founder's ancestors, is against the rest of the human race. Muhammad took the promise in Genesis of one man's struggles against the rest of the world, and turned it into a promise of a whole community of spiritual descendents against the world.

METHOD OF EXECUTIONS

The Bible mentions a method of execution for those to be killed in the end times by the Antichrist and his kingdom.

> I saw thrones on which were seated those who had been given authority to judge. And I saw the souls of those who had been beheaded because of their testimony about Jesus and because of the word of God. They had not worshiped the beast or his image and had not received his mark on their foreheads or their hands. They came to life and reigned with Christ a thousand years. (Rev. 20:4)

Those who had been beheaded were the saints of God who were killed during the Tribulation. The reason we know they weren't beheaded in any other time was because the Antichrist and his mark won't be around until the time of the Tribulation. If Islam is the religion of the Antichrist and Islam is ubiquitous in much of the world at that time, then death by beheading will probably be common.

At various times and places in Islamic history the penalty for leaving Islam has been death, depending on how closely the holy book is followed. One of the six collections within the Hadith (one of Islam's holy books) says specifically, "Whoever changed his Islamic religion, then kill him" (Sahih al-Bukhari 9:84:57).[8]

Today, in Saudi Arabia and in other Muslim countries where Sharia law is in full force, beheadings are a routine method of execution for a number of crimes, including leaving Islam.

CONCLUSION

In addition to seeing two biblical arguments supporting Islam as the empire of the Antichrist and his ethnicity being Arab, we can now also see that Islam is involved with additional various themes in the Bible such as Baal worship, the spirit of antichrist, and even Ishmael.

Now that we understand the Antichrist will be a Muslim and comes from Islam, we can move on in our discussion to the central message of this book—the prophetic Bible passages that reveal the events to occur in the time before the Tribulation. These same events chronicle the emergence of the Antichrist.

SEEING WHAT MUST HAPPEN BEFORE THE TRIBULATION COMES

SECTION TWO

SEEING WHAT MUST
HAPPEN BEFORE THE
TRIBULATION COMES

THE AMAZING WARNING THE BIBLE GIVES US OF THE ANTICHRIST'S COMING

W E SAW IN THE FIRST TWO CHAPTERS OF THIS BOOK THE REINforcement of the idea that the Antichrist is to be Muslim. Knowledge of history showed us in Daniel 2 that the Antichrist's kingdom is Islamic, not Roman. Knowledge of history also showed us in Daniel 9 that the Antichrist will be Arab and likely from the area of Syria, and not a Roman. These discoveries accomplished two things. First, they silenced major biblical arguments supporting a Roman Antichrist. Second, they further confirmed the initial idea that the Antichrist is to be Muslim. Knowing where the Antichrist comes from is a key step to understanding additional prophecy.

In this chapter we now begin the central theme of this book—discovering the signs of the coming of the Antichrist. Having come to expect a Muslim Antichrist with an Islamic empire, I continued on with the journey of exploration into Bible prophecy. To see how Islam might play a role in the end times, I realized I next had to reexamine all passages of prophecy in the Bible. The potential for new interpretations to reveal themselves was an opportunity I didn't want to pass up. I noticed that two passages became open to a radically new interpretation. I saw the visions described in Daniel 7 and 8 with new eyes. And my new understanding of Daniel 7 and 8 in turn gave me new insights into the four horsemen of Revelation 6.

The first passage, Daniel 7, gives us a vision of four beasts. Popular theology today points to these beasts as representing the ancient kingdoms of Babylon, Persia, Greece, and Rome. However, details in the text about the vision in Daniel tell us this view is incorrect and that it takes place in the end times instead of long ago. Since this vision tells of things happening to political entities in the Middle East in the end times, this alone tells us that it may be relevant to the appearing of a Muslim Antichrist from the Middle East. In addition, there is also the fourth beast's eleventh horn in the vision, which is the Antichrist.

The second passage, Daniel 8, gives us a vision of a ram and a goat. The situation here is similar to that of Daniel 7. Popular theology today points to these beasts as representing the ancient kingdoms of Persia and Greece and the prophecy ends with the rise of Antiochus IV (Epiphanes), an ancient Greek king who persecuted the Jews. But on closer inspection, the scriptural text of this vision actually plainly tells us it takes place in the end times instead of long ago. This vision also has a little horn, but instead of growing as an eleventh horn as in Daniel 7, here it grows as a little horn out of one of the goat's four horns. We might then suspect that this vision also tells us of the emergence of the Muslim Antichrist in the Middle East. Knowing the Antichrist comes out of Islam sheds light on the fact that this vision reveals events in the end-times versions of these kingdoms, which leads to this same Antichrist.

The fact that these passages do apply to today instead of the ancient past is nothing short of stunning, because these passages open up for us a whole unwinding script in the end times. Many Christian communities and believers have used the Bible to measure the truth of a teaching. *Now we are given the opportunity to use the Bible to measure the significance of world events and shed light on what season we are in relative to the coming of the Antichrist.*

One example of world events we should watch is the results of the recent riots in various Middle East countries, the largest being in Egypt in 2013. These riots and usurped regimes are actually manifestations of conditions necessary for the exact fulfillment of part of the prophecies in Daniel. Another is the shifting of power within the government of Iran that involves the supreme leader and the Revolutionary Guard. This shift is behind the scenes, being carried on somewhat clandestinely. Again, that shift in power is necessary to exactly fulfill part of the prophecy. This new interpretation will allow us to look at these events and—rather than wondering about them—know that they must happen and why.

Since these passages actually do give us a picture of the rise of the Antichrist, they also answer the question, "Does the Bible give us any warnings or signs of Antichrist's coming?" Up until ten years ago I would have said no, but now I must answer the question with a resounding yes! However, this answer conflicts with a popularly held and cherished idea that nothing more must happen until the time that the Tribulation begins.

This belief is widespread. It has been around since the Israelis took back the Temple Mount in Jerusalem in 1967 after their exile, which started all the way back in AD 70. Bible prophecy does call for the Jews to gather from nations all over the world and to come live in the land of Israel in the end times. Bible prophecy also speaks of a rebuilt temple and a Jewish society again sacrificing at the temple.

These prophecies were partially fulfilled with Israel's declaring independence and retaking the Temple Mount in 1967. It is also believed that the temple will be rebuilt during the Tribulation. So, since 1967 it has become a popular thought that there isn't any other event called out in Bible prophecy until the Tribulation begins, with the exception of the Rapture.

I will not get into a detailed discussion of the Rapture in this book. The Rapture is, of course, the catching away of believers to be with Jesus Christ. Suffice it to say that of those who believe the seven-year

Tribulation is coming, they either believe the Rapture comes before the Tribulation, in the middle, or after the Tribulation. If the Rapture is to occur before or after the Tribulation, it is supposedly very close to the first or last day of the Tribulation.

The point I'm making here is that popular theology says nothing more will happen that fulfills Bible prophecy until the time right at the start of the Tribulation—whether it's the Rapture or the Tribulation itself. We need look no further than the writing of two popular authors who hold to this view to show that it hasn't changed in all these years since just after 1967.

In his landmark book *The Late Great Planet Earth*, Hal Lindsey wrote in 1970, "There's nothing that remains to be fulfilled before Christ could catch you up to be with Him."[1]

And in his fairly recent book published in 2008, *What In The World Is Going On?*, Dr. David Jeremiah confirms Lindsey's written statement thirty-eight years later.[2]

So to move on in our discussion and exploration of prophecy we must bypass that cherished notion that nothing more must occur before the time of the Tribulation. That notion was most likely born from a consensus at the time that no more end-time prophecy existed except that which applied to the Rapture and Tribulation. But now we have the events revealed in Daniel 7 and 8.

As I mentioned earlier, in my exploration I had asked the question, "Does the Bible give us any warnings or signs of the Antichrist's coming?" I have found the affirmative answer to this question very comforting. To me it is much more comforting if God's Word gives us some warning and some signs ahead of the Tribulation. And, wonderfully, it does. The popular view of theology that says we won't see anything being fulfilled until the day the Antichrist appears actually seems, if you'll excuse the expression, appalling to me. The idea that nothing is happening and then "Bam!" one must run for the hills without any prior warning whatsoever runs counter to what I believe I've seen in the Bible (except for the notable case concerning Jerusalem itself in Matthew 24:15–18 midway through the Tribulation).

Jesus always said to "watch." In Matthew 24:32 Jesus said we'd know the *season* of the times we are in. Even of His return Jesus said in Revelation 3:3, "But if you do not wake up, I will come like a thief, and you will not know at what time I will come to you."

As long as you are His you will have warnings available to you, but you must be watchful. In addition, the fact that the Bible tells us of the events leading up to the Antichrist should not surprise us. After all, wouldn't you think that if the Bible talks quite a bit about the Antichrist himself that the Bible would also talk about his emergence?

Once Daniel 7 and 8 are understood to apply to the end times, and to the nations from which a Muslim Antichrist comes, we see a wondrously descriptive and detailed account of events appear, which occur prior to the Antichrist's reign. To me this is just sweet confirmation of how loving God is toward His saints, and how He is in control. These specific events almost organize themselves into four signs or stages, which I call the Four Signposts. They start with the initial sign that we as a world have arrived at the end times. They finish with the last sign in which the Antichrist himself has assembled his empire. I don't know when the Tribulation will begin relative to these Four Signposts, but my guess would be that it would begin almost immediately following the end of the Fourth Signpost.

If you are looking for timetables and years, you are wasting your time. These are signs, not dates. What applies here is just as Jesus said about the fig tree—by watching its blossoms and leaves you know what season you are in. Jesus also said in Matthew 24:36 that no one knows the day or the hour of His return.

After receiving this new understanding of Daniel 7 and 8, I received another wonderful but very unexpected surprise. Continuing on in the journey I reexamined Revelation 6:1–8. This is the passage that tells us of the mysterious four horsemen of the Apocalypse. There is no consensus in popular theology about the four horsemen, what they stand for, and when and how will they come. But when the prophetic events of Daniel 7 and 8 are interpreted as future history involving Muslim nations, the identity of the four horsemen is unlocked!

Together, these three Bible passages are not telling us about disparate and unrelated things and events. All are describing the same set of events, but from different points of view. Together they describe the set of events that show us the path and seasons until Antichrist comes!

The first passage in Daniel 7 gives us a vision of four beasts. It tells us about *the nations that will be involved* with the coming of the Antichrist. The vision given in Daniel 7 functions as an outline of the end times. In this outline there are four parts—Four Signposts—to occur prior to the Tribulation. The Tribulation itself is the fifth part of the vision.

The second passage in Daniel 8 gives us a vision of a ram and a goat. It tells us *the major events, with more detail, involved* with the coming of the Antichrist. The details given in the vision in Daniel 8 fit within the outline of Daniel 7.

And third, through the horsemen in Revelation 6 we are told about *the conditions to occur* during the rise of the Antichrist. The vision given in Revelation 6:1–8 shows the unsealing, or the releasing, of each of the parts of the outline given in Daniel 7.

Figure 4-1 illustrates the flow of the next several chapters in this book and what they will cover. In the next three chapters we will see in detail why these three prophetic passages apply to today and not to ancient times. And we will see why these passages all qualify as telling us about the times leading to the Antichrist. Then in chapter 8 of this book we will see how the passages fit together to form one framework of events. We will assemble the parts of the three visions piece by piece into a framework of four events. These four events, or Four Signposts, chronicle the emergence of the Antichrist. We will then examine each Signpost in detail in chapters 9 through 12.

As I was exploring this subject, and these Four Signposts began to form from the three visions, I realized that the First Signpost was unfolding in the Middle East right in front of my very eyes! Suddenly I saw the true biblical perspective of the events happening in the Middle East. My own discovery of these matters occurred right at the beginning of the process to democratize Iraq, following the invasion of that country that ousted Saddam Hussein. It happened as the first beast in Daniel 7, the lion, was being forced to stand. Also, my human reaction was to fear for the safety of our troops in Iraq, as I realized the terrible Second Signpost could happen at any time.

Figure 4-1 Subjects structured by book chapter

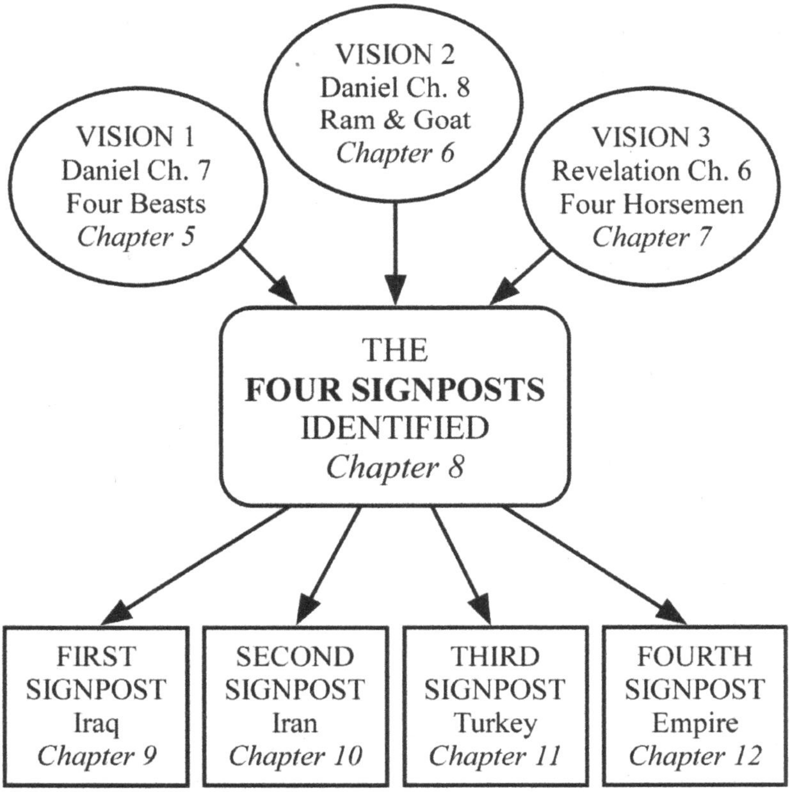

VISION 2
Daniel Ch. 8
Ram & Goat
Chapter 6

VISION 1
Daniel Ch. 7
Four Beasts
Chapter 5

VISION 3
Revelation Ch. 6
Four Horsemen
Chapter 7

THE
FOUR SIGNPOSTS
IDENTIFIED
Chapter 8

FIRST
SIGNPOST
Iraq
Chapter 9

SECOND
SIGNPOST
Iran
Chapter 10

THIRD
SIGNPOST
Turkey
Chapter 11

FOURTH
SIGNPOST
Empire
Chapter 12

I pray that if the material presented here in this book is true, it will encourage and strengthen the saints; that it will show them God has revealed in His Word the events leading up to the Tribulation and that the true significance of these events is not hidden anymore. I pray also that this material provides an opportunity for witness in these last days, and that it shows the Bible written more than two thousand years ago predicts events unfolding before our very eyes and is therefore indeed written by an Intelligence far beyond that of man. And that those who are witnessed to can come to know the Author of these passages, which were provided for His saints in these last days to prepare them for what is shortly to come. In Jesus' name. Amen.

FIVE

THE VISION OF THE FOUR BEASTS

THE FIRST OF THE THREE VISIONS WE WILL EXAMINE IS DANIEL'S vision of four beasts that come out of the sea. As this vision unfolds, it describes a ruler represented as a horn emerging out of the fourth beast. Daniel 7:2–8 relates the vision as follows:

> In my vision at night I looked, and there before me were the four winds of heaven churning up the great sea. Four great beasts, each different from the others, came up out of the sea.
>
> The first was like a lion, and it had the wings of an eagle. I watched until its wings were torn off and it was lifted from the ground so that it stood on two feet like a man, and the heart of a man was given to it.
>
> And there before me was a second beast, which looked like a bear. It was raised up on one of its sides, and it had three ribs in its mouth between its teeth. It was told, "Get up and eat your fill of flesh!"
>
> After that, I looked, and there before me was another beast, one that looked like a leopard. And on its back it had four wings like those of a bird. This beast had four heads, and it was given authority to rule.
>
> After that, in my vision at night I looked, and there before me was a fourth beast—terrifying and frightening and very powerful. It had large iron teeth; it crushed and devoured its victims and trampled

underfoot whatever was left. It was different from all the former beasts, and it had ten horns.

While I was thinking about the horns, there before me was another horn, a little one, which came up among them; and three of the first horns were uprooted before it. This horn had eyes like the eyes of a man and a mouth that spoke boastfully.

In summary, there are four beasts—one like a lion, one like a bear, one like a leopard, and finally a ten-horned beast. The popular theological interpretation of this vision is that the four beasts represent four ancient empires, with the fourth one being ancient Rome. The ten horns represent ten nations that will make up a revived Roman Empire. These four beasts, with the last having ten horns, are viewed as a retelling of the story told by the metal statue in Daniel 2 as a history of the world. What makes the vision of the four beasts different from the metal statue is that the Antichrist makes an appearance as an eleventh horn, the little horn. This interpretation of the vision of the four beasts is consistent with the belief that the Antichrist has to be Roman.

Bible commentators have viewed the first three beasts as the ancient kingdoms of Babylon, Media-Persia, and Greece—showing a progression of empires in history within a couple centuries of Daniel's time. It is thought that since the metals in the statue (gold, silver, etc.) represented empires as they came and left as world history went along, so also the beasts must also be past historical empires. Bible commentators have compared the empires represented by the beasts to the empires represented by the statue in Daniel 2.

The first beast, the lion, is compared to the gold head described in the statue; they are equivalent and are both supposedly ancient Babylon. The second beast, the bear, and the second metal of silver making up the chest go together and are supposedly ancient Persia. The third beast, the four-headed leopard and the bronze belly and thighs are supposedly the ancient Greek kingdom set up by Alexander the Great. And lastly, the terrible fourth beast and the iron legs are equivalent and viewed as ancient Rome. The ten horns of the fourth beast, and the ten toes of the statue each represent the same ten nations that come from Rome, or the ten nations of a revived Roman Empire. So the fourth beast is ancient but the horns are in the end times. The eleventh horn on the fourth beast is the Antichrist, also sprouting out of Rome in the end times.

There are two major problems with this popular interpretation of the vision of the four beasts. The first problem is that if we read Daniel 7 completely and we pay attention to the fate of the four beasts and the details of how the beasts are described, the vision of Daniel 7 should be interpreted as a series of end-time events. It is not a history extending from the time of ancient Babylon to the time of the Antichrist. The distinction of describing centuries of history is reserved for the statue dream in Daniel 2 only.

The second problem, of course, is that the fourth beast is interpreted to be Rome. If the Antichrist is Muslim, as we have evidenced in chapters 1 and 2, and as Joel Richardson shows in his book *The Islamic Antichrist*, then the fourth beast would need to be Islamic—not Roman. However, popular theology does say that the eleventh horn is indeed the Antichrist, and here I agree. So we need to identify what the fourth beast represents to know from which empire the Antichrist comes. Not surprisingly, as we will see, it is Islam.

Let's now look at how Daniel 7 actually describes a series of end-time events only, and not history. Then we will look at the identity of the fourth beast, and finally the identity of all the other beasts.

END-TIME EVENTS—NOT HISTORY

Two passages in Daniel 7 tell us that the vision of the four beasts is a series of end-time events and not history. The first is that the beasts are all contemporaries of the returning Christ, as shown in Daniel 7:8, 11, and 12. The second stems from what the angel told Daniel in Daniel 7:17.

Daniel 7:8 says of the eleventh horn, "This horn had eyes like the eyes of a man and a mouth that spoke boastfully." While that was happening, Daniel 7:9 says that thrones were being set up and that "the Ancient of Days took his seat." The description is one of our Heavenly Father Himself. Daniel 7:10 goes on to say that "the court was seated, and the books were opened." Daniel 7:11 then says, "Then I continued to watch because of the boastful words the horn was speaking. I kept looking until the beast was slain and its body destroyed and thrown into the blazing fire."

Daniel 7:8 and 7:11 say that the little horn is speaking insults, boasts, and blasphemies. This little horn is the Antichrist. While he does these things (see verses 8 and 11), God Himself is setting up court and getting ready to judge. This part of the vision is a picture of God judging the fourth beast with its little horn (the Antichrist) and throwing him (the entire fourth beast, little horn and all) into the lake of fire, upon the return of our King of kings. We know it's at the time of Christ's return because Daniel 7:13–14 says:

> In my vision at night I looked, and there before me was one like a son of man, coming with the clouds of heaven. He approached the Ancient of Days and was led into his presence. He was given authority, glory and sovereign power; all peoples, nations and men of every language worshiped him. His dominion is an everlasting dominion that will not pass away, and his kingdom is one that will never be destroyed.

This is Christ receiving His Kingdom. The beast, the Antichrist himself, is spoken of in the same way in Revelation 19:20 as that of the fourth beast in Daniel 7:11. They are both thrown into a fire, "But the beast was captured, and with him the false prophet . . . The two of them were thrown alive into the fiery lake of burning sulfur" (Rev. 19:20).

The fourth beast in Daniel's vision is to exist at the return of Christ, according to Daniel 7:9–11. It is judged and punished at that time.

The other three beasts are contemporaries of the fourth beast. Daniel 7:12 says of the other beasts, parenthetically, after the fourth beast was thrown into the fire, "(The other beasts had been stripped of their authority, but were allowed to live for a period of time.)"

These three beasts lived just before Christ's return, and were allowed to live for a period of time following the time of Christ's return. So at the time of Christ's return, the fourth beast is judged and thrown into the fire, and the other three are allowed to keep living. This passage cannot be speaking of ancient times. These beasts are in existence at the end times—being allowed to live by the exalted and returning King!

The second reason the vision of the four beasts cannot be considered as history but is applicable to the end times is found in Daniel 7:17. This verse is one of the five unyielding verses of Daniel mentioned in the introduction, which have evaded a proper interpretation. Daniel 7:17 says, "These great beasts, which are four, are four kings, which *shall arise* out of the earth" (KJV, emphasis added). Daniel 7:1 tells us that this vision occurred in the time of the kingdom of Babylon, during the first year of the reign of Belshazzar. Belshazzar was also Babylon's last king according to Daniel 5. So the first beast, the lion with wings, cannot be ancient Babylon as prophecy theologians tell us because the ancient Babylonian Empire was already in existence with its last king reigning at the time Daniel received the vision. Therefore the first beast represents some other king or kingdom that *will* arise in the future relative to Daniel. The text of Daniel 7:17 has been ignored because its true interpretation clashes with the popular idea that the first beast is ancient Babylon.

As to what these beasts are, Daniel 7 says they are both kings and kingdoms. Again, Daniel 7:17 says, "These great *beasts*, which are four, *are four kings*, which shall arise out of the earth" (KJV, emphasis added).

Some translations use the word *kingdom* in place of *king* in Daniel 7:17, but the Aramaic word from which these words are translated is *melek* (Strong's #4430, pronounced meh'-lek) which means "king." The fact that these beasts are kings as well as kingdoms will help us in our identification of what these beasts represent.

However, Daniel 7:23 also says, "The fourth *beast is* a fourth *kingdom* that will appear on earth. It will be different from *all the other kingdoms* and will devour the whole earth, trampling it down and crushing it" (emphasis added).

Since these beasts represent kingdoms, and are contemporaries of each other at the time of the end, these beasts represent modern nations that are involved with or located in the same geographical area as the rise of the Antichrist in the end times. Since we saw in chapter 1 that the Antichrist is Muslim and rising out of Islam, and in chapter 2 that he is Arab, then these nations must be Muslim nations located in or near the Middle East.

THE IDENTITY OF THE FOURTH BEAST

The first three beasts are compared to a lion, a bear, and a leopard—all predators. The beast that is like a leopard has four heads. In prophecy, heads represent government or political authority. These three beasts have a total of six heads between them, and so they represent six modern nations in the Middle East.

I will show later why these beasts are identified with the nations they represent. It is not because of national symbolism. It is because their behavior in each of the vision's unfolding events matches the behavior and properties of each type of beast in nature. While the three first beasts represent contemporary political Middle Eastern nations, the fourth beast is different. About the fourth beast Daniel 7:19 says, "Then I wanted to know the true meaning of the fourth beast, which was *different* from all the others and most terrifying, with its iron teeth and bronze claws—the beast that *crushed* and devoured its victims and *trampled* underfoot whatever was left" (emphasis added).

The word used for *crushed* is the same used to describe the iron legs in the statue in Daniel 2:40 meaning "break into pieces" (*dqaq*, Strong's #1855). It involves pulverizing whatever Islam seizes until nothing recognizable is left, just as we discussed in chapter 1. This breaking in pieces sounds just like what the Empire of Iron did to the other empires in Daniel 2, doesn't it? Even popular theology says that the empire of the iron legs in the statue and this fourth beast are the same, due to the common descriptions used in the Bible to describe them. Popular theology, though, argues that they represent Rome.

Our discussion in chapter 1 about how Islam operates on each tribe and nation it conquers suggests to us that each people group is basically a victim of Islam. It's just as Wafa Sultan wrote in her book, "Islam subjugated all the peoples it afflicted."[1] Islam breaks its victims into pieces just as Daniel 7:19 says the terrible beast does. In history Islam crushed its Babylonian victims, Persian victims, Greek victims, and Egyptian victims and many others as well. Islam will also break into pieces and trample whatever other people groups it manages to subjugate in the end times. The fourth beast is the Islamic Realm.

Where the first three beasts are kingdoms or nations, the fourth beast is *different* as Daniel 7:19 says. Notice that where the first three beasts are described as being "like a lion" or "like a bear," this fourth beast has no such description. The fourth beast has no counterpart in nature. Daniel describes its features and its actions because there is no beast to compare it to. This beast is *terrifying*. What makes this beast different is that it is not just a political sovereign nation. This fourth beast is a religious-political system—it is Islam. Islam does not conquer for national pride or power, but conquers in the name of religion and of their God, Allah. It has been tenacious in its advances and holding on to land. We saw in some detail in chapter 1 how Islam converted a nation's citizenry to another religion and another language. It also changed a people's morals through its written code.

THE OTHER BEASTS IDENTIFIED

So we know the identity of the fourth beast: it is the Islamic Realm. And the fourth beast's head is also Islam. We must now determine the identity of the first three beasts with a total of six heads representing six modern nations. Wonderfully, God has given us key passages that help us identify these countries. We turn for help to three different chapters all in Revelation. A vision of John that begins in Revelation 12 and extends to Revelation 13:1–2 contains elements that are similar to the beasts in Daniel 7. A second vision of John is related to the topic, and is revealed in Revelation 17.

In Revelation 12 we have a vision of a huge red dragon with seven heads, which represents Satan. This dragon confronts a woman who is about to give birth, in order to devour her child as soon as he is born. To understand this vision we must take a step back and remember some things. The theme of the Bible is God's plan of salvation for fallen mankind. Israel and the Jews are of course an integral part of this plan. The Bible is a story of the plan of salvation, and it is also a history of civilization—from its beginning to its prophesied end—but only in relation to Israel and God's plan of salvation. God entrusted Israel as the one nation to keep His Word and to be the nation from whom the Messiah would come.

Since the time of the Garden of Eden, Satan has devoted himself to ruining God's plan for the salvation of the human race. He doesn't want humans to enjoy the forgiveness of sins provided by the sacrifice of Christ on the cross, nor to enjoy communion with God. So Satan has done everything he can to destroy the nation (Israel) and the people (the Jews) through whom God's Son would come. He even tried to destroy Christ Himself. Now after Christ has completed His work and has ascended to heaven, Satan continues to try to destroy the Jews and Christians to somehow prevent the second appearance of Christ.

Revelation 12 is a picture of Satan's attempt to destroy Israel, the Messiah, and Christians. Satan is portrayed as "an enormous red dragon with seven heads and ten horns and seven crowns on his heads" (Rev. 12:3). The head represents authority or government, so Satan has had a sevenfold governing authority on earth, and has ruled from seven significant places. The crowns represent rulers. Horns represent power. It is written of the dragon in Revelation 12:4, "The dragon stood in front of the woman who was about to give birth, so that he might devour her child the moment it was born."

In human history, the dragon has used its authority from these seven places via its seven heads to try to kill the woman, Israel, and devour the male child, the Savior. Verse five confirms for us that the child is Jesus Christ, "She gave birth to a son, a male child, who will rule all the nations with an iron scepter. And her child was snatched up to God and to his throne."

These verses form a brief summary of "Israel-centric" world history. So it was Satan, using these empires, who sought to devour and destroy the male child through one means or another. But as the Bible tells us in Revelation 12, Satan could not destroy the woman, Israel. The dragon with its heads also tried to kill the Messiah (Rev. 12:4–5), but failed. In the end times he will make war on all the saints—those who are the offspring of the woman and are the brothers and sisters of Christ. Revelation 12:17 says, "Then the dragon was enraged at the woman and went off to make war against the rest of her offspring—those who obey God's commandments and hold to the testimony of Jesus."

To make war on the saints, the dragon stands by the sea and waits for a seven-headed beast to come out of the sea. Of the beast coming out of the sea, Revelation 13:1–2 says, "He had ten horns and seven heads, with ten crowns on his horns, and on each head a blasphemous name. The beast I saw resembled a leopard, but had feet like those of a bear and a mouth like that of a lion."

It's as if this is Satan's secret weapon. He could not destroy the woman or the male child from his seven places of authority over many centuries, so his hope during the end times seems to be in this new beast. Notice the similarities between this new beast and the beasts of Daniel 7! This new beast resembles a leopard (the third beast in Daniel). It has a mouth like a lion and feet like a bear (the first and second beasts in Daniel). It even comes out of the sea like the other beasts. This new beast has ten horns like the fourth beast in Daniel. This new beast has seven heads, and there are seven heads among the four beasts in Daniel. Therefore, this new beast is simply a combination of the beasts in Daniel 7—leopard, bear, lion, seven heads, and ten horns.

The key to understanding which modern nations the heads represent on the four beasts in Daniel 7 is to watch the relationship between the dragon, this new beast, and the four beasts. This new beast is the link between the four beasts of Daniel 7 and the dragon. In addition to being an amalgamation of the four beasts, this new, seven-headed beast is also a reflection of the dragon. Look at the descriptions of both the new beast and the dragon. The dragon has seven heads; the new beast has seven heads. They both have ten horns.

(Regarding the placement of the horns, the passage in Revelation 12 does not say from which head(s) the ten horns emerge. But for the seven-headed beast to be a combination of the four beasts of Daniel 7 would suggest that all ten horns come out of only one head of the seven-headed beast, since only the fourth beast in Daniel 7 had the horns. Therefore the ten horns of the dragon would most likely come out of only one head of the dragon as well.)

So we can see that since the dragon is a reflection of the new beast, which in turn is an amalgamation of the four beasts of Daniel 7, it would be reasonable to say that the dragon is somehow related to the four beasts. The relationship is that the dragon's heads represent seven ancient kingdoms and the heads of the beasts of Daniel 7 represent the end-times versions, or inheritors, of each of those same ancient kingdoms. The ancient heads of the dragon are a reflection of the end-times heads of the new beast, which in turn are an amalgamation of the four beasts in Daniel 7. We will see further proof of this concept in this chapter. If we can identify the ancient nations of the dragon, we can identify the end-times nations of the four beasts.

One notable difference between the dragon and the beast is that the crowns have moved from the seven heads on the dragon to the ten horns on the beast. This is significant. The dragon's heads having the seven crowns means that in past history Satan attempted to destroy the woman using seven leaders or kings in seven political places that were historical empires around Israel. Satan tried to devour the woman with each of the seven heads.

The rulers of each of those heads did things to Israel spanning from the time of the Israelites' bondage in Egypt to the time of the independence of the State of Israel in 1948. Satan tried to destroy the woman Israel and God's plan of salvation from his seven political places. But in the end times, the crowns will have been moved from the seven heads to the ten horns of the new beast; they are the ten end times kingdoms and rulers. The rulers of the ten nations will pick up the mantle of the historical seven as the new persecutors of the saints in the end times, and rule with the Antichrist. As we will see in the chapters ahead, the ten end times nations of the ten horns are different from the seven end time nations of the four beasts.

This beast coming out of the sea, which commentators agree represents the Antichrist and/or the Antichrist's kingdom, is described further in Revelation 17. There we find a picture of the same beast as the one in Revelation 13:1–2, being ridden by a woman named Mystery Babylon. I am not going to go into a discussion of Mystery Babylon or who she is. We will instead discuss the beast she is riding. An angel tells John in Revelation 17:9, "Here is the mind which has wisdom. The seven heads are seven mountains on which the woman sits" (NASB).

Some translations of the Bible use the word *hills* instead of mountain*s*. Here is a case where presupposition on the part of the Bible translators gets in the way. There is a long-standing Protestant tradition that says the Catholic Church, based in Rome, is Mystery Babylon. The city of Rome was built on seven hills, and so some people use Revelation 17:9 to argue that the Roman Catholic Church in Rome must be Mystery Babylon.

But the word used for *hill* in some translations, is the Greek word *oros* (Strong's #3735, pronounced with a short o, as in *shot*). *Oros* occurs over sixty times in the New Testament and is always translated "mount" or "mountain." Yet here in this verse it is "hill." If it were hill, then the other verses containing *oros* would mention the "Hill of Olives," "Zion Hill" and "Sinai Hill." This doesn't work. The proper translation of *oros* is "mountain." The NASB and NKJV translate it correctly here as "mountain."

So, in Revelation 17:9, the seven heads are seven mountains. This is significant to understanding prophecy. But what is a "mountain"? In Jeremiah 51:24–25, the Babylonian kingdom or empire is called a mountain.

> "Before your eyes I will repay Babylon and all who live in Babylonia for all the wrong they have done in Zion," declares the LORD. "I am against you, O destroying *mountain*, you who destroy the whole earth," declares the LORD. "I will stretch out my hand against you, roll you off the cliffs, and make you a burned-out *mountain*." (emphasis added)

Why would God call an empire a mountain? Perhaps it can be thought of in the following way. All of human culture, human population, nations, and human achievement can be thought of as spread out in historical time and world geography over a large representative landmass, like a continent. The height of achievement or the density of population or richness of culture in each nation or people group would analogously result in the formation of a plain, or a hill, or a mountain on this continent. Scarcity of human population and achievement would result in a plain. Single nations might form single hills. Just as some nations make more of an impact in history than others, so some hills are bigger and higher than others. But empires—those entities that gather together and unite several nations usually by military conquest—have had the greatest influence in art, literature, and technologies. These are the mountains. Empires have also supported the greatest human populations.

A second passage in the Bible specifically mentions a mountain to refer to a kingdom. Remember the statue in Daniel 2, and how a stone from heaven struck the statue? The stone grew until it became a great mountain (Daniel 2:35) that filled the whole earth. How can a mountain "fill the earth"? This is a picture of Christ's millennial kingdom being the greatest empire in human history in terms of population, achievement, and fruit, because Christ will rule it. The mountain of Christ's kingdom will be the highest and largest mountain, and it will cover the entire earth.

So we can say that the seven heads of the beast, which are mountains, are world empires in past history. These empires reflect the heads of the red dragon as well. We can identify the empires in history represented by the seven heads of the dragon by identifying the empires that attempted to attack the woman Israel and her male child. Since the end-times beast with seven heads is a reflection of the dragon, and is a unification of the four beasts in Daniel 7 which are end time nations, then the identities of the nations of the first three beasts in Daniel 7 are merely the present-day equivalents of each of six of the empires of the dragon. We know the seventh head of the dragon is Islam because it reflects the head of the fourth beast in Daniel, which is also Islam. Once we identify all seven historical empires that tried to destroy the Jews, we can, with some understanding of history, identify the modern nations represented by the beasts in Daniel 7.

If that isn't enough for identification, we are given even more information in God's Word. There is a cheat sheet of sorts in Revelation where the angel continues to tell John about the identity of the heads and mountains. Revelation 17:10 says, "They are also seven kings. Five have fallen, one is, the other has not yet come; but when he does come, he must remain for only a little while."

Look at that! At the time John wrote Revelation in AD 96, the Roman Empire was the current head in history, the current mountain, and the current king. So we instantly know the identity of the sixth historical empire, and the sixth head of the dragon. But there is still more to discover about the true end times identity of the sixth head, as well as all the heads. We know that five empires must precede Rome and one empire must follow Rome—all of these are in history and are heads of the dragon. On a side note, the fact that these mountains are also kings shouldn't surprise us. We saw earlier how the four beasts in Daniel 7:17 are also kings.

This combined seven-headed end times beast itself is further described by the angel in Revelation 17:11–12.

> The beast who once was, and now is not, is an eighth king. He belongs
> to the seven and is going to his destruction. The ten horns you saw are
> ten kings who have not yet received a kingdom, but who for one hour
> will receive authority as kings along with the beast.

The beast out of the sea in the end times, described in Revelation 13:1–2, is the eighth empire, occurring after the seven empires of history run their course. The beast belongs to the seven heads because it will be made up of the seven heads. In other words, the Antichrist's kingdom in the end times will be an eighth kingdom following in history the seven that it has combined. We will discuss in chapter 12 what nations and areas the Antichrist's end-time empire might include.

THE IDENTITIES OF THE SEVEN ANCIENT DRAGON HEADS AND END-TIME BEAST HEADS

We will now review and identify the historical empires represented by the seven heads of the dragon. In parallel, we will also identify the modern nations represented by each of the heads of the beasts in Daniel 7. A look at real world history from the Bible's perspective reveals the identity of six of the empires that existed in the past. All of the heads of the dragon attempted to destroy the woman and devour the male child. Therefore the dragon's heads in history tried to do one or more of the following:

(1) wipe out the Jews;
(2) remove or keep them from their land;
(3) destroy their holy city and holy place of worship;
(4) destroy their religion or their faith.

The first attempt by the red dragon to destroy the Jews was from the ancient Egyptian Empire. In figure 5-1, you can see the location of Egypt marked by the numeral 1 on the map, next to the land of Israel (the small area of dark gray). The area with vertical hatch lines is Egypt at its greatest extent, which included the land of Israel. During this time the Hebrews were in bondage in Egypt as told in the book of Exodus. In the fifteenth century BC, Egypt controlled the Holy Land. At that time Pharaoh gave the order to kill the newborn male children as they were born (Ex. 1:15–22). The woman, Israel, had just become a new nation—growing from twelve brothers to a nation of millions. The dragon was already attempting to kill the male child using his authority in Egypt. But God delivered the Hebrews from this calamity using Moses. The red dragon's first head did not get its target. Satan was stopped the first time. The modern equivalent of this empire, which has a role to play in Daniel's vision of the four beasts, is the present-day nation of Egypt.

Figure 5-1. The Egyptian Empire before the Exodus (1450 BC)

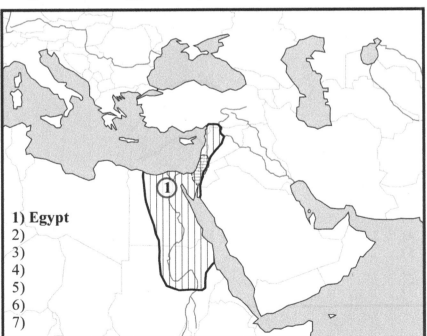

1) **Egypt**
2)
3)
4)
5)
6)
7)

The second empire from which Satan ruled and attempted to destroy Israel was the Assyrian Empire. In figure 5-2, the capital of Assyria, Nineveh, is marked with a numeral 2. The area with the vertical hatch lines shows the greatest extent of the Assyrian Empire. It was Assyria that destroyed the northern kingdom of Israel (2 Kings 17:1–23), and scattered its people. Assyria even whittled away at the southern kingdom of Judah, but could not conquer it because of God's intervention. The dragon was attempting to destroy the woman, but could not quite complete the task from his place of authority in Assyria. God delivered Judah from the Assyrians (2 Kings 19). The red dragon's second head did not get its target. Satan was thwarted a second time. The modern equivalent of this empire, which has a role to play in Daniel's vision of the four beasts, is the nation of Syria.

Figure 5-2. The Assyrian Empire (722 BC)

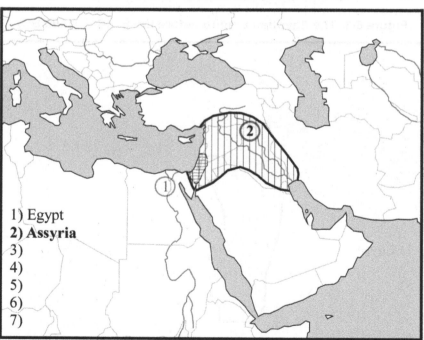

1) Egypt
2) Assyria
3)
4)
5)
6)
7)

The third empire from which Satan ruled and tried to destroy the Jews was the Babylonian Empire. In figure 5-3, the city of Babylon is marked with a numeral 3. It was King Nebuchadnezzar, allowed by God, who destroyed Jerusalem and Solomon's temple and took the Jews into captivity (2 Kings 24, 25). A remnant was saved, however, and they eventually returned to the land and the city and reestablished themselves. The red dragon's third head was not able to devour the woman, though Israel's land and city were conquered. Satan was stopped a third time. The modern equivalent of this empire, which has a role to play in Daniel's vision of the four beasts, is the nation of Iraq.

Figure 5-3. The Babylonian Empire (606 BC)

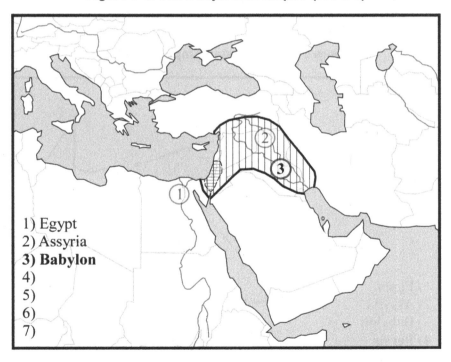

1) Egypt
2) Assyria
3) Babylon
4)
5)
6)
7)

The fourth empire to conquer the Holy Land and attempt to destroy the Jews was that of the Medes and Persians. In figure 5-4, the capital city is labeled with a numeral 4. Cyrus, king of Persia, allowed the Jews to go back to Jerusalem and rebuild their city. For the most part, the Jews lived unhindered throughout the empire. However, at one point, a man within the government, Haman, manipulated the empire's legal system to try to destroy all Jews, and take their possessions (Esther 3:5–15). God prevented this using Queen Esther (Esther 8–9). The red dragon's fourth head was not able to devour the woman either. Persia was the first of the seven empires to conquer all the other empires that existed before it, as you can see in the map in figure 5-4. The modern equivalent of this empire that has a role to play in Daniel's vision of the four beasts in the end times is the nation of Iran.

Figure 5-4. The Persian Empire (500 BC)

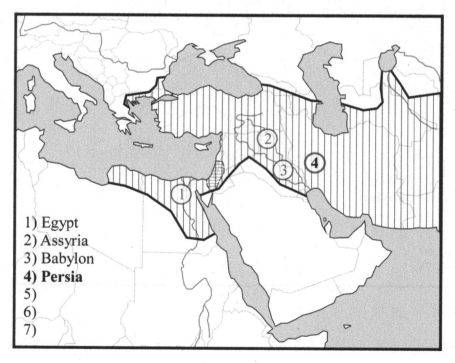

1) Egypt
2) Assyria
3) Babylon
4) Persia
5)
6)
7)

The fifth empire used by Satan to try to destroy the Jews was that of the Greeks. Alexander the Great conquered the Persian Empire and went all the way to India. Alexander's capital city in ancient Macedonia is near the place marked with a numeral 5 in figure 5-5, and the map shows the extent of Alexander's Greek Empire. Like Persia, Greece also conquered all the other empires before it. After ruling only twelve years, though, Alexander died and his empire was carved up into four kingdoms centered around Macedonia, western Turkey and Thrace, Egypt, and Syria. One of Alexander's generals, Seleucus, took control of the fourth piece of the empire that extended from eastern Turkey and Syria out to Afghanistan. He founded the Seleucid Dynasty as Seleucus I Nicator, and made his capital at Antioch. The territory of the Seleucid Empire is shown in figure 5-5.

**Figure 5-5. The Greek Empire (323 BC)
and Seleucid Empire (200 BC)**

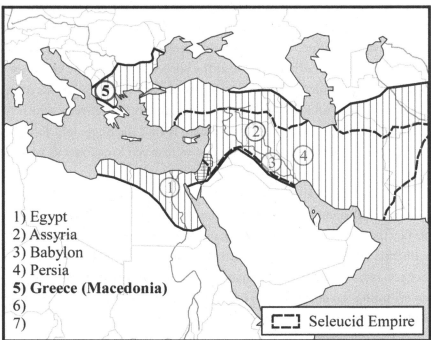

1) Egypt
2) Assyria
3) Babylon
4) Persia
5) Greece (Macedonia)
6)
7)

Seleucid Empire

For the most part, the Jews were allowed to practice their beliefs while in the Greek realm. However, one of the kings of the Seleucid Dynasty, Antiochus IV, thought himself a god and desecrated the Jewish temple and tried to destroy the Jewish faith. This period of time is written of extensively in book 1 of *The War of the Jews* by Josephus, the Jewish historian, and is prophesied in Daniel 11:2–35. Many consider Antiochus IV to be a prototype or foreshadowing of the end-time Antichrist himself. The dragon's fifth head, though it greatly persecuted the Jewish people, was not able to devour the woman either. Copies of the Old Testament were burned, and worship at the temple ceased, yet the Jewish people and faith survived. A Jewish army managed to successfully rebel and end the occupation. The leaders of this Jewish movement were known as the Maccabees.

The modern equivalent of this empire, which has a role to play in Daniel's vision of the four beasts, requires some explanation. For the first four empires, it has been fairly obvious what the modern equivalent nation is. We could use Antiochus IV's capital, Antioch, to find the modern equivalent nation. But that would result in the nation being either Syria or Turkey, since that city is near the border between those two countries. However, both of those countries are already taken (Syria was from the second head and we will get to the explanation for Turkey, which is the sixth head, in a bit). The answer here is that the angel told John in Revelation 17 that the seven mountains were seven kingdoms as well as seven kings.

We have used capital cities of the empires up to now to identify the modern equivalent nations. And in the four kingdoms we have reviewed so far, the kings have been natives of the kingdoms they ruled. Not so with this fifth kingdom. This fifth kingdom covered the areas of the eastern two-thirds of the Persian Empire, as shown in figure 5-5. By determining the ethnic origin of the king, Antiochus IV, rather than by looking at the empire he ruled, we will find the fifth modern equivalent nation. Antiochus IV was of the fifth generation following the founder Seleucus I—a great-great-great-grandson. And the founder of the ruling dynasty, Seleucus, came from the region of Macedonia (which is marked with a 5 in figure 5-5), which is far outside of the empire he founded.

We will use the map in figure 5-6 to help illustrate the investigation into finding Seleucus', and therefore Antiochus IV's, roots. Figure 5-6 shows a map of the region of the present-day nations of Greece, Macedonia, and Albania. The map also shows as an overlay, three ancient kingdoms that emerged in the area during the time of Seleucus' father (about 350 BC): Macedonia, Epirus, and Illyria. To understand where exactly Seleucus' family came from and how it relates to the modern nations in the area today requires some explanation.

First we must understand the ethnicity of the three ancient kingdoms. Prior to the birth of classical Greek civilization, which occurred around 800 BC, Pelasgian tribes inhabited the entire southern Balkan Peninsula.[2] In the area of what is now southern Greece, where cities like Athens and Sparta arose, waves of invasion and migration by people like the Dorians mixed with the native Pelasgians and gave rise to Greek culture and civilization.[3] The Pelasgian tribes further north never mixed with the southern invaders. The ancient kingdoms of Macedonia and Epirus emerged from these northern Pelasgian tribes. Extending further northwest, in what was Yugoslavia, were the Illyrian tribes who were also descended from the Pelasgians.[4] The kingdom of Illyria arose among the southernmost of the Illyrian tribes, in the area of what is now central and northern Albania. These kingdoms of Macedonia, Epirus, and Illyria are shown in figure 5-6.

Now that we have a general background of the ancient kingdoms involved, let's now look at Seleucus and his origins. The founder of the Seleucid Empire, Seleucus, was a commander and general in the army of Alexander the Great. It was Alexander's generals who carved up his empire after Alexander's untimely death in 323 BC. From the information

Figure 5-6. The Three Ancient Kingdoms in the days of Phillip II of Macedonia, and modern Albania

available we know that Seleucus' father was a man named Antiochus.[5] Antiochus was a commander in the army of King Philip II of Macedonia, who was Alexander the Great's father.[6] Shown in figure 5-6 at the west end of the kingdom of Macedonia are three mountainous tribal areas:

Lynkestis, Orestis, and Tymphaia. The Macedonian kings prior to Philip II ruled Lower Macedonia in the lowlands by the coast. The three tribal areas were part of Upper Macedonia, and were independent and ruled by their own tribal kings.[7] King Philip II was the first Macedonian king to conquer and unite these tribal areas with lower Macedonia.[8] The Macedonian kingdom shown in figure 5-6 includes the conquests by Philip II.

Typically, during Philip II's reign, army commanders came from the ruling families in these tribal areas.[9] Antiochus had come from an important family and served in the army as a commander, and so it is believed Antiochus came from one of these three tribes.[10] So now let's take a closer look at these three tribes.

Shown in figure 5-6, Lynkestis was united for many years with the Illyrian tribes to the north, prior to Philip II's conquest.[11] After Philip II conquered them, they were then associated with the Macedonians. If Antiochus were from Lynkestis, he would have been Illyrian or Macedonian.

The second tribal area, Orestis, was an independent tribal state of Molossian descent prior to Philip II.[12] The neighboring kingdom of Epirus was ruled by the Molossians. If Antiochus were from Orestis, he would have been Molossian (from Epirus) or Macedonian. One additional fact that lends support for Antiochus being from Orestis is that a few of the kings of Orestis were also named Antiochus.[13]

The third tribal area was Tymphaia. Tymphaia was, like Orestis, an independent tribe related to the Molossians before being conquered by Philip II.[14] Thus Antiochus would have been Molossian or Macedonian if he were from Tymphaia.

So, in summary, Antiochus was either Illyrian, Molossian (from Epirus), or Macedonian. So his son Seleucus, and also his descendent Antiochus IV, would have also been Illyrian, Molossian, or Macedonian. Now we will look at the descendents of these three tribal peoples in the order listed.

The descendents of the Illyrians today are the Albanians. Edwin Jacques wrote of the Albanian people in his history of Albania:

> With no record or tradition even hinting at their extermination or assimilation or migration, one can only assume their unbroken historical continuity. There seems to be no question but that the present-day Albanians are the historically uninterrupted descendants of the Illyrians who were known to have inhabited that same region in early Greek and Roman times.[15]

The Illyrian homeland originally covered the entire western half of the Balkan Peninsula, including former Yugoslavia and present-day Albania. The Slavs from the north, who began their migrations and invasions of the Balkan Peninsula in the sixth century AD, eventually took over all Illyrian lands except those in present-day Albania. It is thought that due to the difficult mountainous terrain of Albania, the Illyrians there were never displaced.[16] This is in agreement with Jacques' position that the Illyrians are in fact, today's Albanians.

The descendents of the Molossians, or Epirotes, are divided. Figure 5-6 shows this general division. The southern Molossians live in Greece. The northern Molossians live in Albania.

The descendents of the Macedonians live in two countries as well, as shown in figure 5-6. The descendents of those who lived in lower Macedonia near the coast are now part of the present-day nation of Greece. The northern Macedonians became mixed with the same Slav invaders who displaced the Illyrians. Those descendents live in the present-day country of Macedonia. Incidentally, when Macedonia received its independence from Yugoslavia in 1991, it could not be admitted to the United Nations until its name was resolved. Greece objected to it being named Macedonia because it believed it alone had true Macedonians. It insisted that its name be changed to the Former

Yugoslav Republic of Macedonia, due to the distinction that those people were also Slav.

We have now seen why the three present-day nations of Greece, Macedonia, and Albania, as shown in figure 5-6, are the candidate nations for the fifth head. These nations are the home to the descendents of the three tribes, one of which is the place of origin of Antiochus and his son Seleucus. We don't know with certainty from which tribe Antiochus originated. To finally determine which nation of the three is the true candidate, recall from earlier discussions that the nations of the seven heads are Muslim. We will now look at each of the three nations as they exist today: Greece, Macedonia, and Albania.

Greece is traditionally a Christian nation. Though it was occupied for five centuries by the Islamic Ottoman Empire, the people held on to their Christian faith. So Greece is not the final candidate.

The present-day nation of Macedonia is also Christian, but 30 percent of its population is Muslim. However this Muslim community is made up of ethnically Albanian people, who happen to live in Macedonia. Since Macedonia is also Christian, the final candidate cannot be Macedonia either. This leads us to the third nation, Albania.

The only ethnic group in all of the southern Balkan Peninsula that has an overwhelmingly large majority of Muslims is the Albanians. We now have a likely candidate for the fifth modern nation. In summary, this means Antiochus IV, descended from a man named Antiochus six generations prior, was most likely from the tribe of Orestis or Lynkestis. So he was either of the Illyrian people, or northern Molossian people, both of whom have descendants living in Albania. And, of all the nations in the region, Albania is the only one that is Muslim.

The Albanians were Christian before the Ottoman Turks invaded the area in 1481. When the Ottomans retreated in 1912, 70 percent of the Albanian population was Muslim.[17] As I mentioned before in chapter 1 regarding resistance to Islam, if a people have a strong cultural or religious identity, they will resist for a time the conversion to Islam. Of all the Balkan nationalities only the Albanians did not have a singular religious identity.[18] Greece, Romania, and Serbia were Orthodox. Croatia and Dalmatia were Roman Catholic. None of these people groups today are Muslim despite being occupied by the Islamic Ottoman Turks for up to four centuries.

Many in Europe and the United States look upon Albania as a poor, backward, small nation in the southeast corner of Europe. But this state of affairs may be changing for Albania today. Albania was occupied by the Axis powers during World War II. Albania was then taken over by a Communist government in 1944 that officially denied and repressed Islam. The Communists lost power in an election in 1992. Since 1992 Albania has sought ties with, and investment from, the outside world. And since the fall of communism, Islam is resurgent in Albania and its surrounding countries. During the last twenty years, Kosovo (which is 90 percent Muslim) and the Republic of Macedonia became independent following the breakup of Yugoslavia. These developments have allowed the Muslim Albanians to express their faith and to better their situation, having thrown off the yoke of Yugoslavia. Starting in 1990 Turkey began renovating the old Ottoman mosques in Albania and investing in the country.[19] Money from the Wahhabis of Saudi Arabia and the Moroccans began to flow into Kosovo around 2000 for religious funding and the building of mosques.[20] In neighboring Macedonia where the Albanians make up 30 percent of the population, Muslim Albanians account for eighty-nine of one hundred births.[21] This, of course, threatens to overwhelm Macedonia's Christian population in the not too distant future. It is possible that Albania could enlarge in the future to include Albanians living in other territories such as Kosovo, but we will simply assume it is the nation of Albania as it exists today.

All of these unfolding events and trends in Albania may very well result in an Albania that is engaged with the remainder of the Muslim world. These developments, as well as the ties that are developing with Turkey and Saudi Arabia, will help ready that nation for its future role as discussed in chapter 11. In summary then, the modern equivalent of the fifth head, due to the ethnic heritage of its king Antiochus IV, is the nation of Albania. As a side note in chapter 1, I said we should be watching the nations of the Middle East instead of those in Europe, but Albania is the exception.

We have now seen the five empires that ruled and fell before the time of John, and have identified the five modern Muslim nations that correspond to them. To recap, the five modern Muslim nations we have identified are Egypt, Syria, Iraq, Iran, and Albania.

Empire number six, which was the empire in existence during John's time, was obviously the Roman Empire. As was the case with empire five, identifying the modern nation corresponding with empire six is also going to be a bit tricky. The Roman Empire existed over a time span that is longer than many of us may realize. It existed from Augustus Caesar's time in 27 BC to the fall of Constantinople in AD 1453. Figure 5-7 shows the extent of the Roman Empire in AD 330. At that time the empire was divided into the Eastern and Western Roman Empires. The numeral 6 is located at the two capitals: Rome the capital of the west, and Constantinople the capital of the east. Emperor Constantine called his new capital *Nova Roma*, "New Rome," but it was popularly known as Constantinople.

The arrow shown in figure 5-7 shows the seat of Roman government moving from the old Rome to the "new Rome." By the fifth century AD, the city of Constantinople eclipsed the city of Rome politically and commercially as the center of the Roman Empire. After the sack of Rome in AD 476, Constantinople became the only capital of the Roman Empire.

The Roman Empire put down a rebellion of the Jews in AD 70. The result was that Jerusalem and the temple were destroyed as prophesied in Daniel 9:27 and more than one million Jews were enslaved or killed.

The Jews revolted again in AD 132, and three years later that was also put down. Almost 600,000 Jews were killed at that time. Emperor Hadrian forbade circumcision and observances of the Sabbath and other Jewish feast days. Aelia Capitolina was built on the site of Jerusalem. Jews were forbidden from entering the city except for one day a year.[22] But this was not all that the sixth head of the red dragon had in store for Israel.

Figure 5-7. The Roman Empire and its division (AD 330)

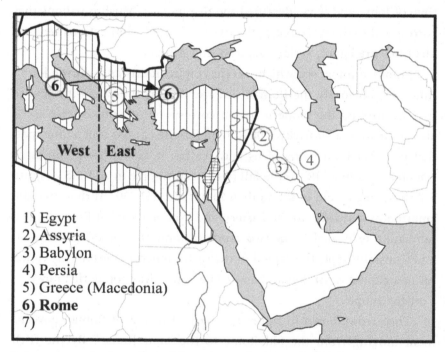

1) Egypt
2) Assyria
3) Babylon
4) Persia
5) Greece (Macedonia)
6) Rome
7)

It is commonly thought in Western civilization that the Roman Empire ended in AD 476. That was the year that Rome was sacked and the last emperor of the Western Roman Empire was deposed. But it was just the western half of the empire that ended. The eastern half continued for another millennium. Edward Gibbon, the author of the landmark work *The Decline and Fall of the Roman Empire*, didn't think the Roman

Empire ended in AD 476 since he called the event, "The Fall of the Roman Empire in the West."[23] Gibbon's book is only half finished at the fall of the Roman Empire in the west. His book *The Decline and Fall of the Roman Empire* doesn't end until the fall of the Roman Empire in the east in AD 1453. Editor D. M. Low wrote in his introduction to Gibbon's book:

> When therefore in 1453 the conqueror Mahomet II rode into Constantinople not merely had that city fallen; the Roman Empire, which may be conveniently dated from 27 B.C., had at last come to total extinction.[24]

Will Durant wrote in his work, *The Age of Faith*, of the Eastern Roman Empire:

> For a thousand years the Roman Empire would here survive the barbarian floods that were to inundate Rome.[25]

And of the people in the capital Constantinople, Will Durant also wrote:

> The population of the city was mainly Roman at the top, and for the rest overwhelmingly Greek. All alike called themselves Roman.[26]

Do not let there be any doubt that the empire that continued on for a millennium beyond AD 476 with its capital at Constantinople was the Roman Empire. The Eastern Roman Empire was called the Byzantine Empire only after it fell. Even the Muslims called them the Romans.

After AD 476 the Roman Empire continued at times the persecution of the Jews that started horrifically in AD 70. Instead of pagan Rome persecuting them, it was a supposedly Christian Rome. In the

seventh century AD, Emperor Heraclius did all he could to extermi-
nate the Jews.[27] Emperor Basil I in the ninth century AD tried to force
Christian baptism on the Jews.[28] Finally, after the ninth century the
persecutions of the Jews from the sixth head of the dragon began to
taper off. The sixth head of the dragon tried for at least eight hundred years to destroy the Jews. Jerusalem was taken, the temple was
destroyed, and the land of Israel was made desolate. But the Jews with
their faith lived on, scattered among the nations.

So what nation is the modern inheritor of the Roman Empire? This
is relatively straightforward if one takes into account that the empire's
final capital was at Constantinople. The Roman Empire centered at
Constantinople continued its persecution of the Jews far longer than
the Roman Empire centered at Rome. Constantinople was then conquered by the Ottoman Empire and renamed Istanbul when it became
the Ottomans' capital city. After the fall of the Ottoman Empire in
the early twentieth century, the nation was reorganized as the modern
state of Turkey. The modern nation that includes Istanbul is Turkey.
Therefore, the modern equivalent of the sixth head of the dragon is
Turkey.

This now leads us to the seventh empire that came after the time of
John. It ruled over the Holy Land from AD 638 to 1948. It is the seventh
head of the dragon and the seventh head of the beast. It is also an empire
that has attempted to destroy the woman, Israel. We saw in chapter 1 of
this book that the seventh empire is Islam.

Figure 5-8 shows the extent of the Islamic Realm at the height of the
Ottoman Empire. The Ottomans ruled from the place marked on the
map with a numeral 6, but the original seat of the Islamic Realm from
the time of Muhammad is in Mecca, marked with a 7. I use the time of
the Ottoman Empire in the map simply to show the extent of Islam into
Europe, but any of the major Islamic Empires could have been pictured
to show the general size of the realm of Islam.

Figure 5-8. The Islamic Realm at the time of the Ottomans (AD 1680)

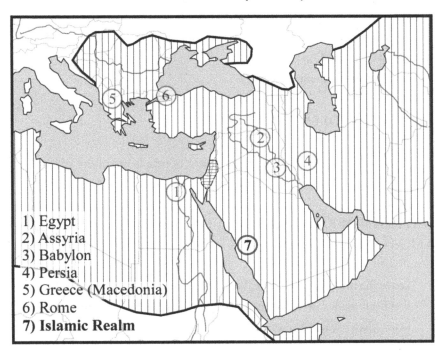

1) Egypt
2) Assyria
3) Babylon
4) Persia
5) Greece (Macedonia)
6) Rome
7) **Islamic Realm**

This seventh empire's actions toward Israel represent a change in strategy on the part of Satan. After Christ came and completed His work on the cross and rose again, salvation was done. As our Lord so rightly said, "It is finished" (John 19:30). So after Christ, Satan had to change his strategy from killing Jews in an effort to prevent Christ from coming to one of "damage control" and attempting to prevent His return. The

Roman Empire over the centuries destroyed the city of Jerusalem and the temple, dispersed the Jews, and tried to stamp out their faith. Islam would pick up where Rome left off. So how did the Islamic Realm attempt to destroy the Jewish nation or prevent the return of Christ?

In summarizing fourteen centuries of history of the Islamic Realm's treatment of the Jews, we must start with the writings of Islam. We saw in chapter 1 that the way Islam is set up caused it to break the older empires into pieces. Similarly, the way Islam is set up causes much of the persecution of the Jews within the Islamic Realm. Islam's writings say several things about the Jews. We will look at some verses from Islam's own holy text, the Qur'an.

Islamic writing says:

JEWS ARE VIOLENT:

> Thou wilt certainly find the most violent of people in enmity against the believers [i.e. Muslims] to be the Jews and idolaters. (Qur'an 5:82)

JEWS HINDER PEOPLE FROM OBEYING ALLAH, THEIR GOD:

> So for the iniquity of the Jews, We forbade them the good things which had been made lawful for them, and for their hindering many people from Allah's way. (Qur'an 4:160)

JEWS ARE MISCHIEF-MAKERS:

> And the Jews say: The hand of Allah is tied up. Their own hands are shackled and they are cursed for what they say. Nay both His hands are spread out. He disburses as He pleases. And that which has been revealed to thee from thy Lord will certainly make many of them increase in inordinacy and disbelief. And We have cast among them enmity and hatred till the day of Resurrection. Whenever they kindle a fire for war Allah puts it out, and they strive to make mischief in the land. And Allah loves not the mischief-makers. (Qur'an 5:64)

JEWS ARE TO PAY THE JIZYA (TAX) AS A SIGN THAT THEY KNOW THEY ARE SUBJUGATED AND ARE SECOND CLASS TO THE SUPERIOR MUSLIM:

Fight those who believe not in Allah, nor in the Last Day, nor forbid that which Allah and His Messenger have forbidden, nor follow the Religion of Truth, out of those who have been given the Book, until they pay the tax in acknowledgement of superiority and they are in a state of subjection. (Qur'an 9:29)

These writings are at the core of Islam's code. Since Islam is a religious-political system it goes without saying that the state religion of the realm is Islam. If the ruling state religion says that Jews are violent, second-class citizens and mischief-makers, and that they hinder Muslims in their faith, there would be innumerable situations over the centuries where Jews in various towns and neighborhoods would be simply looked down upon by the general Muslim population at best, and murdered at worst. I do not know how widespread or common the actual killing or massacre of Jews was during the centuries of Islam. The writings of Islam would have provided a culture of encouragement for harassment of the Jews over the centuries so that it was at least sporadic and not uncommon.

On the other hand, there were some political entities within Islam, like the Andalusian (Spanish) caliphate in the eighth to fifteenth centuries AD, and the Ottomans from the fifteenth to nineteenth centuries, who treated the Jews rather well as citizens and allowed them to have positions of power and importance within the government.

As I've said before about a people resisting Islam, a people with a strong cultural and/or religious identity can withstand centuries of Islamic rule without converting. The Jews are such a people.

One thing that Islam did do over the centuries was prevent the Jews from forming a nation in the land of Israel, or from setting foot on the Temple Mount. Compared with the other heads of the red dragon in history that tried to completely and quickly wipe out the Jews, Islam's strategy has been a war of attrition and prevention: *they tried to discourage them from their faith, and prevent them from taking over their land and city.* This prevention on the part of the Islamic Realm ended in 1948 with the independence of the State of Israel.

Israel was able to come into existence because for the first half of the twentieth century the Western powers, including Russia, had carved up and occupied the Islamic Realm (with the exception of the heart of Persia and Arabia). After Nazi Germany had committed its atrocious Holocaust against the Jewish people, Western powers at the time felt sorry for the plight of the Jewish people. The West was also able to do something about it since they were in complete control of the region.

SUMMARY

In this chapter we saw how the vision of the four beasts in Daniel 7 requires an end time fulfillment. We also saw how it is a narrative of the emerging Antichrist. The seven heads shared among the four beasts required identification so we could know what nations are involved. Noting that the enormous seven-headed dragon in John's vision in Revelation was a reflection of the end times beast, which is a unification of the four beasts in Daniel, we identified the ancient empires of the dragon and therefore their modern equivalents.

Table 5-1 summarizes the list of dragon's heads in historical order, the historical empires represented by those heads, and the corresponding modern Muslim nations. Figure 5-9 shows the locations of the historical empires by number from the earlier maps in this chapter, superimposed on the six modern nations. At this point in our discussion we do not yet know with certainty which nations are represented by the lion or the bear or the four-headed leopard. But we do know that the nations identified here are going to be the main actors on the stage in the Middle East. And we do know the seventh head with the ten horns in Daniel 7 is modern Islam.

Table 5-1. The list of seven ancient empires and modern nations

DRAGON HEAD	HISTORICAL EMPIRE	EQUIVALENT MODERN NATION	BEAST HEAD OF THE FOUR BEASTS
1	Egyptian	Egypt	Not yet identified
2	Assyrian	Syria	Not yet identified
3	Babylonian	Iraq	Not yet identified
4	Persian	Iran	Not yet identified
5	Macedonian	Albania	Not yet identified
6	(Eastern) Roman	Turkey	Not yet identified
7	Islamic Realm	Islamic Realm	Beast with Ten Horns

Figure 5-9. The seven heads surrounding Israel and the six modern nations

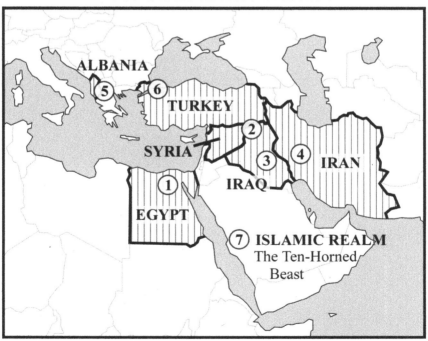

The next two chapters will discuss the other two visions—the ram and goat, and the four horsemen. Then in chapter 8, we will be able to assign the six modern nations to the various beasts of Daniel 7. Also in chapter 8 we will compare this vision to the other two visions and assemble a set of events that show the rise of the Antichrist.

CHAPTER 6

THE VISION OF THE RAM AND THE GOAT

OUR SECOND WITNESS SHOWING THE EVENTS OF THE EMERgence of the Antichrist is given in Daniel 8; it tells of Daniel's vision of a ram and a goat. First the ram charges out; then the one-horned goat charges out and attacks the ram. The goat's one horn then becomes four horns, and out of one of the four horns another little horn grows, representing a ruler. I propose in this chapter that this ruler is the end-time Antichrist. This passage confirms for us not only some of the nations involved as told to us in Daniel 7, but also wondrously, what they will do.

> In my vision I saw myself in the citadel of Susa in the province of Elam; in the vision I was beside the Ulai Canal. I looked up, and there before me was a ram with two horns, standing beside the canal, and the horns were long. One of the horns was longer than the other but grew up later. I watched the ram as he charged toward the west and the north and the south. No animal could stand against him, and none could rescue from his power. He did as he pleased and became great.
>
> As I was thinking about this, suddenly a goat with a prominent horn between his eyes came from the west, crossing the whole earth without touching the ground. He came toward the two-horned ram I had seen standing beside the canal and charged at him in great rage.

I saw him attack the ram furiously, striking the ram and shattering his two horns. The ram was powerless to stand against him; the goat knocked him to the ground and trampled on him, and none could rescue the ram from his power. The goat became very great, but at the height of his power his large horn was broken off, and in its place four prominent horns grew up toward the four winds of heaven.

Out of one of them came another horn, which started small but grew in power to the south and to the east and toward the Beautiful Land. It grew until it reached the host of the heavens, and it threw some of the starry host down to the earth and trampled on them. It set itself up to be as great as the Prince of the host; it took away the daily sacrifice from him, and the place of his sanctuary was brought low. Because of rebellion, the host of the saints and the daily sacrifice were given over to it. It prospered in everything it did, and truth was thrown to the ground." (Daniel 8:2–12)

The popular theological interpretation of this vision is that the ram represents the ancient Persian Empire, which expanded west toward Greece, free to do anything it wanted until it met Greece. The ram's horns represent the kings of the Medes and Persians. The goat is said to represent Greece and the single horn is Alexander the Great. Alexander conquered the Persian Empire starting in the west and did so with great speed for that ancient time—only twelve years. This speed is reflected in the vision by the goat racing eastward with its hooves not touching the ground. And then just as Alexander's kingdom fell apart into four kingdoms, so four horns emerge from where the single goat's horn was. The small horn growing out of one of the four is understood to be Antiochus IV, the king of the Seleucid Empire, who, we saw earlier in chapter 5, was the leader of the fifth head of the dragon.

The problem with this popular interpretation is similar to one of the problems with the interpretation of the vision of the four beasts: it is popularly thought that this vision was fulfilled in the centuries immediately following Daniel. But, just like the vision of the four beasts in Daniel 7 is to have an end-times fulfillment, this vision of the ram and goat is also set to have an end-times fulfillment. How do we know this? The vision in Daniel 8 has some key verses that tell us so, just as Daniel 7 had a couple of keys that told us that vision was also in the end times.

The vision is in fact, still unfulfilled because the angel tells Daniel, "'Son of man,' he said to me, 'understand that the vision concerns the time of the end'" (Dan. 8:17).

It doesn't get any clearer than that. For confirmation, though, a couple verses later Daniel 8:19 says, "I am going to tell you what will happen later in the time of wrath, because the vision concerns the appointed time of the end."

Twice we are told these events pertain to the end times and not to ancient times. Daniel 8:17 and 8:19 are two of the unyielding verses of Daniel mentioned in the introduction. As was the case with Daniel 7:17, their meaning has been ignored because it clashed with the popular interpretation of Daniel 8. Bible commentators have "known" that Daniel 8 was fulfilled in ancient times and so in their commentaries Daniel 8:17 and 19 couldn't have possibly meant what they were plainly saying.

I believe popular theology has assigned Daniel 8 to ancient history for two reasons. The first is because ancient history actually followed the description in the vision fairly well—not exactly but closely enough. One example is Alexander's fast conquest (twelve years was fast by ancient standards) being compared to the goat's hooves not touching the ground. A better fulfillment might be airlifted troops or a modern air force attacking the ram because the goat is airborne. Another example of an ancient fulfillment being close but not quite good enough is that Alexander's empire originally broke into several dozen pieces, but the strongest generals consolidated their gains. There were five kingdoms actually, and then four, and finally two. It could be argued that there were five final kingdoms and not four. A better fulfillment would be for the empire to break up into exactly four pieces.

The second reason might be a matter of default. If one believes the Antichrist to be Roman, then what would a couple of Middle East countries have to do with the emergence of the Antichrist? Even if one knew the ram was modern Iran instead of the Persian Empire, what does Iran have to do with the emergence of a Roman Antichrist? And since popular theology assigns an ancient fulfillment for this vision, the little horn growing out of one of the four horns is taken as Antiochus IV who was a king of the Seleucid Hellenized Realm. He is seen as a type of Antichrist, but not *the* Antichrist. (We discussed Antiochus IV in the last chapter.)

But since the end-time Antichrist will apparently be a Muslim (as we saw in chapters 1 and 2), and the nations involved with his emergence will most likely be modern Middle East nations, this vision of the ram and goat can be interpreted as telling us about the events leading up to the Antichrist.

The vision of the four beasts in Daniel 7 required a lengthy discussion to identify the seven nations represented by the heads of the four beasts. These seven nations will be the only seven nations involved in these events leading to the Antichrist, as told by these three visions. We are indeed only looking for confirmation of some of the nations here in this vision. As it turns out, the angel told Daniel who the nations are later in Daniel 8 when the interpretation is given. Therefore, we need not go into a lengthy discussion of who the ram and goat are, as we did for the vision of the four beasts in the preceding chapter of this book.

Continuing on then, Daniel 8:20 says, "The two-horned ram that you saw represents the kings of Media and Persia."

The language used sounds like an ancient description. It uses "kings" instead of rulers, and "Media and Persia" instead of Iran. Remember though, this prophecy was given in ancient times and an appropriate frame of reference was needed. In the time of Daniel, Iran was the land of the Medes and Persians. So the ram is confirmed as Iran.

There is an additional note to make here regarding the horns in this vision before moving on to the goat. There are a total of eight horns described in this vision: two horns on the ram, followed by one horn on the goat, then four horns on the goat and finally an extra little horn. Since the single horn on the goat, the four horns on the goat, and the little horn are all understood to represent single leaders, then it would follow that the two horns on the ram are single leaders as well. The view of ancient fulfillment of this vision, though, would have to admit that there was only one single king at a time in the Persian Empire, who attempted to conquer Greece. But since this vision indeed has an end-time fulfillment, and because the ram has *two* horns, this suggests there will be two leaders at the same time leading Iran, sharing power, each in their respective positions of power.

Moving on, Daniel 8:21 says of the identity of the goat, "The shaggy goat is the king of Greece, and the large horn between his eyes is the first king."

The Aramaic word for "Greece" is *Yavan* (Strong's #3120, pronounced yaw-vawn'). Yavan first appears in the Bible in Genesis 10 as the name of a son of Japheth, a son of Noah. It is generally agreed that the descendents of Yavan are the people around the Greek Peninsula, the southern Balkan Peninsula, Crete, and the west coast of Turkey. We are told in Genesis 10:5 of the sons of Yavan, "From these the maritime peoples spread out into their territories by their clans within their nations, each with its own language." So to the ancient Israelites they were known as the maritime peoples. In ancient times these people would have included the seafaring Phoenicians.

Going back to our list of identified modern nations in chapter 5, we have two nations in which the descendents of Yavan reside—Albania and Turkey. Recall from chapter 5 that the Albanians are distantly related to the Greeks since the Albanians are descended from the ancient Illyrians— who were a collection of northern Pelasgian tribes. Descendents of Yavan also reside in Turkey not only because of the ancient peoples who once resided there along the Aegean seacoast of Turkey, but also because of a mass immigration in 1923. The new nation of Turkey was emerging from the ashes of the old Ottoman Empire. Greece and Turkey arrived at an agreement called the "Convention Concerning the Exchange of Greek and Turkish Populations" in January 1923. As a result of this agreement, a million Christian Turks moved to Christian Greece and half a million Muslim Greeks moved to Muslim Turkey.

Let's also assume for the moment that Yavan does include two of our seven modern nations—Albania and Turkey. Since Turkey has the largest professional military in the eastern Mediterranean basin and western Middle East, Turkey would qualify as leading any military offensive move.[1] Turkey is also a member of NATO, and even has the largest military of any NATO member except that of the United States.[2] Therefore, a leader of modern Turkey would qualify as "the king of Yavan" in Daniel 8:21, otherwise known in our English Bibles as "the king of Greece."

In this vision though, the goat's horn represents only one king, the first king. This word for "first" in the Aramaic is *ri'shown* (Strong's #7223, pronounced ree-shone'). The word means first in place, time, or rank. The popular theological interpretation that says that Alexander the Great is represented by the goat's single horn would say he is first in time. However, since this vision is at the end time and parallels the vision of the four beasts in Daniel 7, we don't know yet if the horn represents the first king in rank and place, or time.

This vision in Daniel 8 tells of some events that take place involving the ram and goat. First the ram charges from Susa (which is in western Iran). Then the goat attacks the ram in a great rage. Next the goat's horn breaks and is replaced by four horns. And last, a little horn grows from one of the four horns. Overall this vision seems to be in three parts—a start of a war (the ram's charge), a finishing of a war (the goat's charge), and then the unleashing of a leader (the little horn). We will discuss these things and make sense of these details starting in chapter 8 of this book.

CHAPTER 7

THE VISION OF THE FOUR HORSEMEN

G OD HAS GIVEN US A THIRD VISION THAT IS A THIRD PICTURE OF the events leading to the coming of the Antichrist in the end times. This third picture was not given to Daniel as the first two pictures were, but to the Lord's beloved disciple, John. John wrote in Revelation 6 describing the four horsemen of the Apocalypse, as they are popularly known. In John's visions prior to Revelation 6, the Lamb of God Himself, the resurrected Christ, had received the scroll with seven seals. I believe this scroll in the vision to be a representation of the book of Daniel itself, and the seals being broken to be the unsealing of Daniel. No one could break those seals except the Lamb of God who was slain and came to life again. The very fact that these seals are being broken is testament to the fact that it is the end times. In Revelation 6 the Lamb starts breaking the seven seals of the scroll, one at a time.

What are we to think of these seals? What do they represent? The last three seals (fifth, sixth, and seventh) seem to show a future historical progression that many Bible commentators agree on, and I do as well. The fifth seal tells of the saints who are martyred for their faith during the Great Tribulation—the last forty-two months of time before Christ's Second Coming. The sixth seal is the Second Coming, which includes the great earthquake and hailstorm. Other passages in Revelation that describe Christ's physical return also mention an earthquake and hailstorm. The seventh seal is God's wrath poured out on the unbelievers, in the form of the Trumpet and Bowl Judgments. These seals—the fifth, sixth, and seventh—seem to show a progression in events. They are the martyrdom of the saints in the Tribulation, the return of Christ, and God's wrath poured out. But the first four seals, which are the four horsemen are, by and large, mysteries. These four horsemen are described in Revelation 6:1–8:

> I watched as the Lamb opened the first of the seven seals. Then I heard one of the four living creatures say in a voice like thunder, "Come!" I looked, and there before me was a white horse! Its rider held a bow, and he was given a crown, and he rode out as a conqueror bent on conquest.
>
> When the Lamb opened the second seal, I heard the second living creature say, "Come!" Then another horse came out, a fiery red one. Its rider was given power to take peace from the earth and to make men slay each other. To him was given a large sword.
>
> When the Lamb opened the third seal, I heard the third living creature say, "Come!" I looked, and there before me was a black horse! Its rider was holding a pair of scales in his hand. Then I heard what sounded like a voice among the four living creatures, saying, "A quart of wheat for a day's wages, and three quarts of barley for a day's wages, and do not damage the oil and the wine!"
>
> When the Lamb opened the fourth seal, I heard the voice of the fourth living creature say, "Come!" I looked, and there before me was a pale horse! Its rider was named Death, and Hades was following close behind him. They were given power over a fourth of the earth to kill by sword, famine and plague, and by the wild beasts of the earth.

If the fifth, sixth, and seventh seals represent events unfolding during and at the end of the Tribulation, couldn't the first four seals perhaps represent events occurring before the Tribulation? Let's assume for the moment that the first four seals might describe a series of events prior to the Tribulation, the period when events are showing the Antichrist's emergence. We have already seen in chapter 5 how Daniel's vision of the four beasts can be interpreted as a picture of the Antichrist's emergence. It turns out that when these four horsemen are compared to the four beasts in Daniel, we see surprisingly striking parallels between them.

Interestingly, we see in the text of the passage in Revelation that each of these four horsemen is called out by a "living creature." In Revelation 4:6–8 we are told that these four creatures have characteristics like animals such as a lion or an ox, and they have wings. These four living creatures are standing in the throne room of God. Many translations call them "living creatures" in Revelation 6:1, but the Greek word *zoon* (Strong's #2226, pronounced dzo'-on) used there is translated "animal" in other places. I cannot help but notice the similar use of metaphor in the Bible between Daniel and Revelation, echoed and confirmed between these two passages: four animal-like, heavenly creatures each call out a horseman describing four events, the same events represented by the four beasts in Daniel's vision.

Throughout church history there has been much debate about the identity of these four horsemen, or what they represent. The first horseman rides a white horse and wears a crown. It has been said that this first horseman is either Christ Himself, or the Antichrist. The second horseman has a large sword and rides a red horse. He is said to represent war. The third horseman rides a black horse and holds a scale. He is said to represent economic hardship and famine. The fourth horseman rides a pale green horse and is said to represent death and disease. Beyond that, any guesses have been sparse.

The Bible tells us of *four* horsemen who are called out by *four* creatures. We also have *four* beasts in Daniel 7. This could be viewed as nothing more than a coincidence, but we are given two clues in Scripture that the four horsemen are somehow involved with the Islamic Realm in the end times.

THE FIRST CLUE OF THE HORSEMEN: AREA OF AUTHORITY

The first clue is related to their coverage of the earth. Revelation 6:8 says of the riders,

> They were *given power over a fourth* of the earth *to kill* by sword, famine and plague, and by the wild beasts of the earth. (emphasis added)

The popular prophetic picture some commentators speak of is that these riders will kill one-fourth of mankind. But this verse simply does not say that. The riders had power *to kill* within a fourth of the earth—with the purpose of killing, not necessarily that they actually killed. The number of people killed may be significant and large or it may be relatively small, but it will not be a fourth of mankind. The killing will be confined, whatever the intensity, to a fourth of the earth.

It was the phrase "a fourth of the earth" that caught my eye. If Islam is the backdrop for end-times events, wouldn't it follow that the horsemen would operate in the realm of Islam in the end times? And so, just out of curiosity, how much of the earth might Islam cover? I decided to conduct an analysis of the nations of the world, including determining their land areas and populations.

But first I wanted to make sure what the word *earth* in Revelation 6:8 meant exactly. The word for "earth" is *ge* (Strong's #1093, pronounced ghay). It's where we get our word *geology*. *Ge* means the solid land surface of the world, and it suggests the inhabited parts. Next, I determined the list of nations that were Muslim and those that would be considered non-Muslim. Nations and areas that have an affiliation with Islam fell into four categories.

The following forty-seven nations have a population that is 50 percent to 100 percent Muslim (note that our six nations identified as part of the four beasts in Daniel 7 are all uppercase and bold):[1]

Afghanistan	Gambia	Malaysia	Sierra Leone
ALBANIA	Guinea	Maldives	Somalia
Algeria	Indonesia	Mali	Sudan
Azerbaijan	**IRAN**	Mauritania	**SYRIA**
Bahrain	**IRAQ**	Morocco	Tajikistan
Bangladesh	Jordan	Niger	Tunisia
Brunei	Kazakhstan	Nigeria	**TURKEY**
Burkina Faso	Kosovo	Oman	Turkmenistan
Chad	Kuwait	Pakistan	United Arab Emirates
Comoros	Kyrgyzstan	Qatar	Uzbekistan
Djibouti	Lebanon	Saudi Arabia	Yemen
EGYPT	Libya	Senegal	

All forty-seven of these nations I count as Muslim nations, and the land areas of these nations I consider as part of the Islamic area of the earth. All forty-seven of the above listed nations, with the exception of Kosovo, are also part of the Organization of Islamic Cooperation (OIC). The OIC, founded in 1969, is the second largest organization of sovereign governments in the world, second only to the United Nations. Kosovo is not a member yet due to various issues surrounding its fairly recent independence from Serbia in 2008.

Next, the following four nations have populations that are 35 to 50 percent Muslim:[2]

Bosnia and Herzegovina	Guinea-Bissau
Eritrea	Ivory Coast

I count all four of these nations as Muslim since all four have a very strong Muslim presence. I count half of these nations' land areas as part of Islam. Also, as a side note, Guinea-Bissau and the Ivory Coast are even members of the OIC.

The next six nations are 20 to 34 percent Muslim:[3]

Benin	Ethiopia	Mozambique
Cyprus	Macedonia	Tanzania

I do not count these nations as Muslim. But I do count 30 percent of their land areas as included in the Muslim sphere. Benin and Mozambique are members of the OIC.

Finally, I count some of the land area within the nations of China and India. India's population is "only" 13.4 percent Muslim but whole states within India's borders are Muslim states. Also, China's population is only 1.6 percent Muslim, but they live almost entirely within China's western Xinjiang (alternate spellings include "Xinchiang" and "Sinkiang") province and make up a majority of that population.

All other nations in the world have populations that are less than 20 percent Muslim and so are not counted as Muslim, and nor are their land areas.[4]

With these facts taken into account, we can determine the fraction of the earth that Islam covers. There are three ways to count the fraction of the earth that Islam covers: (1) by nation count, (2) by land area, and (3) by population.

By nation count, there are 51 Muslim nations among a total of 208 sovereign independent nations. That is just under 24.5 percent of all the nations by count.

By land area, the total land area of the earth including Antarctica is 56,380,000 square miles. The total land area of the 51 Muslim nations with part of the six additional nations, and the western province of China and Muslim states within India with a majority, comes to 12,451,000 square miles.[5] That is a little over 22 percent of the earth. If we do not include Antarctica, the total increases to 24.4 percent. Because of the definition of *ge* ("earth") in Revelation 6:8 being the generally inhabited land area, the exclusion of Antarctica is warranted.

Finally by population, we will look at a detailed census taken of the Muslim populations of the world by the Pew Research Center in 2009. Though there are many estimates of Muslim populations, this study in particular was methodical and thorough and used the most reliable sources. It found that out of a total world population of 6.8 billion in late 2009, the total Muslim population of the world was 1.57 billion.[6] This is 23.1 percent of the world's population.

So, in summary, 24.5 percent of the nations, 24.4 percent of the populated land area, and 23.1 percent of the world's people are Muslim. These numbers are all very close to the 25 percent of the earth in which the horsemen are to have authority. These numbers are fairly detailed estimates, and though they do not match "one-quarter" exactly, I believe we have a match. The fraction of the countries of the world that are Muslim and the population and land area of the earth could have all been varying fractions, but they are all nearly a quarter.

I find this amazing, and confirming. The four horsemen therefore, given authority over a quarter of the earth, are given authority over the Islamic Realm. Figure 7-1 shows the nations that I indicate as Muslim in this chapter. The cross-hatched areas are also in those countries that are part Muslim, or like India or China, have provinces or states that have a Muslim presence.

One additional thing occurred to me while I was doing this analysis of the world's countries. There is a time dynamic to all of this. A few centuries ago, Islam did not cover nearly a quarter of the earth, while in the future it may very well cover say, a third or more of the earth. Therefore, since Islam covers roughly a quarter of the earth right now, if the prophecy of the four horsemen is to be fulfilled as conditions occurring in the Muslim world in the end times, then it is roughly right now that we should be looking for fulfillment of the prophecy. This is just another indicator that I believe shows that the time is ripe for the end-time events to unfold.

If the horsemen have authority over a quarter of the earth, the Islamic quarter, then I believe that the worst of the chaos in the world leading up

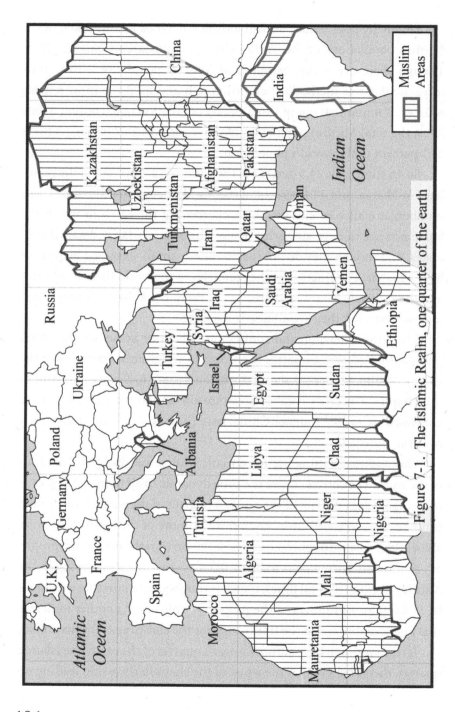

Figure 7-1. The Islamic Realm, one quarter of the earth

to the emergence of the Antichrist will be centered in, and the worst effects contained in, the nations of Islam. The Antichrist may or may not rule over most or all of the earth during his reign, but the events leading up to his reign should be confined to the Islamic Realm.

THE SECOND CLUE OF THE HORSEMEN: COLOR

I mentioned earlier that there are two clues that might hint to us that these four horsemen are involved with the Muslim nations. The "quarter of the earth" was the first clue. The second clue is in the colors of the horses that the horsemen ride. In order, the colors of the horses that charge out are white, red, black, and green. It so happens that every Arab nation today (with the exception of Qatar), and many other Islamic nations in that region of the world, all have flags made up of only those colors (with the exception of the occasional emblem located on a flag). Some may have only two or three of those colors, but those are the colors that are used. We will look more closely at the horsemen and their meaning, including their colors, in the final four chapters of this book.

Each of the four horsemen represents one of the four stages of the emergence of the Antichrist. The political, economic, and social conditions in the Middle East existing at the time of each horseman's release get worse as each horseman rides out. Some Bible commentators have noted that in each of the plagues on Egypt as seen in Exodus, God was using the gods in the pantheon of Egypt as a theme. Likewise, I believe with these four horsemen God is using the colors used in Islam as themes for His own "plagues" on the Islamic Realm.

SUMMARY

When each of the first four seals is broken in Revelation 6, it releases each of the Four Signposts of Daniel 7 and 8 so that its events can proceed. This release is manifested by a horseman on a horse, which in turn, represents a change in conditions associated with that Signpost. There are four riders on four horses, each going out in a sequence in time—chronologically—one after the other. We will see in detail in the next chapter of this book that each of these four horsemen describes the same events as the vision of the four beasts in Daniel 7, and of the vision of the ram and goat in Daniel 8.

HOW THREE VISIONS FORM FOUR SIGNPOSTS

I N CHAPTER 4 WE SAW THAT READING THE THREE PROPHETIC PAS-sages with Islam in mind opens up our eyes to a whole new set of events telling us of the emergence of the Antichrist. We saw three visions in each of the last three chapters, and the reason each of these visions applies to events in the end times and to the emergence of the Antichrist.

Now here in chapter 8 we are going to lay the pieces of these three visions out on the table and see what we get. In our discussion here I will follow the same path of discovery that I originally followed. There may be places in this discussion where there are details that may seem unsubstantiated. I do this here for the sake of brevity. In the four chapters that follow I will lay out all the details.

Each of the three visions seems to be a narrative of a sequence of events in time. Figure 8-1 shows the major events occurring in each of the three visions laid out in parallel on a time line. In one vision we have four beasts, described in order: lion, bear, leopard, and a ten-horned beast. In the second vision we have a ram, a goat, and then four horns. And in the third vision we have four horsemen, riding horses ordered as white, red, black, and green. All these pieces are shown in a diagram in figure 8-1.

The first thing that got my attention was that the bear and the ram shared two things in common. Both have a high side and low side; and both were in the process of starting an incursion, a raid. The bear has one side higher than the other, and the ram has one horn higher than the other. The bear is told to go and consume much flesh and so forages and ravages like a big bear does. The ram begins a charge out to the north, south, and west. The bear and the ram are therefore representing the same nation and the same prophesied actions.

The next thing I noticed was that this incursion or raid is actually the start of a major war, the first phase of a great Sunni-Shia war, in fact. The bear consuming and going from place to place and the ram charging great distances is the equivalent of the aggressor nation attacking many nations. Among the horsemen, the second one on the red horse stands out. He was given authority to make men slay one another. In each of the three visions the key figure—the bear, the ram, and the second horseman—starts a war when he appears on the scene. Figure 8-2 shows the bear, ram, and second horseman all matched together.

TIME	VISION of Four Beasts	VISION of Ram and Goat	VISION of Four Horsemen
	Lion with wings ↓		Rider on white horse ↓
		Ram with two horns ↓	
	Bear with high side ↓		Rider on red horse ↓
		Goat with one horn ↓	
	Four-Headed Leopard ↓		Rider on black horse ↓
		Four horns with little horn	
	Ten-Horned Beast		Rider on green horse

Figure 8-1. The visions laid out together on a time line

Remember, we also have six modern Muslim nations to assign to the first three beasts in the vision of the four beasts. We know the fourth beast is Islam. If the bear is the ram, and the ram is the "kings of Media and Persia," then the bear is Iran. Figure 8-2 indicates that the modern nation of Iran is associated with the bear, the ram, and the second horseman. In this set of events involving Iran, the second horseman signifies that the second seal has been broken. The description of the ram and its actions provide the details that fit within the framework of the description of the bear.

Figure 8-2. The bear, ram and second horseman signal Iran starting a war

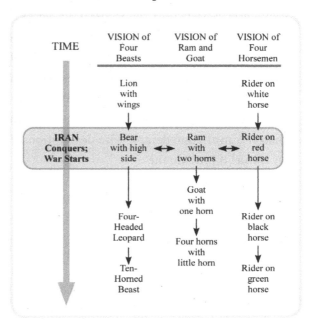

After the ram charges outward, the goat appears in the west and attacks the ram, putting an end to the ram. This is the counterattack by the goat, against the ram. The goat then finishes the war and even takes over the ram's domains. This is the second and last phase of a great Sunni-Shia war. Looking at figure 8-2, the goat and the leopard may seem less connected to one another than that of the bear/ ram/ second horseman connection. The goat follows the ram in the time line, and the leopard follows the bear in the time line. This suggests that the goat and leopard represent similar things. The goat won the war by defeating the ram and takes over the ram's domains; at the same time the four-headed leopard is given authority to rule. Since they were given authority to rule, that means the four nations represented by the leopard didn't have authority to rule before. One thing about the outcomes of major wars is that the "authority to rule" is given to, and taken away from, the nations involved. In this case the four nations of the leopard are the victors and are therefore given authority to rule.

So, who are the four modern Muslim nations represented by the four-headed leopard and the goat? From Daniel's perspective where he sat near the citadel at Susa, the goat appears in the west, beyond the ram's conquests. Susa is near the western border of present-day Iran. The four nations of the four-headed leopard must therefore be the four nations which are furthest west on the map in figure 5-9. These would be Albania, Turkey, Syria, and Egypt. There may be four nations involved as the leopard indicates, but the leading nation of the four is Turkey as shown by the goat. In figure 8-3 we show this next event, which is the attack by a four-nation Sunni confederacy. The description of the goat and its actions in Daniel 8 provide the details that fit within the framework of the description of the leopard in Daniel 7.

Figure 8-3. The pieces assembled for a war's start and end

We will now move further forward in time. The next event after the goat is the four horns that sprout on the goat with the little horn growing out of one of the four horns. The next

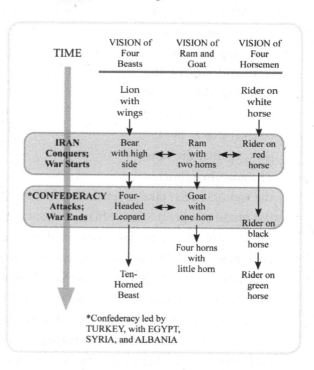

event after the leopard is the eleventh horn that sprouts out of the terrible ten-horned beast and uproots or displaces three of its ten horns. In both pictures we have a little horn, and in both visions it will say and do great things. The little horn in both visions is the Antichrist to come. Hence, the four horns after the goat, and the little horn next to the ten horns after the leopard, both represent the same event—and Islam as a whole will be involved. This seventh head is Islam, which is shown in figure 8-4. Here we see the details of the goat's four horns and little horn, which fits within the framework of the eleventh horn coming up among ten horns on the fourth beast.

Figure 8-4. Most of the pieces fitting into three events

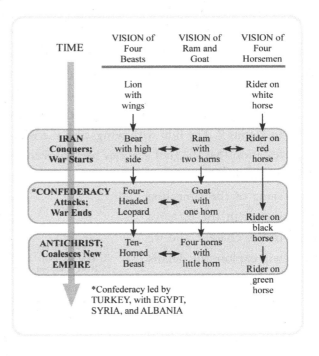

Moving on, notice in figure 8-4 that we still have the lion with wings and the rider on the white horse sitting by themselves at the start of the time line, with no assigned place for the third and fourth horsemen. Up to now, the pieces of the three visions have lent themselves more easily to a solution to the puzzle where we can see more plainly how things line up. To proceed further takes some attention to detail. We only have the lion remaining in the vision of the four beasts, and only one modern nation remaining—Iraq. Therefore by default, Iraq is assigned to the lion. The lion, though, is forced to stand on its hind legs, its wings are ripped off, and its mind (or heart) is changed from a beast's mind to a man's mind. When I saw this description of the lion with Iraq in mind, it dawned on me that the things done to the lion in the vision of the four beasts are the equivalent to what was done to Iraq in the last decade. That age-old culture steeped in monarchies, despots, and theocracies, was unnaturally forced to change into a democracy.

But what of the rider on the white horse? He won a crown, was bent on conquest, and had an empty bow. Could this be Saddam Hussein, the former ruler of Iraq? If these things are true, then we are already in the middle of the events leading to the arrival of the Antichrist! The first stage has happened and the second is ready to go! Looking at figure 8-5 we can see the white horse and the lion with wings together forming the first event. Notice with this first event that, unlike the other three events, there is no detail from Daniel 8 to fit into the framework of the lion with wings in Daniel 7. The lion with wings and the white horseman are the manifestation that the first seal has been broken. In the next chapter we will begin detailed discussions of the time line shown in the pictures in this chapter, and we will explore the details of Iraq and Saddam Hussein and how they fulfill prophecy.

Figure 8-5. Four stages take form

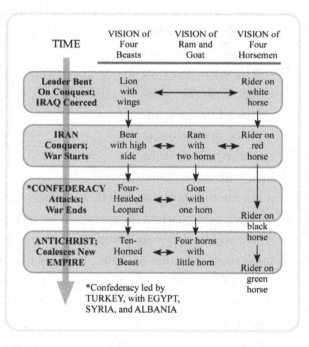

At this point, we still have the third and fourth horsemen unassigned. The third horseman on the black horse represents food shortages and a poor economy. There is food but it requires working all day to get a day's worth of food. If Iran conquers much of the Middle East during the time of the second horseman, who also takes peace from the earth, it is very easy to guess that the world oil supplies would be disrupted. This, of course, would impact just about everything in our world's modern economy including agriculture and food production. Therefore, I assign the third horseman to the time that the four-nation Sunni Confederacy counterattacks, which follows Iran's initial invasion. The third horseman is the manifestation that the third seal in Revelation 6 has been broken, allowing the events of the leopard and the goat to proceed.

Finally, there is the fourth rider, who rides the pale green horse. He represents death and disease. At first glance it is tempting to simply assign him by default to the fourth event, that of the emergence of the Antichrist. However, the assignment is warranted. In prophecy this event calls for more war and territorial expansion through many regions. This could aggravate and prolong the harsh conditions started under the third event, the counterattack. Where conditions included expensive food and a harsh economy, they are then followed in this fourth event with more war and shortages. This would lead to many more deaths and plague. So I assign the fourth horseman to the fourth stage. This fourth horseman is the manifestation that the fourth seal is broken and so the events of this fourth stage can proceed.

In figure 8-6 we have our final framework, with the pieces of the three visions describing four major sets of events leading to the arrival of the Antichrist. Earlier in chapter 4, I called the four major sets of events the Four Signposts. I used this nomenclature because our world is traveling down the road known as time, getting closer and closer to the final destination, which is the return of Christ. As our world encounters these biblically specific sets of events, it is like encountering signposts on a journey to the Tribulation and Second Coming. These Four Signposts precede the arrival of the seven-year Tribulation.

Figure 8-6. The Four Signposts determined by the three visions

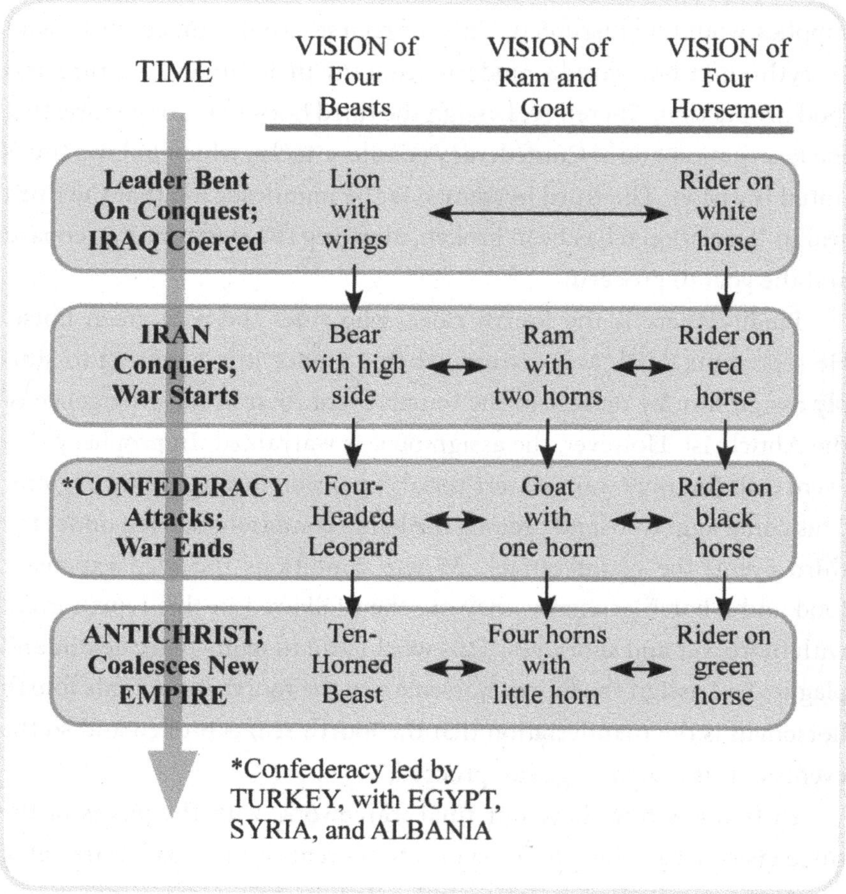

TIME	VISION of Four Beasts	VISION of Ram and Goat	VISION of Four Horsemen
Leader Bent On Conquest; IRAQ Coerced	Lion with wings	←——————→	Rider on white horse
IRAN Conquers; War Starts	Bear with high side	Ram with two horns	Rider on red horse
*CONFEDERACY Attacks; War Ends	Four-Headed Leopard	Goat with one horn	Rider on black horse
ANTICHRIST; Coalesces New EMPIRE	Ten-Horned Beast	Four horns with little horn	Rider on green horse

*Confederacy led by
TURKEY, with EGYPT,
SYRIA, and ALBANIA

SUMMARY

To summarize then where we are in our discussion, we have witnessed the formation of a series of events telling us of the seasons of the coming of the Antichrist. The significance of these events is no longer hidden but is now written across Four Signposts for all who are willing to see.

The First Signpost tells us of a leader bent on conquest who had a bow and was riding a white horse. Saddam Hussein is proposed as the fulfillment of the prophecy of this rider. His country, Iraq, represented by a lion with wings, was forced to go through a process that was unnatural. I call the First Signpost the Coercion of Iraq. We will discuss the First Signpost in chapter 9.

The Second Signpost tells us of the first phase of a major war. A bear and a ram both represent Iran, which starts this major Sunni-Shia war. Going out across many nations in the Middle East, this nation conquers and occupies and triggers the loss of peace and stability in the world. War on a regional scale and loss of economic stability on a global scale are representative of the rider on the red horse. I call the Second Signpost the Conquest by Iran. We will discuss the Second Signpost in chapter 10.

The Third Signpost tells us of a confederacy of four nations starting the second (and last) phase of this major Sunni-Shia war. A new union of four nations forms the Sunni Confederacy and is represented by the leopard. The goat represents leadership of the Confederacy and command of its combined military. This group of four nations reconquers and takes back that which was conquered by Iran. The Confederacy is allowed to govern this region, but only for a short time. The region then falls apart into four new nations. I call the Third Signpost the Confederacy of Four Nations. We will discuss the Third Signpost in chapter 11.

And finally, the Fourth Signpost tells us of an emerging leader represented by a little horn in two different visions, who takes over one of the four new nations that replaced the Confederacy. This leader goes on to conquer a total of three of the four new nations, which are the three horns of the fourth beast that are uprooted. Then, at that point, seven remaining Islamic nations bow to him as their Mahdi—the Antichrist. I call the Fourth Signpost the Coalescing of an Empire. We will discuss the Fourth Signpost in chapter 12.

THE FOUR SIGNPOSTS REVEALED

CHAPTER 9

THE FIRST SIGNPOST: THE COERCION OF IRAQ

IN THIS CHAPTER WE COME TO OUR DISCUSSION OF THE FIRST Signpost. We saw in the last chapter that the events of the First Signpost include the prophecies of the lion with wings and the first horseman, the rider on the white horse. I proposed that the prophecy of the lion with wings was fulfilled by events in Iraq. I also proposed that Saddam Hussein fulfills the prophecy of this rider on the white horse. In this chapter we will see how Iraq and Saddam Hussein are very reasonable, if not exact, fulfillments of the prophecies pertaining to the First Signpost.

Since the First Signpost involves Iraq and Saddam Hussein, then it would be safe to conclude that this Signpost is already in our past. The First Signpost essentially started with Saddam's takeover of Iraq as its leader on July 16, 1979. The Signpost ended when the last large contingent of US soldiers exited Iraq on December 18, 2011. We will see later in this chapter why it can be said the First Signpost ended at that point. If we are witnessing the events of the Four Signposts, then the very fact that these events are occurring is the warning to us saints that we have entered the final times before the Tribulation. Since the First Signpost is already in the past, we are already in the times called out by the Bible leading to the Tribulation. I realize this may not be a surprise for some; for others it may be a cold dose of reality that may be calling them to draw closer to God.

We will see that the major events of the First Signpost involve many of the events that have been reported in the news from 1979 to 2011. The world saw a tyrant named Saddam Hussein take over Iraq, then start a number of wars, and finally get ousted. After that the nation of Iraq that he once ruled was converted into a democracy. During this time when the new government of Iraq was taking form, major issues dominated the headlines. Two in particular were the fate of the weapons of mass destruction (WMD) and the question of whether democracy could survive in a country like Iraq. What we didn't know was that these events and issues were all part of the First Signpost, proclaimed by the Bible, and that the time leading up to the coming of the Antichrist had already begun. Thankfully, the significance of the First Signpost and the others that follow can be plainly seen.

To present a coherent chronology of each of the Signposts we will follow a structured approach. In this, and in each of the following chapters, we will revisit the Signpost summary given in figure 8-6 in chapter 8 by reproducing the relevant portion of that figure for the Signpost we are discussing. That relevant portion will contain the major part of each of the three visions applicable to the Signpost we are examining. Then, we will look at each vision's applicable major part and list the significant details in each part. We will then gather the details to create a list of the events of each Signpost. Finally, we will examine each event for each Signpost drawing on the significant details we captured from each of the three visions in Scripture.

THE THREE VISIONS APPLIED TO THE FIRST SIGNPOST

To help remind us which parts of the three visions are involved here in the First Signpost, figure 9-1 below shows the portion of figure 8-6 from chapter 8 that belongs to the First Signpost. In figure 9-1 we see that this Signpost includes the lion with wings from the vision of the four beasts, and the rider on the white horse from the vision of the four horsemen.

Figure 9-1. The First Signpost: the lion with wings and the first horseman

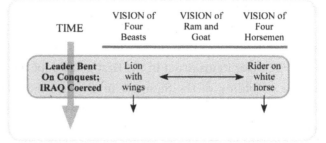

First, Iraq is represented in the vision of the four beasts by a beast that is like a lion, but has wings. Daniel 7:4 says of this lion,

> The first was like a lion, and it had the wings of an eagle. I watched until its wings were torn off and it was lifted from the ground so that it stood on two feet like a man, and the heart of a man was given to it.

This is the extent of the information given of the lion with wings. We can make a list of the things we know about this beast. First, it is like a lion. This may seem obvious, but is important because of the way this nation behaves—it is analogous to the behavior of a lion. Second are the things that are done to it—the tearing off of its wings, being lifted up so it stands, and its mind or heart replaced with that of a man. These are the significant points.

The second vision is the vision of the ram and goat. We see in figure 9-1 that this vision in Daniel 8 has no application to the First Signpost. So we will pass over the ram and the goat in this chapter.

Moving on to the third and last vision, that of the four horsemen, Revelation 6:2 only says of the first horseman,

> I looked, and there before me was a white horse! Its rider held a bow, and he was given a crown, and he rode out as a conqueror bent on conquest.

For such a short verse there is quite a bit said. First, he is on a white horse. Second, he was given a crown. Third, he rode out bent on conquest. And last he held a bow.

We will now arrange the details of each of the three visions that we have noted here into the major events of the First Signpost in table 9-1. The three items listed in the first column of the table are the events of the unfolding of the Signpost in chronological order. We will now explore these three events in the same order as shown in the table, for the remainder of this chapter.

Table 9-1. Vision details form three major events within First Signpost

FIRST SIGNPOST EVENTS TIME LINE	VISION OF LION (DANIEL 7:4)	VISION OF RAM (DANIEL 8)	VISION OF RIDER (REVELATION 6:2)
A) Saddam Like a Conqueror; Iraq Like a Lion	• Like a lion with wings	—	• On a white horse • Given a crown • Bent on conquest
B) What Happened to the WMD?	—	—	• He had a bow
C) Iraq Democratized After Saddam's Fall	• Wings removed • Forced to stand upright • Man's heart given to it	—	—

SADDAM LIKE A CONQUEROR; IRAQ LIKE A LION

Let's start with the beast that looks like a lion. Why would a lion with wings represent Iraq? For that matter, why do the beasts shown in the vision represent any of the modern nations identified in chapter 5?

Bible commentators have only given guesses why the bear and leopard are used as the second and third beasts, but there is a popular consensus about the lion. Popular theology says that the lion with wings represents ancient Babylon. A popular idea is that the symbol of Babylon was the lion with wings, but I have found no evidence to support this view. The drawings and sculptures found in the archaeological ruins of ancient Babylon do contain depictions of lions in many places—all of them without wings. The closest thing to a lion with wings depicted in ancient ruins is a creature called a "lamassu." Depictions of the lamassu have been found both in Assyrian and Persian ruins, but not Babylonian. And though the lamassu has a lion's body with wings, it has a man's head—not a lion's head. If there is any symbol for Babylon that has been seen extensively in its ruins, it would be a regular lion.

I have noticed in this study that these four beasts are not used in Daniel 7 for the nations they represent simply because they might be popular symbols for those nations. For instance, a bear represents Iran in one of the visions, but the symbol of Iran is not a bear. The beasts are chosen because each beast's observed behavior in the wild is analogous to the behavior of the nations they represent. You will see what I mean as we go through each Signpost and look at each nation.

FIRST SIGNPOST EVENTS TIME LINE	VISION OF LION (DANIEL 7:4)	VISION OF RAM (DANIEL 8)	VISION OF RIDER (REVELATION 6:2)
A) Saddam Like a Conqueror; Iraq Like a Lion	• Like a lion with wings	—	• On a white horse • Given a crown • Bent on conquest

The lion is employed to represent Iraq because Iraq under Saddam Hussein, like its ancient predecessor Babylon, behaved among nations like a lion. How is this so? The two significant features of the lion's behavior are the way it hunts prey, and its intimidating roar.

A lion that hunts in the wild will target the smallest or the weakest or the closest animal in a herd. It will then chase it and take it down. The Bible uses this known behavior of the lion in a warning to the saints to watch out for Satan.

Be self-controlled and alert. Your enemy the devil prowls around like a roaring lion looking for someone to devour. (1 Pet. 5:8)

After taking down its prey, the lion will then fill its belly on the animal's carcass and be totally satisfied. It will not go after another animal as prey for a long time. Analogously, this is exactly what Saddam Hussein's Iraq has done with the countries and provinces in its vicinity.

Iraq under Saddam went after its prey one at a time, as shown in figure 9-2. Iraq invaded the oil-rich southwest Iranian province of Khuzestan in September 1980. This was the beginning of the Iran-Iraq War that raged on for eight years. Iraq held Khuzestan for eighteen months before being forced out by the Iranian military. Two years after the end of that war, Iraq then invaded Kuwait in August 1990 and held it for seven months before being forced out by an international coalition of forces led by the United States.

Wings, which suggest flight, are usually used in prophecy to denote physical speed or flight. The wings on the lion would simply mean that whatever Iraq did, it would do it quickly. When Saddam Hussein ordered the invasions of Khuzestan and Kuwait, there was little or no warning for the victims.

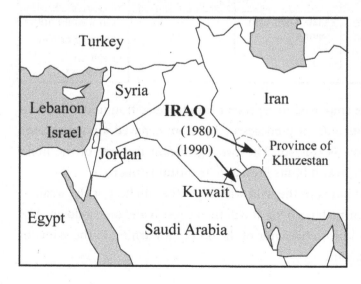

Figure 9-2. Saddam's attempted conquests: Khuzestan and Kuwait

The second key feature of a lion is its roar that instills fear. It is written by the prophet Amos,

The lion has roared—who will not fear? The Sovereign LORD has spoken—who can but prophesy? (Amos 3:8)

Iraq roared like a lion through its leader Saddam Hussein. Not only were its neighbors wary of Iraq, but much of the Western world was concerned about the power Iraq might wield in the form of its possible weapons of mass destruction (WMD).

To allow us better understanding of the lion's behavior, we need to move on to the vision of the rider on the white horse.

Saddam Hussein was Iraq's ruler from July 16, 1979 to April 9, 2003. Comparing the description of the first horseman of Revelation 6 to the career of Saddam Hussein as leader of Iraq, we can see a very close and striking correlation. Of this rider, Revelation 6:2 says, "I looked, and there before me was a white horse! Its rider held a bow, and he was given a crown, and he rode out as a conqueror bent on conquest."

The first thing said about this mysterious figure is that he is riding a white horse. A rider on a white horse has been symbolic in myth and history as a hero or a conquering king. In contrast, the symbolism of a king becoming king by inheritance would be the king riding on a donkey or a mule—as was the case of Solomon (1 Kings 1:38), or our Messiah (John 12:14–15) entering Jerusalem.

I mentioned in chapter 7 how God may be using colors as themes for each of the Four Signposts. In Islam, white is the color of purity and peace. With Saddam Hussein being represented here, there was neither purity nor peace in the First Signpost.

Of this rider on the white horse the Bible says that this king or ruler was given a crown—a victor's crown. The Greek word for "crown" in this passage is *stephanos* (Strong's #4735, pronounced stef'-an-os). This is the same crown won by the winner of a race. This word *stephanos* is used everywhere in the New Testament where it refers to the crown of life or the crown of righteousness that the saints are to receive after having fought the good fight and keeping the faith. Of course, Saddam's "crown" was only a prize for having wrested the leadership position of Iraq from his uncle in a coup. He won the position of ruler of Iraq.

In contrast, the other word for "crown" in the New Testament is *diadema* (Strong's #1238, pronounced dee-ad'-ay-mah) that refers to the crown of royalty. The red dragon of Revelation 12 had seven *diadema* on its heads, and in Revelation 19 the returning King of kings has many *diadema* on His head.

The passage says the horseman was *bent* on conquest. Saddam apparently had a grandiose view of himself. Pictures and statues larger than life adorned many buildings and cities. Saddam even saw himself as a reincarnation of King Nebuchadnezzar.[1] He started rebuilding Babylon. He fancied himself restarting the Babylonian Empire and being the liberator of the Arab people by uniting the areas around Iraq with his nation. Though bent on conquest and having conquered two rather small areas, in the end he didn't retain either of his conquests.

WHAT HAPPENED TO THE WMD?

FIRST SIGNPOST EVENTS TIME LINE	VISION OF LION (DANIEL 7:4)	VISION OF RAM (DANIEL 8)	VISION OF RIDER (REVELATION 6:2)
B) What Happened to the WMD?	—	—	• He had a bow

The last thing Revelation 6:2 says of the rider on the white horse is that the "rider held a bow." This seemed odd to me. Why a bow? Most conquering kings might carry a sword. Swords are mentioned in the New Testament more than thirty times, but this is the only occurrence of a bow. A bow doesn't seem as ominous. At least, it isn't ominous unless you see a quiver of arrows and maybe an arrow loaded onto the bow. But this verse makes no mention of arrows. Of course, if a rider is holding a bow, any observer might *assume* the rider has arrows. After all, what good is a bow if you have no arrows?

Up to this point the comparison between Saddam and the rider of the white horse has been good. They were both bent on conquest, both received a victor's crown, and both could be viewed as heroic, though of course much of the view of Saddam was propagated by Saddam himself. As an example, one of the iconic news events when the coalition forces entered Baghdad back in 2003 was the pulling down of a large statue of Saddam by an angry mob.

But the bow is the part of the comparison that is exceptional. What the bow represents took me by surprise, and then it became rather obvious. What are the major features of Saddam Hussein's career as leader of Iraq, as the world at large might see them? First, he took over leadership of Iraq (he was given the crown). Second, he was bent on conquest and so started wars (hence the white horse). These wars included the Iran-Iraq War, the Gulf War, and finally the Iraq War where Saddam was ousted. There was a third significant theme associated with Saddam that the news media did not stop talking about for years both before and after the invasion of Iraq by American-led forces. The other most significant theme was whether Saddam Hussein was in possession of weapons of mass destruction (WMD). Critics of US President George W. Bush used the subject of WMD for years to try to discredit him as a leader. It was also used as a means of questioning whether or not Iraq should have been invaded. I believe the Bible actually portrays the whole subject with the first horseman's possession of a bow.

Let's start with the word used for "bow" in the Greek text. The word is *toxon* (Strong's #5115, pronounced tox'-on). Ancient Greek archers frequently used poison arrows with their bows. These poisons were toxins that killed or sickened the body. When the Romans conquered Greece, they copied the word *toxon* into Latin, but it came to mean only the "poison" portion, not "bow" or "arrow." Of course today, almost every European language from Spanish to Russian, having been affected by Latin, uses "tox-" as the root in their own words for toxins or poisons. The original Greek root "tox-" has found its way into English with such words as *toxology*, which is the study of archery. But the Latin root "tox-" for poison is much more commonly used. I'd bet if you ask the average person for the definition of *toxology* they would most likely say "the study of poisons."

Today, poisons or toxins can be biological (such as bacteria), or chemical (like mustard gas), or radioactive (like the rays and particles radiated from radioactive elements like uranium or plutonium). Essentially, to be classified as a WMD, a weapon needs to be able to deliver one of these three forms of toxin. The usual form of delivery is via missile. The connection between the first horseman's bow and Saddam's WMD capability I am proposing here is not through the coincidental fact that the word bow comes from the word *toxon*, although it is an attention grabber. Missiles, in ancient times, were arrows shot from bows. Today missiles are self-propelled and have much longer ranges. The connection is through the very fact that the horseman simply had and held his bow. This is strikingly similar to the unfolding story of Saddam Hussein and Iraq's WMD. Let me explain.

After the invasion of Iraq started on March 20, 2003, Saddam Hussein was removed from power April 9. But he escaped and went into hiding. He was finally captured in a "spider hole" in northern Iraq on December 13, 2003, and held by American authorities. On June 30, 2004 he was turned over to the new Iraqi interim government to stand trial for his crimes. It was revealed in January 2008 that during the period from December 2003 to June 2004, Saddam Hussein underwent a series of interviews and casual conversations with an FBI Agent. The FBI agent's name was George Piro, a Lebanese-born Assyrian-American who speaks fluent Arabic. Special Agent Piro was the front man for a team of analysts who were trying to answer many questions, among them, What happened to Iraq's WMD?[2] To Saddam, he was only known as "Mr. George" and he posed as a high US government official who talked to the American president directly.[3] Special Agent Piro treated Saddam as a friend and had casual conversations with Saddam in prison. After five months of conversations with Piro, Saddam Hussein finally told him about the WMD.[4]

According to Piro, Saddam said the UN destroyed most of the WMD in the 1990s. The UN did in fact destroy WMD in Iraq during that time. All remaining WMD were destroyed by Iraq, yet Saddam kept up the appearance that there were more WMD. He would have UN teams wait to inspect an area, then when the teams entered all they would see was an empty room. Suspicions were that the Iraqis had moved the WMD to a hidden location. In the CBS News interview of George Piro by Scott Pelley, Pelley asked Piro the reason why Saddam might risk his life and the security of Iraq by pretending to still have WMD.[5]

The FBI reports of these conversations with Saddam were finally released in July 2009 under the Freedom of Information Act. In one of the reports, the question is answered revealing Saddam Hussein's thoughts and priorities:

> Hussein stated that Iran was Iraq's major threat due to their common border and believed that Iran intended to annex Southern Iraq into Iran.[6]

This concern is not completely unfounded on two counts: (1) Saddam Hussein's regime was secular and Iran was a fundamentalist Islamic state that viewed Saddam more or less as an infidel, and (2) Iran is the major Shia Islamic nation so it might try to unite with the third of Iraq's population that is also Shia, who primarily live in southern Iraq.

The FBI report goes on to show how this concern shaped Saddam's actions:

> Hussein viewed the other countries in the Middle East as weak and could not defend themselves or Iraq from a [sic] attack from Iran . . .

Hussein stated he was more concerned about Iran discovering Iraq's weaknesses and vulnerabilities than the repercussions of the United States for his refusal to allow UN inspectors back into Iraq.[7]

In summary, Saddam Hussein kept up the illusion that Iraq still possessed WMD in order to fend off the possibility of an attack by Iran. Remember that in the 1980s Iraq fought a decimating eight-year war with Iran. It was caused by Saddam's invasion of Khuzestan. But the war it sparked emptied Iraq's treasury and caused the deaths of hundreds of thousands of Iraqis. Apparently, the threat of Iran was fresh and stark in Saddam's mind, and very real to him. One newspaper even noted that the extravagance of the charade maintained by Saddam highlighted the extraordinary lengths that Saddam was willing to go to convince everyone he still held WMD.[8]

So the rider on the white horse had a bow. To those who have ever read or heard this verse in Revelation and who imagined the rider, it must have suggested to them this horseman had the ability to launch arrows. As confirmation, it seems that almost every painting I have ever seen of the first horseman shows his bow with an arrow ready to launch. In ancient Roman times the arrows would have been tipped with poison. Likewise, Saddam Hussein once had WMD. He used them to kill thousands of Kurds in the 1980s. The UN saw the WMD and had them destroyed. Then Saddam kept up the ruse that he still had some. It suggested to any outside observer in the last twenty years that Saddam had the ability to launch missiles tipped with WMD.

Notice what Revelation 6:2 says in detail of the first horseman—and what it doesn't say. It says, "its rider held a bow." That's it. The crowned rider rode a horse, was bent on conquest and held—maybe even waved around a bit—a bow. Saddam supposedly confessed the true status of Iraq's WMD. He waved an empty potential to launch WMD. I see no reason that he would have lied to his jailors. His reasoning for maintaining the charade, if true, does make some sense. In this lifetime we will probably never know with absolute certainty if this is the truth about the WMD. But the point is, this is the picture of Saddam Hussein and his WMD that the world saw.

Likewise, the Bible doesn't say the rider had arrows. And remarkably it doesn't say the rider didn't have arrows. The Bible is silent to the truth of the rider's arrows. But maybe that's the point the Bible is trying to make. By the Bible itself being silent about the arrows, it matches perfectly the lack of absolute knowledge of the fate of Saddam's WMD. There is still a little mystery as to the absolute truth of Saddam's holding the threat of WMD in front of people's faces. Likewise, there is some mystery as to the absolute truth of the first horseman holding a bow in Revelation's readers' faces.

Earlier in this chapter I talked about the lion's two major traits: the way it hunts and its roar. The threat of WMD was part of this lion's roar. The world feared the lion's roar so much that the US led a lion hunt with the participation of other world nations.

To me, Saddam Hussein, his coming to power, his desires, his wars, and how he handled the threat of WMD is an extraordinarily detailed fulfillment of every aspect of the prophecy of the first horseman—both what is written in Revelation, and what is specifically not written.

IRAQ DEMOCRATIZED AFTER SADDAM'S FALL

FIRST SIGNPOST EVENTS TIME LINE	VISION OF LION (DANIEL 7:4)	VISION OF RAM (DANIEL 8)	VISION OF RIDER (REVELATION 6:2)
C) Iraq Democratized After Saddam's Fall	• Wings removed • Forced to stand upright • Man's heart given to it	—	—

If you read the entire prophecy about all four beasts in Daniel 7, this first beast is different from the remaining beasts in one regard: this is the only beast of the four that has something *done to* it. All the other beasts *do* something to others—the bear consumes, the four-headed leopard rules, and the terrible beast crushes and tramples. This beast is shorn of its wings, made to stand up, and its heart or mind is replaced.

We already saw why Iraq is represented as a lion in the prophecy. Since the actions of this lion with wings are not mentioned in the Bible, the only hint we have from the Bible of what this first nation did was that it was represented by a lion. We saw what lions do in general, and saw similarities in behavior to what Iraq did.

However, the Bible mentions specifically what in turn was done *to* the lion. The lion had its wings torn off, it was forced to walk like a man, and given a man's heart or mind. Bible commentators generally reflect the popular theology that this vision was fulfilled in ancient times. They compare what was done to the lion to a story in the Bible to identify it with Babylon. Daniel 4 is the story of how King Nebuchadnezzar was punished by God for his pride, by being brought low. He was made insane and made to act like a grazing animal in a meadow eating grass like an ox for seven years. After the seven years were over God restored Nebuchadnezzar to his position as king. The popular theory is that King Nebuchadnezzar's restoration to sanity (in Daniel 4) is the lion receiving a man's heart, and standing upright like a man (in Daniel 7).

But there are three key problems with assigning the fulfillment of the lion with wings to Nebuchadnezzar. First, the vision of the lion only matches the second half of the story where Nebuchadnezzar is restored to sanity and his kingship. It ignores the fact that Nebuchadnezzar started out as a man. Second, Daniel 4:25 says that Nebuchadnezzar would "eat grass like cattle." This is hardly lionlike behavior. He was not made like the king of beasts but rather brought lower, like a grazing animal. And third, in the vision, the lion was forced to stand unnaturally and was not restored to a former natural state as was Nebuchadnezzar. So this is an imperfect fulfillment of Daniel 7:4.

When empires and nations act with no accountability they do tend to act like wild beasts—attacking and devouring each other rather than acting civilized. The Iraqi government under Saddam Hussein ruled like any one of the beasts—a beast that was unruly, acted with complete power and authority in its country, and attempted to conquer the countries around it.

But in the Bible, the lion with wings was changed, and unnaturally at that.

What we saw happen to the "lion with wings" was that Saddam Hussein was removed from power in March 2003 in the invasion of Iraq, and the nation got a new government. Iraq was given a fledgling democracy, ruled by law rather than the whims of a conqueror or beast. There is an experiment going on since the fall of Saddam to change Iraq so that it becomes more "civilized"—at least in the eyes of Western democracies. I believe that the prophecy of the tearing of the wings off the lion, forcing it to walk upright, and giving it the heart of a man, was fulfilled by the United States' attempt to turn Iraq from a monarchy or empire into a Jeffersonian democracy.

First, the wings of the lion were "torn off." The Aramaic word used in the text is *mrat* (Strong's #4804, pronounced mer-at') meaning literally "to pluck." In May 2003, after the invasion of Iraq, the Iraqi army was disbanded. Also, all of the fighter aircraft that existed at the end of Saddam's reign were scrapped.

Next, the lion was "lifted from the ground." The word used in the text is *ntal* (Strong's #5191, pronounced net-al') which is "to lift up." It takes a conscientious effort by a force other than the lion to do this. The effort is in lifting the beast's chest off the ground so its hind legs were left on the ground, thereby forcing it to stand. The text also uses the Aramaic word *quwm* (Strong's #6966, pronounced koom), and it means "to make to stand." The Bible uses this word in other places in regard to people "arising" to stand—but they do it on their own, under their own power. But in this case, others forced this beast up so that it could stand. This was unnatural for a lion, so who forced it? Who provided the outside force to lift the lion? It was the international coalition of forces led by the United States. Lastly, this lion was basically given a heart transplant. The way this creature thought and acted was changed from "let's devour our neighbor" when it had a beast's heart, to "let's try to get along with everyone" when it was given a man's heart.

Iraq, containing basically the land of Mesopotamia, has a heritage of anything but democracy. From the beginning of civilization that region was part of various empires like the Babylonian and Assyrian Empires. Then it was part of various empires ruled from Persia before Islam conquered it. Then it belonged to various Islamic empires, the last being the Ottoman Empire. So, before 2005, the region of Iraq had never been governed by a democracy. More importantly, because Iraq is a thoroughly Muslim nation, any democracy will have a difficult time establishing and sustaining itself. Indeed, for democracy to begin in a Muslim nation, democracy must be forced on it.

As we saw in chapter 1, Islam has as its central code the Qur'an, the Hadith, and the Sira. The people must be obedient to what is written in its holy writings as interpreted by a group of clerics. In any typical Islamic nation or empire, the clerics interpret the writings to create the code of Sharia law. Politically, fundamental Islam does not foster an educated and well-informed population, nor would it want one. A properly educated and well-informed population would be resistant to Sharia law and jihad.

The Muslim nation of Turkey was able to make the transition to a democracy because of unique conditions. For centuries, the Muslim Ottoman Empire had threatened Europe. Following World War I, what remained of the empire, which today is Turkey, was vulnerable to being completely vanquished by the victorious European powers. It took Ataturk, a powerful and charismatic leader, to insist on and lead reforms to shape the nation to look and act like any other European nation so it could survive as a nation. In a way, Ataturk taught another beast how to act like a man. But now after ninety years there are signs Turkey is reverting back to its old Islamist ways.

For a democracy to develop on its own, its people need to be educated, informed, and willing to work together. These factors also tend to create wealth for its people when a free market economy and trade are allowed within the democracy. Recent examples since World War II are nations of East Asia such as Japan, Taiwan, and South Korea, as well as European nations such as Germany. When the United Kingdom gave up its colony of India and Pakistan in 1947, it left a democratic government in both new nations. Hindu India retained its democracy. But, in contrast, Muslim Pakistan did not. It is now a dictatorship with terrorist organizations operating within its borders. Hamas, which rules in Gaza, has no priority on development of the Gaza territory but only on jihad with Israel.

Since 2003 a topic of discussion on news shows and in academia here in the United States has been the question of how out of place a democracy is in Iraq, and whether Iraq can keep a democracy. Marine General Anthony Zinni, former head of US Central Command, summed up the situation in Iraq well when he said,

> If we think there is a fast solution to changing the governance of Iraq, then we don't understand history, the nature of the country, the divisions, or the underneath suppressed passions that could rise up. God help us if we think this transition will occur easily . . . There is no history of Jeffersonian democracy here.[9]

From what we know of political Islam, as well as examples of fledgling democracies in Muslim and non-Muslim nations, we can say that a classical Greek or modern American-style democracy is at odds with the very nature of Islam. The picture the Bible gives in Daniel 7:4 actually describes the situation well. A Muslim nation such as Iraq being made into a democracy is like a lion being taught to think like a man and walk like a man. I would say the Bible views the whole scene of what is happening in Iraq as unnatural. It's as unnatural as forcing a lion to walk and to think differently.

Please do not misunderstand me. If Iraq can keep a civil democracy and by doing so improve the lives of millions of Iraqis, more power to them. I am simply saying that if the picture in Daniel 7:4 is indeed describing democracy being forced on Iraq, then the Bible is saying the whole picture is unnatural. There is nothing in Daniel 7:4 that says the process is slow or difficult or even impossible. It simply implies that it is unnatural.

Today, the lion with the man's heart continues to walk on its hind feet. The democratic government was set up per election results in December 2005 and then had its second and third parliamentary elections in 2010 and 2014. So far, so good. Despite the Islamic State occupying large areas of Iraq starting in 2014, the Iraqi government continues to function democratically.

We can also say that the First Signpost ended officially on December 18, 2011. That was the day the last large contingent of American troops on the ground left Iraq. Saddam Hussein was removed from power in April 2003 by international coalition forces led by the US. After his removal, those same military forces provided the outside force to make the lion stand and to change its mind. It could be argued that any end to the First Signpost would be the completion of the action to force the lion to do what was done to it in Daniel 7:3, and then the removal of the outside force. Iraq, the former lion with wings, is now standing erect somewhat like a man, and indeed has a heart of a man, rather than that of a beast. It was reported that the last contingent of American troops numbering three thousand left for Kuwait in a convoy of five hundred vehicles on Sunday, December 18, 2011.[10]

In addition, I am thankful to God that most of our men and women on the ground will now be out of harm's way when the Second Signpost begins. According to the Bible, when the ram comes storming out of Iran, no country will be able to stand up to it, and no country in the ram's path will be rescued.

As a side note, many have wondered why the United States of America is not mentioned in end times prophecy in the Bible. Well, it may not be specifically mentioned by *name*, but if the interpretation of prophecy is true as given in this book, then the Signposts mention the actions of the United States directly in prophecy.

SUMMARY

During the time of the First Signpost the world was to watch for a leader of the end-time inheritor nation of Babylon, bent on conquest, acting as a conqueror, and threatening the use of a bow. The deeds and career of Saddam Hussein from 1979 to 2003 are an extraordinary fulfillment of the description of the first horseman in Revelation 6:3, even down to the status of the WMD.

If Iraq and Saddam Hussein are the fulfillment of the lion with wings and the first horseman, then we know exactly how the lion was forced to walk upright and why, and why the horseman was carrying his bow. Could these passages (Revelation 6:3 and Daniel 7:4) be fulfilled any better or any closer than by Saddam and Iraq? Time will tell.

If Saddam is the fulfillment of the first horseman, what about the three horsemen that follow? Some people may say that the release of the horseman on the white horse should be a more significant event—after all, it's one of the four horsemen of the Apocalypse—as ominous as that sounds. Perhaps there should have been more destruction or awful times with the horsemen of the Apocalypse on the loose. But remember, Revelation 6:8 says of the horsemen:

> They were given power over a fourth of the earth to kill by sword, famine, and plague, and by the wild beasts of the earth.

The horsemen have authority in the Islamic quarter of the earth. Also, the second horseman, who was given the power to allow men to slay each other, can be linked with the killing by the sword in the passage.

With the third horseman holding a pair of scales in his hand, and with the words spoken about the high cost of food, this can be linked to the killing by famine. Death, who is the fourth horseman, can be linked with the killing by plague. But what can the first horseman be linked with in that list? Nothing it seems. So compared to the other horsemen with their war, famine, and plague, the Bible may be saying that the coming of the first horseman will be a more benign event than the remaining three.

Saddam Hussein was responsible via sword and plague for the deaths in the Islamic quarter of the earth of tens of thousands of Kurds via mustard gas, and the deaths of hundreds of thousands of Iraqis and Iranians from his triggering of the Iran-Iraq War of the 1980s. And if these events, caused by Saddam, are to be more benign than the events caused by the next three riders, we as a world are soon to be exposed to much more violence and death than that caused by Saddam Hussein. Remember, however, the words of Jesus when He said that events in the end times would increase in sorrow before His return, by comparing them to birth pains of a woman in labor. He said in Matthew 24:7–8, "Nation will rise against nation, and kingdom against kingdom. There will be famines and earthquakes in various places. All these are the beginning of birth pains."

Ominously, if Saddam was the fulfillment of the first horseman who has come and gone, we are already on the doorstep of the calling out of the second horseman. *May the Lord protect all those who are His.*

CHAPTER 10

THE SECOND SIGNPOST: THE CONQUEST BY IRAN

I N THIS CHAPTER WE COME TO OUR DISCUSSION OF THE SECOND Signpost. As we saw in the last chapter, looking at the visions of Daniel with new eyes has shown us some surprising things. Due to the First Signpost, we saw from the Bible that recent events in Iraq have more significance than we first thought. It shouldn't surprise us then that these visions are telling us of things going on right now that are related to the Second Signpost—things so significant we need to watch them with a great deal of urgency.

The Second Signpost is the invasion of the Middle East by Iran. Ominously, this Signpost could begin at any time.

We saw in chapter 8 that the events of the Second Signpost include the prophecies of the bear, the ram, and the second horseman, which is the rider on the red horse. I proposed that the prophecies of the bear and the ram are to be fulfilled by the forces of Iran invading the Middle East. I also proposed that the prophecy of the rider on the red horse represents the conditions during this war—the loss of life in the Middle East and the loss of peace of mind worldwide. In this chapter we will see how Iran and its potential near-term actions could in fact fulfill the prophecies pertaining to the Second Signpost.

If these Four Signposts are the correct interpretation of biblical prophecy, then we are presently waiting and watching for the Second Signpost to begin. We saw in chapter 8 that this Signpost is mostly about Iran starting (or possibly escalating) a major Sunni-Shia war. Indeed, in the years since 2005 when Mahmoud Ahmadinejad, the sixth president of Iran, was in office, Iran has been threatening to unleash war on the Middle East. This great war that begins in the Second Signpost will change the world and over a number of years set it on its path to the Tribulation itself. Now is the time to be awake and watching. Astonishingly, Iran's supreme leader and the Revolutionary Guard are showing us that Iran is on the threshold of fulfilling the ram's role in Daniel 8.

While on center stage as the nation of the First Signpost, Iraq dominated the international news headlines through the 1990s and well into the 2000s. As one might expect for the approach of the Second Signpost, Iran is now dominating the news headlines.

Figure 10-1. The Second Signpost: the bear, the ram, and the second horseman

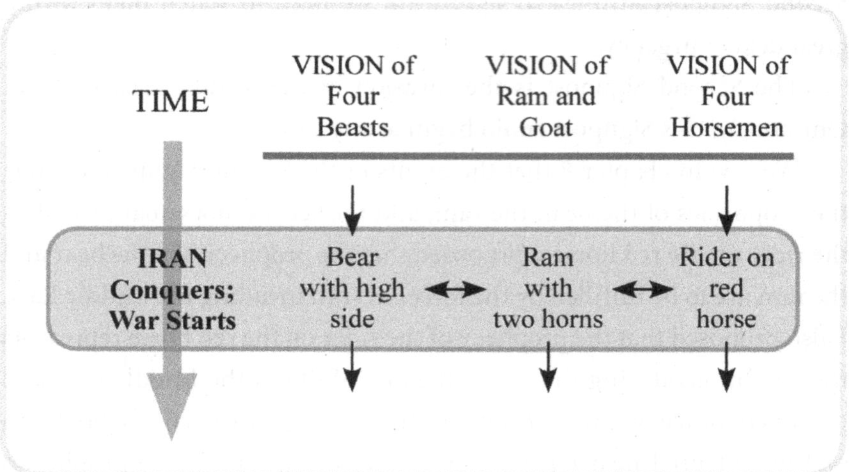

TIME	VISION of Four Beasts		VISION of Ram and Goat		VISION of Four Horsemen
IRAN Conquers; War Starts	Bear with high side	◄►	Ram with two horns	◄►	Rider on red horse

THE THREE VISIONS APPLIED TO THE SECOND SIGNPOST

To help remind us which parts of the three visions are involved here in the Second Signpost, figure 10-1 below shows the Second Signpost's portion of figure 8-6 in chapter 8. From figure 10-1 we see that the Second Signpost has the bear from the vision of the four beasts, the ram from the vision of the ram and the goat, and it has the rider on the red horse from the vision of the four horsemen.

We will now review the various details of these three visions and collect them into a scenario for the Second Signpost.

First, Iran is represented in the vision of the four beasts by a beast that is like a bear. Daniel 7:5 says of the bear,

And there before me was a second beast, which looked like a bear. It was raised up on one of its sides, and it had three ribs in its mouth between its teeth. It was told, "Get up and eat your fill of flesh!"

This is all the Bible says about the second beast. The first thing we see is this second beast is like a bear. This is obvious but significant. Second, this bear is raised higher on one of its sides. Third, it has three ribs in its mouth. And last, it is told to eat much flesh.

Second, Iran is represented by a ram in the vision of the ram and goat. Regarding the ram here in the Second Signpost, Daniel 8:3–4 reads:

I looked up, and there before me was a ram with two horns, standing beside the canal, and the horns were long. One of the horns was longer than the other but grew up later. I watched the ram as he charged toward the west and the north and the south. No animal could stand against him, and none could rescue from his power. He did as he pleased and became great.

We can gather three things here. First, the ram has two long horns; the longer horn is the newer horn of the two. Second, this ram charged out in three directions—north, south, and west—with little or no resistance from any other nation. Third, the ram did as it pleased and became great.

The third vision reflects the ongoing condition of the Second Signpost—the start of a war. Of the second horseman riding the red horse, Revelation 6:4 reveals,

> Then another horse came out, a fiery red one. Its rider was given power to take peace from the earth and to make men slay each other. To him was given a large sword.

This one verse about the second horseman says he rides a red horse and is given a large sword. It also says he will make men slay one another. We saw that a major war starts during the Second Signpost. So the sword given to the rider and the very color of his horse are all appropriate for war. If you'll recall, in chapter 7 we saw that this horseman, like all the horsemen, only has authority to operate in one quarter of the earth. Therefore he can only make men slay one another in one quarter of the earth. However, he is given power to take peace from the entire earth.

We will now arrange the noted details of each of these three visions into the major events of the Second Signpost. This is shown in table 10-1. The six events in the first column of table 10-1 are the events of the unfolding of this Signpost in chronological order. We will explore these six events in the same order as shown in table 10-1 for the remainder of this chapter.

Table 10-1. Vision details form six major events within Second Signpost

SECOND SIGNPOST EVENTS TIME LINE	VISION OF BEAR (DANIEL 7:5)	VISION OF RAM (DANIEL 8:3-4, 20)	VISION OF RIDER (REVELATION 6:4)
A) A Shift in Power in Iran's Government Prior to War	• One side higher	• Newer horn is longer • Horns are kings of Medes and Persians	—
B) Iran's Military Prepares for War	—	—	• Given a large sword • Red horse
C) Iran Starts War with a Massive Invasion	• Like a bear • Told to eat	• Ram charges out from Susa	—
D) Iran's Advance Into Many Nations	• "Much" flesh • Three ribs in mouth	• Ram charges north, south and west • Did as he pleased	
E) Iran Removes Worldwide Stability	—	—	• Makes men slay one another • Takes peace from the earth
F) Iran Feared, Respected	—	• Becomes great	—

A Shift in Power in Iran's Government Prior to War

We begin our examination of the Second Signpost by looking at the higher and lower sides of the bear, and the two horns of the ram. We know from chapter 8 that the bear and the ram both represent modern Iran. We will also see that the sides of the bear and the horns of the ram also represent the same thing relative to each other: the leadership of Iran.

Daniel 7:5 tells us about the bear's sides where it says, "It was raised up on one of its sides." Bible commentators, supporting the fulfillment of this vision in ancient times, have said that the bear's two sides represent the two powers within the ancient Persian Empire—the Medes and the Persians. The Medes ruled first and then the Persians, who were stronger, ruled later. Hence the Persian side was the higher side in the bear over the Mede side. But, of course, the problem with this idea is this vision is to be fulfilled in the end times. So, instead of the two sides representing kings of two ethnic groups within the old Persian Empire, I believe the two sides represent two positions of power within the government of modern Iran. These positions of power either presently hold or will hold the most power in that country, sharing power, with one leader being greater than the other. Today, most Iranians are descended from the Medes and Persians and so can be considered Medes and Persians themselves. Therefore, the two leaders will indeed be the kings of the Medes and Persians in these end times.

SECOND SIGNPOST EVENTS TIME LINE	VISION OF BEAR (DANIEL 7:5)	VISION OF RAM (DANIEL 8:3-4, 20)	VISION OF RIDER (REVELATION 6:4)
A) A Shift in Power in Iran's Government Prior to War	• One side higher	• Newer horn is longer • Horns are kings of Medes and Persians	—

In addition to the bear having two sides with one higher, we have more information due to the ram's two horns. Daniel 8:3 says, "there before me was a ram with two horns." Daniel 8:20 gives us the interpretation of the two horns of the ram: "The two-horned ram that you saw represents the kings of Media and Persia." Again, the popular view that supports an ancient fulfillment would say that these are kings of the ancient Persian Empire ruling one after the other, just as with the bear. But, with the modern fulfillment, these kings must represent individual leaders in Iran who are contemporaries of each other. As mentioned in chapter 6, just as the horns on the goat represent single leaders, so do the horns of the ram. The symbols used within a vision must be consistent.

Therefore, when the ram charges out having two horns, Iran will be led by two leaders who are sharing power. The two leaders will be occupying two positions of power that will be the two highest in Iran at the time of the start of the war. A position of power can be officially recognized like a government office, or it can be less official but nevertheless present, such as a high-ranking general supported by his military where power is behind the scenes. The ram's horns and the bear's sides "agree" and can both support the same interpretation of two leaders ruling together and sharing power.

We have even more information about the horns from Daniel 8:3. In addition to the ram merely having two horns, the growth and establishment of the horns relative to each other is astonishingly similar to what has been happening in Iran for the last thirty years or so. Daniel 8:3 says of the ram's two horns, "one of the horns was longer than the other but grew up later." In other words, at the beginning we start with one long horn and one short—maybe even stubby—horn. At the end of the growth phase there will be two long horns on the ram. The short and stubby horn in the beginning becomes the longer one in the end. The long horn in the beginning stays that way all the time while the short horn becomes the longest horn. The long horn in the beginning therefore ends up having his power exceeded by the growing second horn.

Astonishingly, this describes the situation perfectly between the supreme leader and the Iranian Revolutionary Guard Corps (IRGC). I believe the supreme leader of Iran is the first horn that was initially longer—the horn that in the end will be exceeded in length by the second horn. The IRGC is the power behind the second horn, the horn that grows up and becomes longer in the end. We do not yet know who the man will be who is the second horn, but his power will come directly from the IRGC. He may be a representative of the IRGC or an IRGC commander.

The supreme leader appeared first as the top leader of Iran back in 1979. The second horn—the other position of power—in reality has been growing up quietly for thirty years behind the scenes. We do not yet know what form this second position of power will take, but we do know it will come about as a consequence of the IRGC's growth in power relative to the supreme leader. Just as Julius Caesar established his praetorian guard as a bodyguard of the emperor, and a couple centuries later that guard ended up deciding who would be emperor, so now the Iranian guard (the IRGC) seems to be on the same path. The IRGC has grown from being merely the supreme leader's bodyguard in 1979 to being a body that in some ways exercises greater control over Iran than the supreme leader does.

Following the revolution in Iran in February 1979, a constitution was approved in Iran in October of that year establishing the supreme leader as the highest office. The supreme leader is not elected by the people but by a special committee of clerics—much as the cardinals in Rome elect the pope. The office of the supreme leader is considered to be the highest governing position of the land and the religious leader of the nation. The supreme leader sets national policy and is the commander-in-chief of the military forces.

(As a side note, three additional lower offices were established at the same time. These three offices are the president, the head of parliament, and the head of the judiciary. The president is the executive who merely carries out the direction set by the supreme leader, and is elected directly by the people. The supreme leader also decides who can run for president. The president only has power with the people, but no real power over the matters of state.)

The first man to hold the office of supreme leader was Ayatollah Ruhollah Khomeini, who founded the Iranian Revolution. The second and current man is Ayatollah Ali Khamenei who took over in 1989. When the office of supreme leader was established in 1979, Ayatollah Khomeini was seen by many in Iran as speaking in the very name of God and so had near absolute power over Iran. The first horn was, as Daniel 8:3 says, indeed long.

At the same time, Ayatollah Khomeini himself sowed the seed for the second horn when he started the Iranian Revolutionary Guard Corps (IRGC) in April 1979. A statute legally defining the IRGC was ratified toward the end of April 1979, by the Council of the Revolution, the highest de facto governing body at the time in Iran.[1] In this statute the functions of the IRGC were defined: (1) to guard the Islamic revolution in Iran, which included defending the supreme leader, and (2) to export the Islamic revolution to other countries.[2] To execute these functions the statute also gave the IRGC the role of army, police, and intelligence. The IRGC, also known as the Pasdaran, has its own army, navy, and aerospace force apart from Iran's regular armed forces. The aerospace force controls the country's nuclear and missile programs. Iran's regular armed forces, also known as the Artesh, have an army, navy, and air force whose function it is to defend Iranian territory from outside aggression.

In addition to the IRGC's own army, navy, and aerospace force, it has a fourth branch known as the Basij paramilitary. The Basij began as a separate force, but the Iranian parliament formally incorporated it into the IRGC in 1981.[3] The Basij has fulfilled the role of internal religious police since 1979, but during the Iran-Iraq War the Basij was also called to fight on the battlefield. It was the Basij that provided the human waves of zealots that threw themselves against Saddam's army in the 1980s during the Iran-Iraq War. It is the Basij that has suppressed rebellions that have threatened the regime over the years. The Basij is an all-volunteer force and the IRGC recruits its members for its other branches from the Basij.[4] Finally, the IRGC has a fifth major branch known as the Quds Force which is named after the Arabic word for "Jerusalem." It is presently "exporting the Revolution" by funding, training, and arming many of the Islamist and terror groups in Iraq, Syria, Lebanon, and the Gulf states.

The growth of the IRGC as the power behind the second horn started in 1980 when the war with Iraq began. The IRGC fought the Iran-Iraq

War from 1980 to 1988. During these years the IRGC was transformed from an undertrained bodyguard of the supreme leader into an organized fighting force.[5] One author has made the claim that the IRGC may not have achieved all the power it has if it were not for the Iran-Iraq War of the 1980s that gave it the boost it needed.[6] It is here we see that the actions of the lion in the First Signpost directly sowed the seeds for the Second Signpost.

Following the war, and during the presidency of Akbar Hashemi Rafsanjani from 1989 to 1997, the IRGC first became involved with the economy of Iran.[7] The Iranian government wanted to create jobs for the returning war veterans in order to contribute to the country's stability. The IRGC's engineering corps was reorganized into a major civil engineering company that built houses, roads, and bridges.[8] Besides building houses, the IRGC has grown to the point that it also speculates in real estate abroad.[9] The IRGC took over many of Iran's high-tech businesses and now produces consumer goods. It later took over seaports and border areas to control trade and border security. The IRGC has taken over the telecommunications industry.[10] Most recently it has even taken over part of the oil industry.[11]

In summary, the IRGC is now involved with every major money-making business in Iran.[12] The IRGC's economic position has even continued to improve in recent years despite the international sanctions against Iran. The sanctions caused many foreign companies to leave Iran allowing the IRGC to win the equivalent of multibillion-dollar contracts in Iran with no competition.[13] It is not known with certainty how much of the Iranian economy the IRGC directly controls, but 40 percent could be a fair figure derived from a consensus of various sources.[14] The profits derived from all of these industries are used in part by the IRGC to acquire weapon systems, pay IRGC salaries, bribe politicians, fund terror groups, and recruit new members using financial incentives such as cheap housing.

During the presidency of Mohammad Khatami from 1997 to 2005, the IRGC first became involved with both state security and national politics. IRGC Intelligence and the Basij replaced the older security and intelligence ministries. The IRGC's involvement with politics came as a consequence of its growing power. The IRGC was directly represented in national politics when it supported Mahmoud Ahmadinejad, a former Basij commander, to be president in 2005 for his first term. Against popular opposition, the IRGC also made Ahmadinejad the president for a second term, having him "win" the election in 2009. It was indeed the Basij stuffing ballot boxes in some of the provinces that allowed Ahmadinejad to win a second term.[15] At that point it could be said that the IRGC had the power to control who could be president. Though the supreme leader chooses the candidates who will run for president in Iran, the IRGC can effectively decide who will be president. They do this to place a man in office who will most push their agenda. The election of Mahmoud Ahmadinejad as Iran's sixth president greatly benefitted the IRGC. Ahmadinejad appointed a record two-thirds of the cabinet positions to former IRGC commanders. This allowed the IRGC to continue to expand in domestic influence, and in particular, banking and the oil industry.

Add to the IRGC's control over the presidency the control of intelligence, the military, and much of the economy, along with the fact that the supreme leader relies on the IRGC to suppress rebellion to stay in power, and we see why the IRGC can be said to be at least as powerful as the supreme leader himself. Even when the "moderate" candidate and cleric Hassan Rouhani surprisingly won the election in June 2013 and became Iran's seventh president, it is because the supreme leader and IRGC allowed it.[16] I believe the supreme leader and the IRGC let Rouhani win so the majority of the public of Iran would be pacified long enough to allow the regime to complete its plans.

My first hint that the second horn was possibly getting ready to take power was in the actions of Iran's former president, Ahmadinejad, starting in 2010. He was always outspoken with his own ideas on what

Iran's domestic and foreign policies should be, much to the dismay of the supreme leader. In the last three years of Ahmadinejad's administration he belligerently increased his challenges to the supreme leader's policies. For a while it looked like he might exceed the supreme leader in power, making him the second horn. If this were true then the Second Signpost was about to start back in 2011. However, Ahmadinejad was a false alarm, and the IRGC itself fits the description of the second horn much better. The IRGC has been growing nonstop for more than thirty years, and has real power that only now rivals the supreme leader, while the presidency always had the same minimal power it does now, and that has not changed.

It has recently become apparent that Ahmadinejad, not formerly one of the core IRGC leaders, acted on his own beliefs. He may have challenged the supreme leader's positions thinking he had the backing of the IRGC. The IRGC, however, stopped supporting Ahmadinejad and came to the aid of supreme leader Khamenei.[17] At the end of Ahmadinejad's second term, the IRGC labeled his administration as containing a "deviant current."[18] With continued observation and research, it has become apparent to me that Ahmadinejad was a red herring that the IRGC used to further its own agenda, and that the IRGC leadership is the real power that is the second horn.

The IRGC's power has increased to the point where one could debate that it rivals or exceeds that of the supreme leader. However, differences in ideology with the supreme leader will finally cause the IRGC to be the driver and planner for the invasion by Iran. We will look at the IRGC's ideology in the next section.

Now we are at the place where observers and analysts watching Iran wonder who really is in charge of Iran—the supreme leader or the IRGC.[19, 20] From a prophetic viewpoint, has the second horn already grown longer than the horn that is the supreme leader, or does the IRGC have a final move to make to establish the second horn as longest? I believe the position of power that is the second horn, the IRGC, will come into its own as the longest horn when it takes the power to declare war away from the supreme leader. But this transfer of power may be hidden and may have already happened. The IRGC may either operate with this power behind the scenes with its leadership overruling the supreme leader, or it may establish an official government office. We probably will not know until the first overt and significant event happens—whether a new office in Iran takes greater power, or the great invasion itself begins. How I wish it were the former, since in that case we might have the luxury of extra time to warn and prepare, but I fear it is the latter.

Positions of power in the IRGC are somewhat veiled, and so the invasion could happen tomorrow with the IRGC already having exceeded the supreme leader in power, or there may be a visible shuffle of power in Iran first. We simply cannot know. Therefore, we do not really know how much more time we have until the great invasion. If the position of power stays hidden in the leadership of the IRGC, this makes the great invasion by Iran in the Second Signpost imminent—the next thing to watch for in Bible prophecy.

In summary, Iran has its first horn, the first king. One author wrote about the supreme leader's position in Iran as that of "a Platonic philosopher *king*."[21] Regarding the IRGC's rise and becoming the premier de facto power in Iran, another author wrote that the IRGC is "a *king maker*" in Iranian politics.[22] This second quote relates to the IRGC's ability to allow whomever it wants to be president. But when the time comes, its leader will in fact be the second king, and the IRGC will have made him king. It is interesting to me that two secular authors speak of the two horns of the ram just as Daniel 8:20 does when it says, "the two horns are the *kings* of the Medes and the Persians."

When the position of the second horn is finally established with power exceeding that of the supreme leader, then the prophecy in Daniel 8:3 that says the second and longer horn "grew up later" will be fulfilled. At that time, in addition to Saddam Hussein and the democratizing of Iraq that fulfilled the prophecies pertaining to the First Signpost, we will see prophecies pertaining to the Second Signpost starting to be fulfilled.

IRAN'S MILITARY PREPARES FOR WAR

SECOND SIGNPOST EVENTS TIME LINE	VISION OF BEAR (DANIEL 7:5)	VISION OF RAM (DANIEL 8:3-4, 20)	VISION OF RIDER (REVELATION 6:4)
B) Iran's Military Prepares for War	—	—	• Given a large sword • Red horse

In this section, we note that the second horseman of Revelation 6:4 is given his great sword, and he rides out. War is to begin on a large scale once the second horn finally finishes its growth. In terms of territory covered, this war will likely be akin to the European theater of World War II in geographic extent. Some journalists may even call it World War III, but it will be confined to the Middle East. I believe that the wars of the Second and Third Signposts may be called the Great Sunni-Shia War in retrospect. At least a dozen nations now existing will be directly involved in this war.

For Iran to carry out the invasion of the Middle East, which the ram and bear in prophecy are showing that Iran must do, Iran must have the leadership with the ideology to do so, as well as the military to execute it. Again, as an example from World War II, the aggressor nation Nazi Germany had an ideology at the time which made invasion of Europe a given. They also had the military to do something about it. In this section we will look at the ideology of Iran's leadership, and in later sections we will go on to Iran's military.

To begin with, you might recall from chapter 1 that Iran is a Shia Muslim nation. The vast majority of its people are Shia Muslims. Let me explain why this is significant. The difference between Shia and Sunni sects in Islam centers on their beliefs about who should have succeeded Muhammad, the founder and original prophet of Islam. This split started soon after Muhammad's death. The majority of Islam—the Sunni sect— believed that the successor should be in the family of Muhammad. The minority—the Shia sect—believed it should be someone who had unique spiritual qualities from God, a "spark" if you will, as Muhammad is believed to have had.

According to Shia belief within the Twelver sect, there were eleven imams who were supposed to rule Islam. The Twelfth Imam disappeared in the tenth century and is to reappear toward the end of the age and rule all of Islam. It is this Twelfth Imam who is to be the Mahdi. Joel Richardson's book *The Islamic Antichrist* compares the Islamic Mahdi with the Bible's end-time Antichrist and shows that they are one and the same. About 85 percent of all Shia Muslims are Twelvers. The minority sects within Shia Islam believe in a different number of imams, or a different role for them. So the fact that Iran is a nation of Twelver Shia Muslims means that many are expecting the coming of their Mahdi (our Antichrist).

The founder of the Iranian Revolution, Ayatollah Ruhollah Khomeini, was a Twelver.[23] His successor, current supreme leader Ayatollah Ali Khamenei is also a Twelver, and so is the leadership of the IRGC.

Khomeini founded what he called the Islamic Revolution using the book he wrote containing his philosophy of how to run an Islamic society. His book was titled *Velayat-e Faqih* (in English the *Guardianship of the Jurisprudent*). In this book Khomeini wrote that there should be one highest leader—the *Faqih*, or the Guardian—who rules the flock of Muslims while they wait for the Mahdi to appear. Khomeini also believed that his Islamic Revolution should be exported to all the countries of Islam, so that all of Islam could wait for the Mahdi and the restoration of the caliphate could be ushered in.[24] Tangible proof of Khomeini's desire to export the Revolution is twofold. First he founded the Quds Force within the IRGC in 1981, whose sole purpose is to export the Islamic Revolution to other Muslim countries. Second, it is believed that the only reason Khomeini did not call for ending the Iran-Iraq War in 1982 after the IRGC expelled Saddam Hussein's forces from Iran, was to immediately export the Revolution to Iraq. The war continued for six more years, but the Iraqi army contained Iran's attempts.

Ahmadinejad's outspoken beliefs about the Mahdi and how the IRGC responded positively to him can be thought of as a litmus test of what the IRGC believes. At his first swearing-in ceremony in 2005, Ahmadinejad told Supreme Leader Khamenei that his own presidency was temporary and that he would be handing power over to the Mahdi. Ahmadinejad even told him that the Mahdi will come soon.[25] He said in official meetings that the end of history (when the Mahdi arrives it is the end of history according to the Twelvers) is only two or three years away.[26]

Ahmadinejad began each of his major campaign speeches with a prayer for the early return of the Mahdi.[27] As president of Iran, he spoke at the UN each year about the coming of Mahdi.[28]

Ahmadinejad said that everyone should work toward the hastening of the return of the Mahdi. He said that he is proud of his beliefs, and that they are not radical or superstitious.[29] Ahmadinejad also claims that he regularly receives help and direction from the Mahdi.[30]

According to the Twelvers' belief, the Mahdi, the Twelfth Imam, will unite all of Islam and extend Islam to the ends of the earth. Ahmadinejad likewise said that the Revolution in Iran is not just to change the government of Iran, but the Revolution wants to be a world government.[31] He also said that the Iranian Revolution's primary mission is to make the appearing of the Mahdi possible, to pave the way.[32]

One might think these statements are bold or extraordinary, and yet these were all said before the 2009 presidential election. Not only did the supreme leader support Ahmadinejad for his second term in 2009, but the IRGC supported him directly also. They supported him to the degree that some sources in Iran noted that the 2009 presidential election was the most fraudulent in their history. Among other things, the Basij was accused of stuffing the ballot boxes in various provinces.[33]

All of this shows the IRGC did not object to Ahmadinejad's beliefs. What eventually caused the IRGC to abandon support of Ahmadinejad after 2010 were his challenges to the supreme leader's directives. The IRGC looks upon the supreme leader as its reason for existence, and so they came to his defense.

The supreme leader uses the Quds Force to export his idea of the Revolution (the Guardianship) to other countries. However, the IRGC's slight differences in ideology with the supreme leader, I believe, will ultimately cause the IRGC to plan and execute the massive invasion that is the Second Signpost. Even news sources have noted a distinction between the supreme leader's and the IRGC's ideologies. They label the supreme leader and his political allies as "principalists." IRGC commanders and others such as Ahmadinejad are known as "neo-principalists." Neo-principalists are considered more radical by the principalists.

Any community of believers will have various sects and shades of belief, and Twelver Shia Islam is no exception. A particular belief system held by some in the neo-principalist camp is mentioned from time to time. This belief system is a group known as the Hojjatieh. Founded in 1953 to combat the Baha'i faith in Iran, the Hojjatieh Association goes beyond the supreme leader's belief of only waiting for the Mahdi. They believe that the coming of the Mahdi can *only* be brought about by physically spreading chaos to nations in the Islamic Realm. Ayatollah Khomeini "officially" ended the Hojjatieh Association in 1984 because he viewed their beliefs as a threat to his Guardianship of the Jurisprudent, or one ruler ruling the people waiting for the Mahdi. However, the Hojjatieh (also spelled "Hojjatiya") believers have moved their association into hiding. It is thought that counted among Hojjatieh believers are former Iranian president Mahmoud Ahmadinejad, and various IRGC commanders.[34] I believe that this faith of the Hojjatieh is what drives people like Ahmadinejad and the IRGC leadership on a slightly different path from that of the supreme leader.

In addition, IRGC ideology has been insulated somewhat from the ideology of the supreme leader because its own internal indoctrination process reinforces its ideology. Early on following the Revolution in 1979, IRGC officers were made responsible for IRGC troop indoctrination. In essence the IRGC was allowed to provide philosophical guidance for itself.[35] The IRGC has been able to keep its ranks ideologically pure and uniform, and to expel those who think differently. Indoctrination of guardsmen and officers is carried out at various Iranian universities.

So what does the IRGC teach itself? Unlike most Shia Muslims who are allowed to choose their own Ayatollah to learn from, all IRGC members follow a cult of the supreme leader. Their cult may be more of a following of Khomeini himself rather than of the supreme leader's office. The IRGC has been called to intervene many times to defend the supreme leader. This cult of the supreme leader has therefore reinforced disrespect among the IRGC for elected officials.[36]

The IRGC is also more paranoid than the supreme leader that the US or Israel is trying to bring down the regime.[37] This contributes to their militarism and their perceived need to intervene in politics. Where the supreme leader may lean more toward clerical means or, when needed, terrorist means to export the Revolution, the IRGC may be leaning more toward outright military conquest. Hojjatieh belief within the IRGC leadership would reinforce this idea.

The commanders of the IRGC today were soldiers and junior officers during the Iran-Iraq War thirty years ago, and fought on the front lines. This would also contribute to a greater feeling of nationalism in the IRGC. Where the supreme leader believes the Revolution needs to be exported, the IRGC also believes that Iran is specifically the country that needs to do it. Finally, the IRGC, being Shia, believes their religion is superior to Sunni Islam and so would spread the Revolution not only for Iran, but also for Shia Islam.

It should be evident at this point that the significance of Iran being Shia Muslim and not Sunni, with Shia's internal sects and beliefs in the Mahdi, is that God has prepared the Iranian nation to be the main actor of the Second Signpost.

In summary, the massive invasion of the Middle East during the Second Signpost is consistent with IRGC ideals. But the invasion will not start until the IRGC's power has exceeded that of the supreme leader. The greatest visible indicator of IRGC ideology is the military buildup in Iran over the last several years. More advanced weapon systems are being built and fielded domestically in Iran. The IRGC also carries out several large-scale military exercises. One of those exercises a number of years ago reminded me of the prophecy of the second horseman, which also represents Iran's war.

Revelation 6:4 says that the rider on the red horse was given a large sword. A few years ago there was an interesting news story that called to mind the prophecy of that sword. Israel fought a "mini-war" on its border with Lebanon in August 2006 against Hezbollah militants who were also supported by the Iranian military. On August 19, the day after the cease-fire in Lebanon, Iran began a huge and unprecedented military exercise called the "Blow of Zolfaghar." Zolfaghar (also spelled "Zulfiqar") is actually the name of the sword used by the first of Shia's twelve imams, Imam Ali (one of the first Four Caliphs mentioned in chapter 1). During the exercise, Iran placed its entire military on high alert. Military exercises were carried out in fourteen of Iran's thirty provinces (all the border provinces). Iran tested several new rockets and cruise missiles as well.[38] One of the news articles reporting the story even referred in its headline to Iran getting its sword ready.[39] It seems that the rider of the red horse is receiving his sword and, through the IRGC, will wield it.

There is one last note to be made about the sword known as Zolfaghar. Except for one distinguishing feature, physically it is no different than any other medium-length and slightly curved sword: its tip is bifurcated. That's right; the tip of the sword has two points, frequently drawn with one slightly longer than the other. It is probably the most important sword in Shia Islam. Iran uses that name for its military tank and for many other purposes. I cannot help but notice that the two tips of this sword are a "signature" feature. If indeed this can be thought of as the sword of the second horseman, it is very much related to the two horns of the ram. There are two horns—two tips—on the ram where one is higher than the other. The sword that Iran hails as their sword also has two tips with one slightly longer than the other. How amazing is that?

Regarding the color of this second horse and of the four colors mentioned in chapter 7, the significance of the color red in Islam is least agreed on. There is no universal meaning for red in Islam. Red is simply one of the four colors and is appropriate for war, which is indeed the theme for the Second Signpost.

In the sections ahead, we will next look at Iran's military capabilities.

Iran Starts War with a Massive Invasion

SECOND SIGNPOST EVENTS TIME LINE	VISION OF BEAR (DANIEL 7:5)	VISION OF RAM (DANIEL 8:3-4, 20)	VISION OF RIDER (REVELATION 6:4)
C) Iran Starts War with a Massive Invasion	• Like a bear • Told to eat	• Ram charges out from Susa	—

As I mentioned in chapter 5, each of the nations represented by the four beasts of Daniel 7 will behave like the beasts that represent them. In chapter 9 we saw how Iraq, represented by the lion, attacked like a lion and attempted to hold its prey. The prey was a single country or province. We will now see why Iran will behave like a bear when it goes to war and how this behavior is different from a lion's behavior.

Bears will generally eat anything as opportunities come along—insects, fish, small mammals, and deer, to name a few. A bear will eat berries on bushes, then move on to eat fish it catches out of rivers, and then moving on still take down newborn calves of deer and elk. A hungry bear will go from place to place and feed and gorge on what it finds. The Bible makes reference to this behavior of bears in two places. The first is in Proverbs 28:15 where it says, "Like a roaring lion and a rushing bear is a wicked ruler over a poor people" (NASB).

The Hebrew word for "rushing" in the text is *shaqaq* (Strong's #8264, pronounced shaw-kak'). It conveys the idea of running about, being eager and greedy, and rushing back and forth. The verse is saying that a wicked ruler is like a bear running about taking from everyone, and doing damage in one form or another to everyone he meets.

The second reference is in the story of how the prophet Elisha, who was Elijah's successor, was being taunted by a group of boys to follow Elijah up to heaven. The Bible says in 2 Kings 2:23–24 (NKJV):

Then he went up from there to Bethel; and as he was going up the road, some youths came from the city and mocked him, and said to him, "Go up, you baldhead! Go up, you baldhead!" So he turned around and looked at them, and pronounced a curse on them in the name of the LORD. And two female bears came out of the woods and mauled forty-two of the youths.

The Hebrew word for "mauled" is *baqa* (Strong's #1234, pronounced baw-kah') and it means to be ripped open, to be mauled, and therefore killed. Those two bears went from person to person to person mauling a total of forty-two!

The bear in the vision of the four beasts is told to "eat your fill of flesh!" We may understand what the "flesh" is by looking at the corresponding vision of the ram and the goat. Daniel 8:4 says of the ram, "No *animal* could stand against him, and none could rescue from his power" (emphasis added). This passage suggests that all other nations in the area are to be considered as animals or beasts as well. So, to carry the metaphor of these visions further, if the nations around Iran are beasts, then this bear will attack any nation, consuming the flesh of any other beast where the opportunity presents itself.

So, also like a bear, when Iran starts its war it will rush from country to country to country doing damage, mauling governments and societies everywhere it goes. Bears are also known to intimidate with their large size. Many smaller nations like the Gulf states may simply surrender. As revealed in Daniel 8:4, no other nation in the area will be able to stop the bear.

Moving on in the passage about the ram, Daniel 8:4 tells us what the ram of Iran does: "I watched the ram as he charged toward the west and the north and the south. No animal could stand against him, and none could rescue from his power. He did as he pleased and became great."

Backing up a bit in Daniel from Daniel 8:4, Daniel 8:2–3 says that before the ram's charge, the ram was standing near the citadel of Susa. The ruins of Susa can still be found today and are just 150 miles or so east of Baghdad. This verse suggests that Iranian forces will begin their charge out from Susa. Now Susa may just be a point of reference in the vision, and they may or may not do so. However, the geographic area would be a good staging area just inside the Iranian border. The border between Iran and Iraq is mountainous and not very traversable. But Susa is west of these mountains and on the plains, still within Iranian territory. Anyway, the verse says that Iranian military forces are to charge and conquer to the north of Susa, to the west of Susa and to the south of Susa.

Figure 10-2. Iranian ground force advances and ground force military strengths in the region[40, 41]

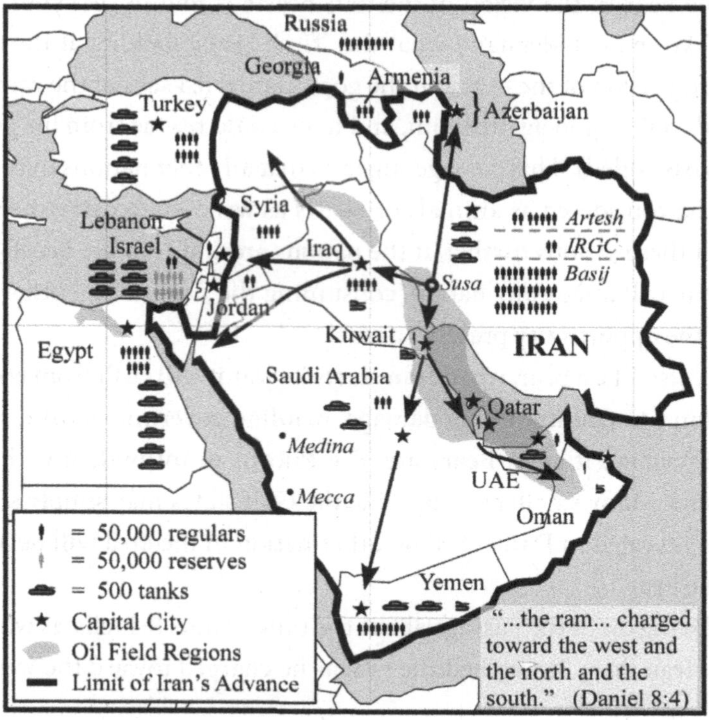

The present-day countries in the Middle East and the possible routes Iranian forces may take are shown in figure 10-2. Note the arrows that go almost exactly in north, south, and west directions. If you'll recall in this chapter, we saw that the supreme leader and the IRGC both want to carry the Revolution in Iran to other countries.

What better way than to target the capital cities of each of those countries. The most significant capital cities of these countries lie along lines in these three directions.

As a Shia nation, Iran would have as its objective the subjugation of the Middle East to Shia Islamic rule, and to export its Islamic Revolution. It would also have in mind as part of this to take the two holiest cities in Islam—Mecca and Medina. In order to best export the Revolution and cause chaos in the world it would also have the strategic objective of capturing all the Gulf oil fields. The IRGC's conquest of many targets perfectly fits the Bible's description of Iran as a hungry bear running from place to place.

In the next section we will discuss the military capability of Iran and further discuss the strategic situation in the region. We will be referring again to figure 10-2.

IRAN'S ADVANCE INTO MANY NATIONS

SECOND SIGNPOST EVENTS TIME LINE	VISION OF BEAR (DANIEL 7:5)	VISION OF RAM (DANIEL 8:3-4, 20)	VISION OF RIDER (REVELATION 6:4)
D) Iran's Advance Into Many Nations	• "Much" flesh • Three ribs in mouth	• Ram charges north, south and west • Did as he pleased	

We have seen so far in this chapter that Iran will begin a large invasion of the Middle East. We also looked at its leadership and its ideology and can see that an invasion of this scale could definitely be in their sights. In this section we will look at the possible territorial extent of the invasion, and at the military situation in the region.

Continuing on in Daniel 7:5 in the NIV, the bear is told to eat its fill of flesh. Other translations say "much" flesh. The word in the text of Daniel for "much" or "your fill" is *saggiy* (Strong's #7690, pronounced sag-ghee'). It means exceedingly large or many. The word *much* or the phrase "your fill" in English doesn't quite capture the sense of quantity displayed by this word in the text. We will see that many countries will be involved. We saw earlier that the vision of the ram and the goat mentions the nations around Iran as animals that might rescue others from the ram, or might themselves need rescue from the ram. So the use of *saggiy* essentially says that the bear will not just get its fill, but will *gorge* on many animals, thus many nations, to the point of bursting.

Continuing on in Daniel 7:5, the bear is said to have "three ribs in its mouth between its teeth." This part was a bit of a challenge to understand. I can remember as a young person seeing illustrations of this vision. The ribs were always curved up out of the bear's mouth and all three were together. I had always thought of the ribs in this way. But the Bible makes no distinction as to how the ribs are oriented in its mouth. The passage simply says they are between its teeth, most likely fixed or stuck in their orientation. I believe the three ribs represent the same thing as the three directions in which the ram will charge—north, south, and west. It is in these three directions that the bear will charge and consume much flesh. The ribs could very well be sticking out of his mouth in those three directions. From the ram's perspective in Susa the ribs could each be sticking out of the bear's mouth to the right (north), the left (south), and straight ahead (west). The ribs stand for the animal/nation carcasses to be stripped clean by a hungry bear in each of the three directions—one direction for each rib.

Before going any further in our discussion to understand Daniel 8:4 and its brief description of the invasion, let us take a look at the military situation in Iran and the neighboring countries that are targets for invasion.

This will help in our understanding of how Daniel 8:4 might be fulfilled. Look again at figure 10-2 at the end of the last section. Of the military forces represented in figure 10-2, only ground forces, or armies, are shown. Each "man" symbol represents fifty thousand troops—both regular and reserves. Most of the larger militaries have reserves, but only Israel's are shown because they are the only ones that can be ready on extremely short notice; and most of Israel's troops are indeed reserves. Each "tank" symbol represents five hundred tanks. The types and ages of tanks vary greatly within each country. A country's armies may have Russian, American, or locally made tanks, and vary in age from new to 1960s vintage.

Starting with Iran, its regular army (the army of the Artesh) has 350,000 troops, and the IRGC army numbers roughly 100,000.[42] In addition, there is the paramilitary Basij with perhaps 1.5 million volunteers (an average of rough estimates). One official in Iran boasted that the Basij numbers anywhere from ten to thirteen million, but we won't assume those numbers.[43] The Artesh and IRGC have roughly 1,600 tanks between them.

As the reader can see in figure 10-2, Iraq is the nation that Iranian forces would have to go through to carry out its invasion to the west and south. But Iraq no longer has the sixth largest military, one capable of containing Iran as it did under Saddam Hussein. Iraq now has only 150,000 troops.

However, in the end, the size of Iraq's military will probably not matter. The reason is that Iran, via its Quds Force, has built and maintains a network of control in "allied" countries continuing west to Lebanon, which includes Iraq. These allied countries are those with Shia communities, whether a minority as in Syria or a majority as in Iraq. Iran maintains control in Iraq and Lebanon, and is currently the only ally (other than Russia) of the Assad regime in Syria.[44] By doing all this Iran maintains a pathway leading to the Mediterranean Sea (with the exception of the newly emergent Islamic State) and to Israel through Iraq, Syria, and its Hezbollah partners in Lebanon.

Iran also supplies materiel to Iraq's army.[45] Iran supplies arms to the Syrian regime, and is even helping Assad maintain power by providing some of the pay for Assad's troops. It also does so by coercing Iraq to provide the money.[46] Today, Iran moves men and materiel through porous borders to Iraq and Syria into Lebanon.[47] When Iran invades en masse, the only enemy it will encounter when heading west will be the Islamic State.

Looking south from Susa in figure 10-2, all the nations of the Saudi Peninsula with the exception of Yemen have militaries that are much smaller than Iran's. Here as in Iraq, Syria, and Lebanon, there are also Shia communities and militant groups in Qatar and east Saudi Arabia supplied by the IRGC. The large Shia minorities in the Gulf countries may very well act as Trojan horses, causing societal instabilities when Iran invades. Between these groups causing disruptions and Iran's rocket attacks from their large arsenal of rockets on the Iranian side of the Gulf, there should be enough diversion for Iran's ground forces to roll through.

Yemen in the extreme south of the peninsula is a divided country in the midst of a civil war with roughly 100,000 fighters on each side. This could otherwise be seen as a real problem for Iran, except Iran does not need to go so far south to capture its strategic targets, which are the oil fields and the holy cities (Mecca and Medina). Yemen is roughly half Shia and half Sunni. Only about twenty years ago North Yemen (Shia) and South Yemen (Sunni) united. Since 2005 there have been repeated civil wars and/or rebellions. Recently, Shia rebels supplied by Iran, known as Houthis, have taken over a large portion of western Yemen. Iranian forces may advance into Yemen or may use the Houthis to keep the nation of Yemen from interfering with Iran's objectives on its southern flank, much as Hitler used Franco's Spain to secure his southern border during World War II.

So, now having seen the military situation in Iran and surrounding nations, we go back now to Daniel 8:4. It says of the charge of the ram, "the ram . . . charged toward the west and the north and the south." Now the original Aramaic words in Daniel for "north" and "south" mean just that, and so we can't say for sure how far the Iranian forces will go—it's just in the general directions of north and south. Looking again at figure 10-2, forces going north probably would not go past Azerbaijan, though Azerbaijan itself would be an easy target for the IRGC. If you will recall the discussion at the end of chapter 7 regarding the four horsemen, their authority should be confined to the Islamic Realm. Russia, Armenia, and Georgia are not Muslim countries and so may be spared from any invasion by Iran. This is also why I believe Israel will be spared. This war will be a war among Muslims.

Looking again to figure 10-2, Iranian ground forces going south could take most of the Arabian Peninsula, including the Gulf oil fields, the holy cities of Mecca and Medina, Qatar, the UAE, and Oman. Unlike the northern direction, there is no limit going south. The Arabian Peninsula has strategic objectives for Iran with the exception of Yemen. First there are the oil fields (see figure 10-2). If Iran occupies them, Iran could literally affect the world economy and take down the US dollar at the same time. All they would have to do is stop the selling of oil in US dollars to end the petrodollar system, and so bring down the dollar. Second, there are the holy cities of Mecca and Medina, which Shia Muslims have longed for centuries to take away from Sunni control. As part of assuring control they would also take the Saudi capital of Riyadh.

The Bible does not suggest any limits going south. As I mentioned before, figure 10-2 shows that Yemen has a large military, but Shia Muslims known as Houthis are an ally of Iran in this war. The entire Arabian Peninsula could be within the Iranian sphere either by alliance or by occupation.

The Bible gives "north" and "south" as general descriptions but does give us a clue about the ram charging west. The word for "toward the west" or "westward" is interesting. The word is *yam*, (Strong's #3220, pronounced yawm) and comes from a root word meaning "crash" as in the waves on a beach. The word *yam* means "westward" but it can also mean "seaward." In other words, the Iranian ram will go west as far as the east end of the Mediterranean Sea. This is also the extent of the terrorist network maintained by the Quds Force.

So in its western advance as shown in figure 10-2, Iran would be able to pass through Iraq and into most of Syria after dealing with Islamic State. Iranian forces are far larger than those of Islamic State and would be able to advance through the area quickly. Many are worried by Islamic State, its tactics and ideology. When Iran invades not only will Islamic State likely melt away, but Iranian forces will likely use many of the same tactics. So people should be more worried about Iran than IS. It is unknown how far in to Turkish territory Iranian forces might go. The Turkish military is formidable, but roughly two-thirds of it is based in the western part of the country. Iran would be conducting its invasion based on exporting the Revolution and causing worldwide chaos. The territory in eastern Turkey would give diminishing returns. Nevertheless, as we will see in the next chapter, the fury and speed with which Turkey counterattacks suggests that Iran may indeed occupy Turkish territory for a time. Iran may occupy much of Syria, eastern Jordan, and perhaps even the Sinai Peninsula of Egypt, but go no further. The eastern shore of the Mediterranean Sea is the limit of its western advance. Figure 10-2 shows the extreme limit that I believe Iranian forces can advance.

And, as I said before, I believe Israel will not be conquered at this time, though it will probably be threatened and possibly attacked. The Bible shows in other passages in prophecy that the nation of Israel will still be there for later events including the Tribulation. Iranian armies may threaten Israel with invasion, and they might force their way through southern Israel on their way to Egypt, but, by and large, Israel should be spared. It is possible that with the large Iranian forces coming from the east, Israel may need to assist in the defense of Jordan in order to ultimately help itself. The western half of the country of Jordan would provide a bulwark or buffer against a massive Iranian invasion. Daniel 11:41 also speaks of "Edom, Moab and the leaders of Ammon" being delivered from the armies of the Antichrist when he consolidates his empire. These three areas make up the whole of western Jordan. We will discuss this subject in more detail in chapter 12.

As the reader can see in figure 10-2, the nation of Russia in the north, and Israel, Egypt, and Turkey in the west, which have large enough military forces, should all form barriers in the region to stop Iran's advance. Notice that the forces of Turkey, Egypt, and Israel form a "wall" for Iran at the eastern end of the Mediterranean—where the "west" is in Daniel 8:4. These nations together will form a containment area to which Iranian forces will be limited.

Though Iran has a regular standing army (called the Artesh) of 350,000, I do not believe this force will carry out the invasion. It will most likely be the IRGC that will use its forces to deal with various strategic targets when the invasion begins. I believe the Basij's potential to overwhelm with its numbers will be behind the bulk of the invasion. The Basij forces are shown on the map in figure 10-2. As stated before, most estimates place Basij reserves at one to three million. It would be quite an undertaking to call up, say, 1.5 million reserves. To call and recruit a force of 1.5 million will require conditions similar to those during the Iran-Iraq War, with an enemy that is encroaching on Shia Muslim territory. Islamic State forces in western Iraq encroaching on, say, Baghdad, could provide such an opportunity. The Iranian regime may take advantage of some crisis and argue that it is critical to Shia Islam in order to call up 1.5 million Basij volunteers to go into battle. It is possible that such an opportunity could come about from the current civil war in Syria. That war started with rebels trying to expel Assad, who is the president of Syria. But, it is being seen more now as a Sunni majority trying to expel the Shia leader who is part of the Shia minority in Syria.[48]

The civil war in Syria is already triggering an escalation in hostilities between Sunnis and Shias. But, with mutual Sunni and Shia hostilities generally approaching a boiling point in the Middle East, if it isn't Syria it may be some other hotspot in the near future that provides the trigger. If all-out war between the two major factions of Islam erupts, this would be consistent with prophecies regarding both the Second and Third Signposts. It would contribute to allowing Iran to call up the Basij reserves that it needs to kick off the Second Signpost. We will see in the next chapter that a religious war between the Sunnis and Shias would fulfill part of the prophecy in Daniel 8 regarding the Third Signpost.

We do have an example of the Basij's capabilities. The outside world saw it in operation in the Iran-Iraq War of the 1980s. Human wave after human wave of hundreds of thousands of the Basij pressed and strained Iraqi forces, which were at the time the sixth largest military in the world. Saddam Hussein's Iraq provided containment of Iran since it was large and well equipped. The war ended in a stalemate. One could say that God was not going to allow the Second Signpost to begin in the 1980s.

But Saddam's army was dissolved when coalition forces removed Saddam from power in 2003. Though Iraq has an army again, not only is it not nearly as large as it was under Saddam, but it is equipped and to a degree controlled by the IRGC itself. As an example of the IRGC's awareness of this situation, back in 2008 General Suleimani, the commander of the Quds Force, told US General Petraeus in a letter that he was the most powerful man in Iraq.[49]

The Iraqi army may very well give the IRGC a free pass to points west and south. Imagine 1.5 million (and perhaps more) Basij in a war in the near future running up against not a military like Iraq's under Saddam Hussein, but against all the relatively smaller military forces on the Arabian Peninsula and in the Gulf. The nations of the Gulf would be invaded and occupied in short order.

Going back to the biblical text, Daniel 8:4 says about the ram that "no animal could stand against him, and none could rescue from his power." It goes on to say, "He did as he pleased." In the geographical area shown in figure 10-2 where Iran is allowed to conquer, no nation will stop it; Iran will be allowed to do all it wills.

It is on this point that I believe Iran's nuclear weapons program becomes relevant. Of course, Iran will be able to do all it wants because the Bible says so, but typically there is a physical means by which a prophecy is fulfilled. As of 2013, Iran had between thirty and fifty GHADR-1 medium-range ballistic missiles.[50] These missiles are upgraded from their standard workhorse medium-range rocket, the Shahab-3. The GHADR-1 is capable of carrying a nuclear payload and has a range of up to two thousand kilometers. The range and payload capacity of the GHADR-1 would allow Iran to strike with a nuclear weapon anywhere in the Middle East.

As far as the nuclear warheads themselves are concerned, in 2013 Iran had enough fissile material to produce one or two bombs, and was producing enough material every six months for additional bombs.[51] Iran has enough fissile material to eventually produce up to ten bombs.[52] Processing the material is only a matter of time. The last hurdle technologically would be to weaponize this material into a warhead and construct it so it could be carried on its missile. The bottom line is that Iran could have a missile that could deliver a nuclear warhead anytime in the near future.

An international agreement between Iran and world powers such as Russia and the US was reached on July 14, 2015; the so-called Nuclear Deal. This agreement does not include inspections of Iran's military facilities—only its uranium enrichment facilities. In the end this agreement will not make any difference for Iran's success in its invasion, for according to Daniel 8:4 Iran will be able to do all it wants to do.

I mention all this because if Iran possessed nuclear-tipped missiles capable of striking anywhere in the Middle East, indeed it would be able to do all it wills for it could threaten the Gulf oil fields. Typically, nuclear powers are not harassed to the extent non-nuclear powers are. It would also take only two or three missiles to threaten the entire Gulf oil field region.

The Bible says the ram will be free to do as it pleases to the north, south, and west of Susa. Regretfully Daniel 8:4 says, "No animal could stand against him, and none could rescue from his power." The nations surrounding Iran will not *stand*, and forces caught in the ensuing melee will not be *rescued*. I have heard many times that the United States would never allow Iran to successfully invade the Middle East. But, the Bible says what it says, unfortunately in this case. Anyone who tries to stop Iran will fail.

When I first saw these Signposts in my journey of exploration, I became grieved over the possible fate of our own American men and women in Iraq. Back in 2003 when I first discovered this, the United States had 130,000 soldiers in uniform over there. If they were caught in the invasion of the Second Signpost we could have lost the entire force. I am glad to see that the last major contingent of troops was removed from Iraq in December 2011.[53] If the interpretation of Bible prophecy contained in this book is true, Iran will overrun Iraq—indeed much of the Middle East—and do as it pleases.

IRAN REMOVES WORLDWIDE STABILITY

SECOND SIGNPOST EVENTS TIME LINE	VISION OF BEAR (DANIEL 7:5)	VISION OF RAM (DANIEL 8:3-4, 20)	VISION OF RIDER (REVELATION 6:4)
E) Iran Removes Worldwide Stability	—	—	• Makes men slay one another • Takes peace from the earth

The bear and the ram in the two visions tell us that Iran will unleash an invasion of the Middle East. Here we revisit the vision of the four horsemen. This invasion will have a twofold effect according to Revelation 6:4. Remember, the horsemen can be thought of as the prevailing condition of the times. The first effect is that men will slay one another in the Middle East, as we saw all-out war begin in the last two sections. The second is that in the rest of the world security and peace of mind will be taken away. We have seen in this chapter that Iran is willing and capable of fulfilling the prophesied role of the bear and of the ram.

Since the four horsemen have authority over the Islamic quarter to kill men (as we saw in Revelation 6:8), the second horseman will make men slay one another by the sword in the Islamic quarter. This is why we saw earlier that the war may not come to Armenia, Georgia, Russia, and Israel. But Revelation 6:4 says the red horseman will take peace from the earth. Note that this phrase "take peace" applies to the *whole* earth, not just a quarter of it. How can men slay one another in just one quarter of the earth but peace is taken from the whole earth?

To "take peace" suggests starting war all over the earth. But in this passage the Greek word from which "peace" is translated is *eirene* (Strong's #1515, pronounced i-ray'-nay). This word is used almost one hundred times in the New Testament and in only one place, Luke 14:32, does "peace" definitely mean "absence of war." In all the other places in Scripture, the word *eirene* is translated in the New Testament as peace of mind, rest, security, and stability, like when Jesus says, "My peace I give you."

The second horseman will make men kill each other in the Islamic quarter of the earth, but peace of mind and stability will be taken from the entire earth *because* of the war in the Islamic quarter of the earth. Look again at figure 10-2 to see where Iran's Basij and other IRGC forces could go. An army of Islamic fundamentalists would be unleashed on most of the major oil fields of the Middle East. Can you imagine the impact on the world financial markets and the oil market if Iran were to attack and occupy those regions and cut off one-fourth of the world's oil supply? Nations such as Japan, South Korea, and Taiwan who physically depend almost entirely on those oil fields would be scrambling for alternate supplies, and so would bid up the price of oil from other foreign sources.[54] The foreign oil that the US, Germany, France, Italy, and China receives from sources like Canada, Venezuela, Nigeria, and North Africa would triple or more in price overnight. When the supply of oil was cut by only 6 percent in the 1973 oil embargo, the price "only" doubled. Everything that depends on oil—from agriculture to building materials, transportation to power, in other words practically everything—would become more expensive. Iranian leadership is serious about starting an Islamic revolution in other Muslim countries and causing chaos; this would be an effective way to maximize chaos.

Today most people throughout the world have a reasonable assurance they will be able to commute to work, earn a wage at a job, and put food on the table. With a spike in oil prices or a cut-off in oil exports from the Middle East, all these things become topics of concern. Since everything including food is moved by land and sea transportation that requires oil, the price of food and everything else will skyrocket.

Back in the 1970s when OPEC enacted two oil embargoes, the United States imported only fifteen percent of its oil. When OPEC cut off their exports to the United States there were lines of people in their cars waiting for hours to get gas at their local stations. There was a lot of uncertainty and worry. Today the United States imports 40 percent of its oil. Imagine how much greater panic, uncertainty, and loss of peace of mind would occur if oil prices spike or supplies are cut off. There will be greatly increased market competition for any oil provided outside of the Middle East. Not only would oil be much more expensive, but supplies of various products like gasoline may not be counted on to be consistent. In short, a cut-off of oil from the Middle East would be disastrous for the world's economy. This economic instability would indeed set the stage for the conditions of the third horseman on the black horse, who we will see in the Third Signpost in the next chapter.

In addition to a massive oil shortage and commensurate skyrocketing price, there is a second thread to all of this that will only add more to the misery and loss of peace of mind. The United States will most likely at this time lose its ability to project power at will beyond its shores. Why do I say this? Because wars cost money. The US government has had the ability to deficit spend with no restraint. This is because the US dollar is the reserve currency of the world. Unlike other countries that print money at will and cause hyperinflation in their currencies (Zimbabwe is the most recent example), the US has avoided hyperinflation up to now because other nations have created a demand for dollars. Most nations carry a large reserve of dollars because most of the oil worldwide is bought using dollars, though this situation even now is changing. The backbone of this immunity to great inflation is the petrodollar system, where Saudi Arabia and the small Persian Gulf states agreed back in the 1970s to sell all their oil in US dollars in exchange for US military protection. If Iran takes these oil fields and cuts off the oil, that will be the end of the petrodollar system, which in turn spells the end of the dollar currency reserve system.

Nations will no longer need so many dollars, and so those dollars will come back to the shores of the US. In recent years, the Federal Reserve itself has become the greatest buyer of US debt.[55] It has done this by printing an extra trillion or so dollars per year (it's officially called Quantitative Easing, or simply QE) to buy US Treasury bonds (or debt).[56] If the Fed keeps printing money—and it will—the dollar will fall in value to a fraction of what it is now because the printing will combine with the dollars returning from abroad. To save the dollar, the Fed may raise interest rates like it did in the 1970s, but if it does that it would kill what is left of the US economy. Ben Bernanke of the Federal Reserve announced in 2013 he was keeping interest rates low for as long as the economy performs poorly. Even as recently as September 2015, the Federal Reserve has decided to wait to raise rates because the US economy is not showing the signs of recovery the Fed wants to see.

The US government would either have to curtail spending if it raises interest rates because paying the extra interest on the debt would be prohibitive, or not raise interest rates and watch the dollar evaporate into worthlessness. In any event, that would be the end of America's ability to project power anywhere across the world. The United States itself will lose its superpower status. The one nation that will fall hardest is the United States. Its people will no longer be able to enjoy the standard of living they have had for most of the twentieth century.

In addition, the 2008 financial crisis and bankruptcy of Lehman revealed that there are literally hundreds of trillions of dollars of bad debt (or derivatives gone bad) weighing on the balance sheets of the large banks.[57] This is why the banks keep tens of billions of cash from the bailouts and do not lend it out—it's to keep minimum cash reserves against their hundreds of trillions of dollars of derivatives. The banks and their depositors (that's you and me) would see the value of their stored wealth in dollars evaporate. In addition, to keep the borrowing going for as long as possible, it is possible the US and other Western governments could seize retirement plans or take a percentage of depositors' money as we saw in Cyprus in 2013.

This invasion by Iran would be the "black swan event" that would take down the US dollar house of cards, and take down America's unique position in this world in which it has been blessed for so many years. A "black swan event" is considered to be something big affecting the world that no one sees coming but afterward everyone claims was easy to see coming. Written about in Nassim Nicholas Taleb's book *The Black Swan,* the term is commonly used now in financial circles.[58]

IRAN FEARED, RESPECTED

SECOND SIGNPOST EVENTS TIME LINE	VISION OF BEAR (DANIEL 7:5)	VISION OF RAM (DANIEL 8:3-4, 20)	VISION OF RIDER (REVELATION 6:4)
F) Iran Feared, Respected	—	• Becomes great	—

Finally, the Bible also says in Daniel 8:4 that the Persian ram "became great." The Aramaic word is *gadal* (Strong's #1431, pronounced gaw-dal') and is defined as becoming rich, most important in the region, and magnified, praised, or respected. If Iran did conquer Iraq to the west, the Arabian Peninsula to the south, and a couple of nations to the north, as shown in figure 10-2, it would indeed have over half of the world's oil reserves and over one-quarter of the world's oil production within its grasp. Its territory would stretch from eastern Turkey and Jordan in the west, to Yemen in the south, to Azerbaijan in the north, and to Pakistan in the east.

With a nuclear capability coupled to this, Iran would be a nation that other more powerful nations would have to negotiate with simply because it could threaten to bomb the oil field distribution points with nuclear weapons. It could also threaten to simply detonate a nuclear weapon over all the Gulf oil fields causing an electromagnetic pulse (EMP) effect that would most likely knock out all the electronics controlling the pumping and distribution of oil. The world's powers would take the threat seriously coming from a regime like Iran's. For a time, Iran would be by far the most powerful nation in the Middle East, and have a regime the world would have to bargain with.

SUMMARY

Israeli scholar of Arabic and Islam, and lecturer at Bar-Ilan University, Dr. Mordechai Kedar elegantly summed up the Iranian leadership's current mindset and its view of the Middle East region when he wrote,

> Iran will continue to be what it is—a dark and radical state, controlled by a group of narrow-minded ayatollahs who are stirring up the Sunni-Shi'i conflict and who threaten world peace with doomsday weapons that are meant to impel humanity into uncontrolled chaos, thus bringing about the return of the Mahdi—the hidden imam—to impose the Shi'ite religion on the Sunni Islamic world in the first phase, and on all other parts of the world in the last phase. This is their world view, and it is their declared goal.[59]

Dr. Kedar describes what Iran intends to do. According to the visions in Daniel, this is what Iran will succeed in doing. As we will see in the final chapters of this book, all of Iran's goals will be accomplished because the chain of events it starts will achieve what they want. This will only occur, though, long after the current Iranian regime is ended and in a way they did not anticipate.

Presently, we are at the threshold of beginning the Second Signpost. The leaders that are the two horns of the ram will give the command for the great invasion to begin, and for the Islamic Revolution to spill in earnest over Iran's borders into all other countries in the region, to the north, south, and west. At that time the ram will charge out, the bear will eat, and the rider of the red horse will "take peace" from the earth. All we are waiting for right now is for the first sign of that invasion.

CHAPTER 11

THE THIRD SIGNPOST: THE CONFEDERACY OF FOUR NATIONS

I N THIS CHAPTER WE COME TO OUR DISCUSSION OF THE THIRD
Signpost. We saw in chapter 8 that the events of the Third Signpost
include the prophecies of the leopard, the goat, and the third horseman—the rider on the black horse. I proposed that the prophecies of the
leopard and the goat are to be fulfilled by four nations forming a nation
I call the Sunni Confederacy. This Confederacy would reconquer the
territories taken by Iran in the Second Signpost, and conquer Iran itself.
I also proposed that the prophecy of the rider on the black horse represents the conditions during this time—famine and economic hardship.
In this chapter we will see what it would take for the prophecies pertaining to the Third Signpost to be fulfilled; what the Confederacy of four
nations would be required to do to fulfill the prophecies of the Third
Signpost.

After Iran's forces have pushed out across the Middle East as far as
God allows them to go, and Iran has extended its military across much of
the Middle East, the scene will be set for the Third Signpost. Since we are
only waiting now for the Second Signpost to begin, the Third Signpost is
reserved for some time in the future. As always, we will not be guessing
at any dates in this book. Instead, the prophecies we have been looking at

provide signs God is giving us to tell us what season we are in. The Third Signpost is to include the finishing of the great Sunni-Shia war started in the Second Signpost. It will include a counterattack by the Confederacy that not only retakes all the lands conquered by Iran, but will also remove the current government of Iran. This Confederacy will then administer the lands that it takes back from Iran, until the Confederacy falls apart.

THE THREE VISIONS APPLIED TO THIRD SIGNPOST

To help remind us which elements of the three visions are involved here in the Third Signpost, the appropriate portion of figure 8-6 is repeated here in figure 11-1. This Signpost is made up of the four-headed leopard, the goat that attacks the ram, and the rider on the black horse.

**Figure 11-1. The Third Signpost: the leopard,
the goat, and the third horseman**

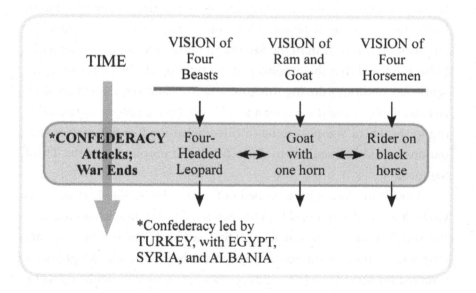

We will now review the various details of these three visions and collect them into a scenario for the Third Signpost, summarized in table 11-1.

In the first vision, the vision of the four beasts, the Confederacy of four nations is represented by a beast that is like a leopard but has four heads and four wings. Daniel 7:6 says of this leopard:

> After that, I looked, and there before me was another beast, one that looked like a leopard. And on its back it had four wings like those of a bird. This beast had four heads, and it was given authority to rule.

There are four things to note about this leopard. The first is that it looks like a leopard. Like the beasts before, the nations that it represents will behave as the beast does in nature. Second, it has four wings. Third, it has four heads. These are clues, as we discussed in chapter 5, that this beast is a four-nation Confederacy. We have also identified the four modern nations that will most likely make up this Confederacy. And fourth, this leopard is given authority to rule.

The second vision, of the ram and the goat, describes the goat in Daniel 8:5–8:

> As I was thinking about this, suddenly a goat with a prominent horn between his eyes came from the west, crossing the whole earth without touching the ground. He came toward the two-horned ram I had seen standing beside the canal and charged at him in great rage. I saw him attack the ram furiously, striking the ram and shattering his two horns. The ram was powerless to stand against him; the goat knocked him to the ground and trampled on him, and none could rescue the ram from his power. The goat became very great, but at the height of his power his large horn was broken off, and in its place four prominent horns grew up toward the four winds of heaven.

There are several things to note in this text. First, the goat has a prominent horn. Second, the goat comes from the west. Third, as the text moves on to talk about the charge of the goat, we are told that the goat crosses the whole earth without touching the ground. Fourth, the goat attacks in a great rage. Fifth, the goat tramples the ram and shatters the two horns of the ram. Sixth, the goat becomes great. And seventh and last, the large horn breaks off and four horns replace it.

And finally in the third vision, we have the third of the four horsemen. Revelation 6:5–6 says of this horseman:

> When the Lamb opened the third seal, I heard the third living creature say, "Come!" I looked, and there before me was a black horse! Its rider was holding a pair of scales in his hand. Then I heard what sounded like a voice among the four living creatures, saying, "A quart of wheat for a day's wages, and three quarts of barley for a day's wages, and do not damage the oil and the wine!"

In this last vision there are three things to gather. The first is that the rider is riding a black horse. The second is that the rider is holding a balance—a pair of scales. And third is the high cost of food.

We now arrange the noted details of each of these three visions into the major events of the Third Signpost, as shown below in table 11-1. The six events in the first column of table 11-1 are the events of the Third Signpost. The events are in chronological order except for the sixth one. We will explore these six events in the same order as shown in table 11-1, for the remainder of this chapter.

Table 11-1. Vision details form six major events within Third Signpost

THIRD SIGNPOST EVENTS TIME LINE	VISION OF LEOPARD (DANIEL 7:6)	VISION OF GOAT (DANIEL 8:5-8, 21)	VISION OF RIDER (REVELATION 6:5,6)
A) Four-Nation Confederacy Headed by Turkey's Leader	• Four-headed	• "Suddenly" Goat with one horn • From the west	—
B) The Charge to Take Back the Middle East	• Like a leopard • With four wings	• Charges without touching ground • In a great rage	—
C) Iran's Government Ended	—	• Trampled ram; broke its horns	—
D) Confederacy Rules the Middle East	• Given authority to rule	• Became great	—
E) Realm Divided into Four Sectors	—	• Four horns replace big horn	—
F) Food Shortage and High Food Prices	—	—	• Black horse • Held a balance • Day's wage for food

FOUR-NATION CONFEDERACY HEADED BY TURKEY'S LEADER

We begin the Third Signpost with the appearance of a four-nation Confederacy. The third beast the prophet Daniel saw that came out of the sea in Daniel 7:6 was a beast that was like a leopard, but had four heads. It had four wings as well, but first we are going to look at the heads. We have seen from chapter 8 of this book that the four modern nations to be represented by this leopard are most likely Turkey, Egypt, Syria, and

Albania. Unlike the lion and the bear, which had one head, one government, and one leader each, this beast will have a fourfold authority—four governments and four leaders. For a while I had thought of these four nations as forming a coalition or an alliance. A coalition would be like four nations working together but each still completely sovereign. However, the way Daniel speaks of the leopard ruling as one entity but having four governments reminded me more of a confederacy. It suggests that these four nations are four states within some sort of political union, even if it is temporary. This Confederacy would be a union of four states working as one, under one leader.

We also saw in chapter 6 of this book that Turkey will most likely be the dominant and most powerful nation of the four, and that the leader of Turkey will head this Confederacy of nations.

THIRD SIGNPOST EVENTS TIME LINE	VISION OF LEOPARD (DANIEL 7:6)	VISION OF GOAT (DANIEL 8:5-8, 21)	VISION OF RIDER (REVELATION 6:5,6)
A) Four-Nation Confederacy Headed by Turkey's Leader	• Four-headed	• "Suddenly" Goat with one horn • From the west	—

Bible commentators supporting the ancient fulfillment of the prophecy of the four beasts have said that the four-headed leopard (representing the ancient Greek realm as it existed after Alexander the Great) and the four horns that sprout from the one great horn of the goat in Daniel 8 are the same thing.

For the modern end-time fulfillment of this vision, I do not believe the comparison can be made between the four horns of the goat and the four heads of the leopard. They are different from each other. The four heads of the leopard were there as it emerged from the sea, and it never changed its form. For the goat however, the four horns are a development from the one single horn. Both horns and heads being four in number is, I believe, only a coincidence. I will talk more about this later in the chapter when we discuss the fifth event (Event E from table 11-1) where the realm is divided into four sectors.

We also see at the start of the Third Signpost a future leader of Turkey in the form of a large single horn on the goat in Daniel. This leader is ready to lead a counterattack eastward toward the ram of Iran. Daniel was given the interpretation of the goat in Daniel 8:21, "The shaggy goat is the king of Greece, and the large horn between his eyes is the first king."

Recall from chapter 6 of this book where we saw how the word Greece is actually Yavan, who is the ancestor of all the peoples in that region. Also recall that the argument was made that Turkey qualifies as including the descendents of Yavan. So the leader of Turkey could easily qualify as the "king of Yavan." We also saw in that chapter some of the military potential of Turkey and how its armed forces are world class. It is possible that there could be a surprise and that the "king of Yavan" could actually be the leader of Albania, but I doubt it. Its military will most likely be by far the smallest of those of the four nations.

Now the argument could be made that Egypt and Syria—two nations of the Confederacy—have nothing to do with Yavan. Mizraim was the ancestor of the Egyptians, and one of the ancestors of the Syrians was Aram, for example. The descendents of Yavan do not live there. So how could the leader of the entire Confederacy be called the "king of Yavan"? The leader of Turkey isn't named the King of Yavan because he is the leader of Egypt and Syria. The leader of Turkey merely needs to be heading up and leading the most militarily and economically powerful nation of the descendents of Yavan. In the entire region of the Balkan Peninsula and the eastern Mediterranean basin where the descendents of Yavan live, this is clearly Turkey.

Daniel 8:21 tells us that the "king of Yavan" is the goat, but that its horn is also a king—the "first" king. We also saw in chapter 6 how the word for *first* could mean first in time or place or importance. Since the leader of Turkey is leading the most powerful military in the geographical region, and he is the first leader of this four-nation Confederacy, he would be the first in time and the first in importance. This situation is equivalent to the idea of this prophecy being fulfilled in ancient times by Alexander the Great who also was the first and greatest king of that realm.

So is there anyone in the political scene in Turkey today who might be the first horn of the goat? After all, if the invasion by Iran starts within the next few years, the Confederacy counterattacking with its leader as the single horn of the goat could be seen in just five to ten years from now, more or less. Any leader who is the horn would have to be influential, popular, have a track record for getting things done, and be an Islamist. This doesn't leave much time for political newcomers. That man may very well be in power now and, if this is so, it can only be Turkey's current prime minister Recep Tayyip Erdoğan (pronounced Red-chep Ta-jip Aerdo-an). He indeed seems to be someone who is the one leader in a hundred, and who stands out.

Erdoğan has changed his country for good in a dynamic way, and is popular with the half of the population that voted for him and his party. After having founded the Justice and Development Party (AKP in Turkish), he won elections starting in 2003 and subsequent elections in 2007 and 2011, with ever-increasing percentages of the vote. No one has achieved that since Ataturk himself. One reason for his popularity is that he has tripled the average wage of the Turkish worker and Turkey's GDP also, where double-digit growth has been the norm during his watch. Even the 2008 financial crisis did not slow down Turkey's economic growth.

On the other hand, Erdoğan showed his heavy handedness as an Islamist in his handling of the demonstrations in Taksim Square in June 2013 and other similar events. His actions seem to have tarnished his image among secular Turks. However, in the big picture, Erdoğan seems as popular as ever.

He became Turkey's first directly elected president in 2014, as he had reached his term limit as prime minister. But the presidential post is relatively powerless, so he and his AKP are attempting to rewrite the constitution giving the president much more executive power. Since his own party does not quite have enough votes to approve a new constitution by itself, it is attempting to work with other political parties, with no success so far.

In foreign policy, during his 2011 election victory speech he said that not only has Turkey benefited from his election victory, but so did a number of capital cities which he named—all of countries within the old Ottoman Empire—and that his country was ready to expand its influence in the area.[1] These statements of course can be taken as imperialistic and in line with what the first horn of the goat is indeed destined to do—be the founder of the vast Sunni Confederacy.

Of course, the leader of the Confederacy may not be Erdoğan, but he seems to be the most likely candidate among Turkish leaders today.

The last thing we are told in regard to this first event of the Third Signpost is where the goat comes from before he charges eastward. Daniel 8:5 says, "Suddenly a goat with a prominent horn between its eyes came from the west." The word for "west" used here in the text is *ma'arab* (Strong's #4628, pronounced mah-ar-awb'). It means westward, as well as extreme west, even "setting sun west." For example, the word *ma'arab* is also used in Psalm 103:12, "as far as the east is from the west, so far has he removed our transgressions from us."

"East" and "west" in this verse, of course, are two extremes in distance. I call this west, *ma'arab*, "sunset-west." Contrast this with the word in the text, *yam*, used for "west" in Daniel's description of the ram which charges west, which we saw in the last chapter which was "sea-west" or "seaward." From Daniel's location in his vision in western Iran, the ram charged seaward to the Mediterranean, but the goat comes from sunset-west—way beyond the limits placed on the ram's charge. Most likely then, the main military charge from the leader of Turkey, the "king of Yavan," will be from western Turkey.

Back in chapter 5, figure 5-9 shows the modern nations represented by the beasts of Daniel, which are the inheritor nations of the seven ancient empires as described in chapter 5. Since the lion is Iraq, and the bear is

Iran, and the terrible fourth beast is Islam, then the four-headed leopard is Turkey, Egypt, Syria, and Albania. Figure 5-9 also readily shows that the four nations of the leopard are the farthest west among the seven. The forces of Albania, Egypt, and Syria would be ready to join Turkey in its advance. Egypt and Syria will also charge eastward, with Turkey and Albania's charge.

THE CHARGE TO TAKE BACK THE MIDDLE EAST

THIRD SIGNPOST EVENTS TIME LINE	VISION OF LEOPARD (DANIEL 7:6)	VISION OF GOAT (DANIEL 8:5-8, 21)	VISION OF RIDER (REVELATION 6:5,6)
B) The Charge to Take Back the Middle East	• Like a leopard • With four wings	• Charges without touching ground • In a great rage	—

We now have an idea what this third beast will be—the four-nation Confederacy. As we continue in the prophecies in Daniel we'll see what this Confederacy will possibly be capable of and what it will do.

The fourfold Confederacy that is the third beast is described as being like a leopard. We saw in chapter 9 how Iraq fulfilled the role of a lion, attacking single prey and not moving on. We also saw in chapter 10 how Iran will fulfill the role of the bear, ravaging many nations and pressing on to feed its "hunger." But this third beast is a leopard. What does being represented by a leopard mean in terms of how this Confederacy behaves? First, a lion and a bear are large carnivores. A male lion can weigh five hundred pounds and a large brown bear can weigh five- to eight hundred pounds. But the leopard usually gets no larger than two hundred pounds. These sizes can be compared to the size of the military of each nation. At five hundred pounds, the lion of Iraq was once the sixth largest military in the world, under Saddam Hussein. And an eight-hundred-pound bear could be indicative of the million-man or more Iranian Basij we saw in the last chapter. But at just two hundred pounds the leopard is smaller. It may have just fought to keep Iran's forces back from Egypt proper and from western Turkey. The very reason it becomes a confederacy may be to consolidate thinned ranks in the military of these four nations. This also may be the reason that even Albania with its small military is asked to help.

So the third beast's forces will be smaller than its two predecessors. This is in line with the leopard being smaller in size than the bear or lion. But the leopard's tactics to catch prey are different than those of the lion or bear as well. Where a lion chases down prey and a bear simply wanders and ravages, a leopard will stealthily creep in the underbrush or in a tree, and lie in wait and watch. When its prey gets close then it leaps and pounces! It leaps onto its prey in such a way that it is completely surprised. We saw some Bible passages reflecting the behavior of lions and bears, and so we have two for the leopard as well.

> Therefore a lion from the forest will slay them,
> A wolf of the deserts will destroy them,
> A leopard is *watching* their cities.
> Everyone who goes out of them will be torn in pieces,
> Because their transgressions are many,
> Their apostasies are numerous. (Jer. 5:6 NASB, emphasis added)

> Therefore I will be unto them as a lion: as a leopard by the way will I *observe* them. (Hos. 13:7) KJV, emphasis added)

In both passages the leopard is said to watch. The word translated "watching" in Jeremiah is *shaqad* (Strong's #8245, pronounced shaw-kad') and it means "to watch." The word for "observe" in Hosea is *shuwr* (Strong's #7789, pronounced shoor) and it means "to watch while waiting, to observe, and to behold." That is what a leopard does. It will wait and watch until the right moment.

As a side note, I find it remarkable that the Bible itself tells us some of the natural behavior of all these animals. Besides their use in the context of the verse itself, who would have thought they could also be used as hints as to how prophecy might play out in Daniel 7? I take this as yet another wonderful blessing that is in God's Word.

Moving on in the text of these visions we get some more information. Remember that the four-headed leopard and the goat with the single horn are part of the same entity. The leopard represents the nations, while the goat represents its leadership. The way both the leopard and the goat are described suggests that the forces of the Confederacy will be very mobile. We are told in Daniel 7:6 that the leopard has four wings. We are also told in Daniel 8:5 about the goat that "suddenly . . . came from the west, crossing the whole earth without touching the ground." Having four wings suggests that the leopard will fly when it leaps. But the goat crossing the earth from the west without touching the ground definitely denotes flight.

The lion will give chase to its prey but the leopard will stealthily wait and watch until it finally pounces. The prey of a lion may see the lion coming from a distance and start to run, but the prey of a leopard is totally surprised. We know that this beast will behave like a leopard—catching its prey by leaping. The word *suddenly* in the text indicates, I believe, how both this goat and this leopard will move. The nations that are the leopard will wait and watch for the right strategic moment when Iran is most vulnerable. Just as the leopard's sudden movement surprises a leopard's prey, the forces of the Confederacy will attack from the air—suddenly—and by surprise.

The goat will apparently travel at very high speed—not touching the ground. The current popular theology, which assigns this whole prophecy to fulfillment in the days of Alexander the Great, notes that Alexander conquered the civilized world from Greece to India in only twelve years. This was indeed very fast by ancient standards, and so it is said to resemble the goat not touching the ground. But this is still an imperfect fulfillment. Alexander's forces were still earthbound. Today's modern air forces with their air transports could literally not touch the ground. This would be a literal fulfillment. This would also greatly resemble the leopard's surprise leap and pounce. The conquest of Iran and all of its new territory in the Middle East could be completed in days or weeks.

Figure 11-2 shows a map of the Middle East and the general paths that the four-nation Confederacy's forces could take.

It is possible that since Iran's forces will be stretched thin and somewhat exhausted in manpower, having expended itself fighting across many nations, that the leopard will not need a large land invasion. All it would need is an airlift from major city to major city to take out both the Iranian garrisons and the new governments set up in the various capitals of the old countries.

Figure 11-2. Confederacy forces (the goat)
attack Iran and its holdings (the ram)

Finally, about the goat's charge to the east, we are told by Daniel 8:6–7 that the goat "charged at him [the ram] in great rage . . . I saw him attack the ram furiously." The word for "rage" in the text is *chemah* (Strong's #2534, pronounced khay-maw'). It means fury, wrath, burning anger, and even indignation. The first time it is used in the Bible is in Genesis 27:44 to describe Esau's rage against Jacob for being tricked out of his birthright. It is used in many places to describe God's wrath and anger at sin and evil. This terrible fury on the part of the goat and the leopard for that matter, results in the goat attacking the ram "furiously." The word in the text behind "furiously" is *marar* (Strong's #4843, pronounced maw-rar'). Perhaps a better translation, one that is used elsewhere in the Bible for *marar*, is "bitter." *Marar* is used in Exodus 1:14 to describe the bitter bondage of the Hebrew slaves. It is also used in Ruth 1:20 where Naomi says to call her "Mara" because she said God had dealt bitterly with her in the death of her husband and both sons.

In summary, the goat is so enraged, so wrathful, and so full of indignation, that it would make the goat embittered so it will deal very harshly with the ram—in an "embittered" way. To be bitter suggests intensity and severity of feeling, great animosity toward someone or something, and expressing extreme grief and pain. The goat may act in a way to exact revenge on the ram for what the ram did. Esau probably felt this same need for revenge—an attack on his birthright, on his person. The great rage and bitterness that is spoken of in the text speaks to an avenging, I believe, that goes beyond the revenge fed by mere nationalism and patriotism. I suspect that the people of the Confederacy will feel this great rage and even indignation personally. The only way I can think of for that to happen in this war with Iran is that it will affect everyone's personal religion and faith.

Both the Confederacy's purpose and motivation to conquer would be quite different from that of Iran's. Iran would have started a war to bring chaos to the region in hopes of allowing the emergence of the Mahdi. Many of the nations of the Middle East—Saudi Arabia, Iraq, Kuwait, Oman, Azerbaijan, and others—would have recently been victim to a

Shia-backed push to start Islamic-backed revolutions in each of these countries. Most Muslims are Sunni, not Shia. In contrast, the purpose of the Confederacy, being made up of four Sunni Muslim nations, would be to push back the advance of Shia Muslim conquests by retaking territory, and punishing the leaders of Iran, who started the whole mess. Would a group of Sunni Muslims take it as a personal attack to have the Middle East swept through by Shias?

Imagine Europe in centuries past. If a Roman Catholic kingdom conquered great swaths of Protestant territory and declared these new lands to be changed to Catholic (or vice versa), don't you think the natives of the conquered lands would rally and attack rather vehemently? So I believe the answer to the question is yes. As we saw in the last chapter, the civil war that started in Syria in 2011 is visible proof that Sunni and Shia hostility toward one another is increasing.

Also, while we are watching the power shuffle within Iran's government prior to the start of war in the Second Signpost, we are also watching the preparation for the Third Signpost even though it is further in the future. Today the nations that are to be the Confederacy—Albania, Egypt, Syria, and Turkey—share a commonality in Islam in that they are mostly Sunni Muslim. But all also had a secular form of government until a few years ago. But, in the last few years and presently, we are witnessing the transformation of the governments of Egypt, Turkey, and Syria from secular to Islamist.

If the secular Turkey, Egypt, or Syria from a few years ago had been attacked by Iran, we might have seen a similar response to what happened when Saddam's Iraq was attacked by Iran in the Iran-Iraq War of the 1980s. It would be a rallying, a call to arms, and a defending of the nation. If any one side of that war could be said to have been in a great rage and embittered, it would have been Iran with its Basij, pushing back Saddam's advance into Shia Islam territory that started the war. So, if these nations had been attacked in past years, we may have seen only nationalism and patriotism.

I believe that for the Third Signpost to take place and the prophecy of the goat's rage be fulfilled, the nations of the Confederacy have to become by and large Islamist governments with increasing Sunni Islam fundamentalism among the population. In this way, these four nations would take revenge on Iran's attack with great rage and take it personally from a standpoint of faith. We are already witnessing this transition to Islamist governments in Egypt, Turkey, and Syria.

Egypt's Hosni Mubarak and his secular government were removed from power in February 2011. The Muslim Brotherhood, illegal under Mubarak, won a majority of seats in Egypt's parliament and so began to change that country's government and laws. Muhammad Mursi, the former head of the Muslim Brotherhood, was elected president in June 2012. With Mursi then being removed by the army in July 2013, Egypt's road to Islamism may be bumpy. However, the Islamist half of the population who voted him in didn't just go away with that act. At this time, Egypt seems to be on course for a civil war of its own.

Syria's Bashar al-Assad, currently leading a secular (and Shia) regime in that country, may yet fall in the months and years ahead. Protests and unrest that started in January 2011 at the time of the "Arab Spring" riots in many countries in the Middle East became all-out civil war by January 2012. Now Syria's territory is divided between Assad-held, rebel-held, and Islamic State-held areas.

As mentioned before, the Syrian civil war seems to be contributing to the rising tide of hostilities between Shia and Sunni Muslims. This enmity has gone on for thirteen centuries, and is resurging. Iran is supporting the Syrian regime at the current time, and imams in Sunni countries are calling for Muslims to fight the regime in Syria. Indeed, the Second and Third Signposts can be thought of respectively as the start and finish of a great Sunni-Shia war.

A secular government currently leads Albania. It may change in the future, but it doesn't really need to since it is the smallest of the four nations.

Egypt's and Syria's governments becoming Islamist fits with the goat being in a great rage. But, since the goat is the leadership of Egypt and Syria, Turkey's government will most likely also become Islamist to fulfill prophecy. This, of course, would have great ramifications for both the Middle East and Europe.

Turkey is unique among all the Muslim nations that have existed in the twentieth century. All other Muslim countries have had governments that are monarchies, theocracies, or dictatorships. Only Turkey established a secular democracy on its own. Iraq, of course, had help from the outside and this is an exception.

Turkey's heritage is from the Ottoman Empire, which existed for seven centuries. In the early 1920s after World War I, Western Europe's anger at centuries of invasion by Islamic Ottomans was being vented on the last vestiges of the old empire. The European powers were about to carve up the heart of the old Ottoman Empire, which was Asia Minor proper. To save the core of the empire, a leader arose. Mustafa Kemal Ataturk is considered the father of modern Turkey, having built the modern nation on the ruins of the old empire. He led military campaigns to save the territory that makes up the nation of Turkey that we know today. He forced and led reforms to make Turkey a secular democratic state in order to calm the concerns of the European powers about a major Islamic state being allowed to survive on Europe's doorstep. In 1924 he officially abolished the office of the caliph that had survived continuously since the death of Muhammad thirteen centuries earlier. He even changed the way Turkish was to be written—from Arabic characters back to a Roman character alphabet.

Ataturk (which means literally "father of the Turks") was modern Turkey's first president. Kemal Ataturk set up the government with the military leaders as a vanguard defending his institutionalization of secular ways. Ataturk was their model, and following secular ways came to be known as Kemalism. Over the many years from 1924 to 1997, whenever the government began to lean toward fundamentalist Islam again through popular elections, the military was free to step in, cause a coup, and "reset" the government. It would then step back and let the democratic process continue with new elections. So far there have been four coups—in 1960, 1971, 1980, and 1997. However, there are obvious signs that Islamism is creeping in. The Turkish people seem to be leaning more towards a return of the old Islamic and Ottoman ways.

The office of the prime minister has the greatest executive power in Turkey. Recep Tayyip Erdoğan, the current president of Turkey, founded the Justice and Development Party (AKP) in 2002 and it is known to lean toward Islamism. The AKP won 34 percent of the vote in 2003. That allowed him to become prime minister, and his party to control a majority of the 550-seat Turkish parliament. His party won 46 percent in 2007 and 49 percent in 2011. No other Turkish politician since Ataturk himself has won an increasing share of the vote in successive elections.

Erdoğan then managed to end the secular threat from the military. In February 2010 more than forty military officers were arrested and charged with the "Sledgehammer Plot" to overthrow the current government. Evidence (there is debate as to whether it was real or created, and from what I have read, I believe much of it was the latter) was gathered and used in court. Trials began in December 2010. The verdict was handed down on September 21, 2012. About three hundred officers were given sentences of sixteen to twenty years. On September 30, 2012, Turkish Prime Minister Recep Erdoğan declared, "The era of coups in this country will never return again."[2] He went on to say, "Anyone who intervenes or tries to intervene in democracy will sooner or later go in front of the people's courts and be made to account."[3] My translation would be, "Anyone who tries to interfere with Islamist power and politics will fail." Erdoğan has succeeded in ending the era of Kemalism. Turkey is now free to drift to a more Islamist form of government.

It would not be a stretch to say that if Iran starts its war and the Second Signpost begins, Shia Muslims would occupy what is thought of as Sunni territory. Religious fervor could be further fanned into flame among the Turkish population.

To summarize, and this is speculation on my part, I believe that for the goat to truly charge the ram in a "great rage" and bitterly and furiously attack, the governments of Turkey, Egypt, and Syria need to be Islamist just as Iran's government is. This is needed so that those nations will respond to Iran's invasion the way Daniel 8 says they will respond—with a great rage. Indeed they are headed that way. With Egypt already becoming Islamist, Assad's secular government teetering in Syria, and Turkey having overcome obstacles to its government becoming Islamist, the required conditions for the governments of these nations to fulfill the prophecy of the goat's rage are being set up. Though Albania is still secular, its forces would be much smaller than those of the other three nations and would most likely be under the command of the Turkish leader.

Iran's Government Ended

THIRD SIGNPOST EVENTS TIME LINE	VISION OF LEOPARD (DANIEL 7:6)	VISION OF GOAT (DANIEL 8:5-8, 21)	VISION OF RIDER (REVELATION 6:5,6)
C) Iran's Government Ended	—	• Trampled ram; broke its horns	—

Continuing on in the vision of the ram and goat, Daniel tells us about the goat in Daniel 8:7, "I saw it attack the ram furiously, striking the ram and shattering its two horns. The ram was powerless to stand against it; the goat knocked him to the ground and trampled on it, and none could rescue the ram from its power."

As you might recall from the last chapter, the two horns of the ram will be the two highest positions of power in the Iranian government. The goat is to break the two horns, meaning that their power is completely removed. This most likely would mean the Iranian government in its current form would come to an end, and be replaced by another government set up by the Confederacy. Starting from that time there would be no more Iranian supreme leader, and no more IRGC. This would also mean the Confederacy's forces would need to invade and take over Iran itself.

The text also says the goat "trampled" on the ram and none could rescue him from the goat's power. As a result of that bitter rage, the goat will dominate the Middle East and completely take back all the lands conquered by Iran, the ram.

CONFEDERACY RULES THE MIDDLE EAST

THIRD SIGNPOST EVENTS TIME LINE	VISION OF LEOPARD (DANIEL 7:6)	VISION OF GOAT (DANIEL 8:5-8, 21)	VISION OF RIDER (REVELATION 6:5,6)
D) Confederacy Rules the Middle East	• Given authority to rule	• Became great	—

After the Confederacy has retaken the Middle East, it will have had a great military victory. It might be similar to the one experienced by the Allied powers in World War II once it had reconquered lands taken by Nazi Germany, though perhaps with fewer men and less military hardware involved. Of this Confederacy represented by the four-headed leopard, Daniel 7:6 says, "it was given authority to rule." God will allow the Confederacy to rule and have authority over the lands it reconquered, including Iran itself.

For an idea of the extent of this new large nation's territory and its resources, which would lend to the influence of the Sunni Confederacy on world affairs, the reader can refer to figure 11-3. All of the gray vertical-hatched territory on the map would belong to this nation. At 385 million, its population will make it the third most populous nation after China and India and ahead of the United States. With a territory of 7.3 million square kilometers it will be the seventh largest nation in land area after Russia, Canada, China, the US, Brazil, and just behind Australia.

And, of course, it will possess one quarter of the world's oil production capacity and half of its oil reserves.

Moving on to the vision of the goat, Daniel 8:8 tells us that "the goat became very great." When the goat—the Turkish-led Confederacy—takes back the Middle East from Iran, it will also take back all the oil fields. The Confederacy will also likely be the only military power in the region between Libya and Afghanistan, except for Israel.

The ram became "great" in Daniel 8:4, but Daniel 8:8 says, "The goat became *very* great" (emphasis added). The word for "great" in the text is *gadal* (Strong's #1431), the same word used earlier in Daniel 8:4 to describe the ram: "He did as he pleased and became great." However, about the goat the text says he became "very great." The word for "very" is *m'od* (Strong's #3966, pronounced meh-ode') and means "exceedingly" or "abundantly."

Just from the language one might say that the goat will become greater than the ram ever does. It is actually rather easy to see why. Iran will be viewed as an invader by most countries. Iran will become "great" based on a series of revolutions using coercion, and due to possible nuclear blackmail of targets such as the oil fields.

However, the Confederacy will be seen as liberators restoring order. One of its main tasks will be to establish government order. If Iran did indeed behave like a bear, ravaging the governments from country to country trying to start Islamic revolution, there will be chaos. Its second task would be to get the oil to flow again if it can. In this circumstance, the Confederacy could become much greater than the ram in power and influence.

In addition, we saw the size of the population of this new nation and the great extent of its territory. For a time, it would be "very great" alongside other nations that rank among the greatest population and territory such as the United States, Russia, China, and India. As of 2013, the region had a combined GDP of roughly $2.5 trillion. I speculate that it might even displace Italy, Russia, or Canada to become the newest member of the G8. The eight nations of the G8 produce roughly half of the GDP of the entire world.

REALM DIVIDED INTO FOUR SECTORS

THIRD SIGNPOST EVENTS TIME LINE	VISION OF LEOPARD (DANIEL 7:6)	VISION OF GOAT (DANIEL 8:5-8, 21)	VISION OF RIDER (REVELATION 6:5,6)
E) Realm Divided into Four Sectors	—	• Four horns replace big horn	—

The leopard was given authority to rule. From the vision of the goat we do have a clue for how long that might go on. Daniel 8:8 says of the goat after it finished its conquest of the ram, "The goat became very great, but at the height of his power his large horn was broken off, and in its place four prominent horns grew up toward the four winds of heaven."

Remember the prominent horn of the goat is the "king of Yavan." This is literally one person. At the height of the power of the goat, the horn was broken. Just as the broken horn is ascribed to Alexander the Great's death by those who are seeking an ancient fulfillment of this prophecy, in the current-day fulfillment, it will most likely mean the dying, or possibly just the removing, of the leader of Turkey. When that happens, the Confederacy of four will fall apart. The lands of the Middle East, which had up to then been briefly united under the rule of the Confederacy, will fracture into exactly four pieces. Daniel 8:8 says, "four prominent horns grew up" in place of the one.

As I mentioned earlier, I do not believe the four horns will be the same as the four heads of the leopard. The four heads of the leopard at the time of Iran's initial invasion will be Albania, Egypt, Syria, and Turkey. These four nations will be much as they are today, except some of them will have had territory conquered by Iran. United into the Confederacy, they will rule as one sovereign entity over the Middle East. The four nations to rise after the Confederacy will be very different.

In figure 11-3 I illustrate what I believe to be the territories and boundaries of these four new nations. It is my guess that these four new

nations will set up boundaries roughly along ethnic and/or old geopoliti-
cal lines. In the Middle East there are three major ethnic groups—Arab,
Persian, and Turk. The Arabs are Semitic peoples. The Persians are Indo-
Europeans. The Turks originated from Central Asia but migrated into what
is now Turkey and western Iran. Turkey, being the dominant military in
the region and in the Confederacy, may also include in its territory some
of the Syrian and Kurdish lands of former northern Iraq that border the
Turkic areas. In the south, the Arab area may very well fracture between
the Arabs of the Arabian Peninsula, and the Arabs of Egypt. Daniel 8:8
mentions that these four new realms are in the four compass directions as
seen from Daniel's perspective in Susa ("toward the four winds of heaven").
This is shown in figure 11-3. Note the boundaries of the four new nations
radiate out from the vicinity of Susa.

Figure 11-3. The Lands of the Sunni Confederacy and the four new nations

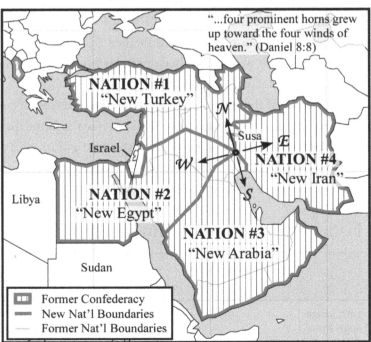

231

I give the four new nations generic names and labels for the purposes of our discussion in the next chapter. Referring to figure 11-3, the territory of Nation #1 covers the present-day nations of Turkey, Syria, Lebanon, Azerbaijan, and northern Iraq. I call this nation New Turkey. The lands of the Kurds are within its borders.

Nation #2 is present-day Egypt combined with some territory in northern Arabia and perhaps parts of Jordan and western Iraq. I call it New Egypt.

Nation #3 is basically the Arabian Peninsula, the cradle of Islam, along with southern Iraq and the Gulf states, which I call New Arabia.

Finally, Nation #4 will basically be Iran, but its territory will only include that inhabited by ethnic Persians. I call it New Iran.

These new nations are shown in figure 11-3. I find it interesting that the ethnic boundaries between Turkic, Persian, and Arab peoples come together roughly in the vicinity of the ruins of Susa. This is consistent with Daniel saying that the four new nations were in the directions of the four winds from his location at Susa.

In all, there will be four new nations birthed from the huge area of the Confederacy. There would have been perhaps fifteen nations in the region that Iran invaded, and four will emerge.

The boundaries of these four new nations are just guesses, of course. However, their number and arrangement will provide the foundation for the last Signpost, the Fourth Signpost. It is the configuration of these new nations that will force the Antichrist to emerge along a path that is actually called out for in these prophecies in Daniel.

FOOD SHORTAGE AND HIGH FOOD PRICES

THIRD SIGNPOST EVENTS TIME LINE	VISION OF LEOPARD (DANIEL 7:6)	VISION OF GOAT (DANIEL 8:5-8, 21)	VISION OF RIDER (REVELATION 6:5,6)
F) Food Shortage and High Food Prices	—	—	• Black horse • Held a balance • Day's wage for food

If the interpretations of prophecy are correct in this book, then the major condition that occurs during the time of the rule of the Confederacy is one of inflation in food prices, and possibly famine. The fourfold Confederacy may rule and become great in much of the Middle East, but an ever-present and pressing problem will be its economy and the availability of food. Whether there could be similar conditions in much of the world is unknown. The Bible here says it will occur in the quarter of the earth in which the third horseman has authority (the Islamic quarter). There may be famine or high food prices in other parts of the world but it will be extreme in the Islamic Realm.

The reason for the color of the third horseman's mount is a bit of a mystery. Black could mean mystery, or darkness, or worsening conditions. If the horse preceding the black one symbolizes war and the horse after it symbolizes death, than this third horse could easily mean worsening conditions. Revelation 6:8 does say that people will die of war, famine, and plague in the quarter of the earth where the horsemen have authority. As we saw in chapter 7, black is one of the colors used in Islam and by the Muslim nations in their flags. Black is the color of mourning. It's also worn by the ayatollahs in Shia Islam. With deaths increasing during this time, black is an appropriate color.

The rider of the black horse holds a balance or scale. This represents an issue of an economic nature. This is the theme of the third horseman just as the second's theme is war. Balances were used in ancient times to weigh a commodity like grain against known weights, in order to know how much was being purchased and what the price should be. When this horseman rides, Revelation 6:6 says, "A quart of wheat for a day's wages, and three quarts of barley for a day's wages, and do not damage the oil and the wine!" There is a temptation to say that this is representative of famine, perhaps from natural causes such as lack of rain. However, certain crops such as olives and grapes will be unaffected. Therefore if there is any famine it won't be from natural causes alone. A lack of rain would affect grapes just as much as it would wheat or barley. I think there is a case to be made that the famine during the Third Signpost is man-made.

Revelation 6:6 says that the cost of certain staple foods will rise such that a day's labor pays for perhaps what a small family might eat in a single day. And yet oil and wine will not be affected. I believe that in 2008 the world had a taste of these very economic conditions to come during the Third Signpost. In the first half of 2008 food prices of staples rose dramatically. From the start of 2006 to early 2008, the average worldwide prices of rice rose 217 percent, wheat rose 136 percent, corn 125 percent, and soybeans 107 percent.[4]

The causes were many. First, losses in the financial markets, particularly in 2008, caused investors to get out of stocks and sink their money into commodities, including agricultural commodities. This drove up prices. A second cause was the increase in the production of biofuels, which made less food available. As an example, worldwide corn production went up by fifty-one million metric tons from 2004 to 2007, but it was all taken up by increased conversion of corn into ethanol, particularly in the United States.[5] During this time the world population continued to increase. A third cause was a 370 percent rise in the price of fertilizers worldwide from 2004 to 2008.[6] Most fertilizer is made from petroleum, which increased in price by 180 percent during that same time.

And yet, there were no drastic reductions in harvests during this period. Some news sources called this the "food price crisis" instead of the "food crisis." Various man-made factors conspired to drive the price of staples up. In developed nations like the United States even the poorest families may spend one-sixth of their budget on food, but in a third-world nation like Nigeria it's closer to three-fourths.[7] A doubling of food prices then would cause some families to buy less food, or cheaper alternatives. Social unrest and riots resulted in many nations across North Africa and South Asia in 2008.

If Iran does cut off much of the oil supply coming from the Middle

East, even though the Confederacy tries to restore it, the price of petroleum will skyrocket. Fertilizer prices along with a shortage of petroleum to run modern farm equipment would cause this tremendous rise in food prices.

The foods that increased in price to create this food crisis in 2008 were foods such as wheat and barley as spoken of in Revelation 6:6. But what happened during 2008 to foods that make oil and wine, like olives and grapes? Were they untouched like it says they will be in Revelation 6:6? During the year 2008 worldwide olive oil prices fell roughly 20 percent. In India it was reported that olive oil prices were stable and would not fall.[8] As for the reasons why olive oil prices fell worldwide, Simon Field wrote of olive oil prices in late 2008:[9]

> Compared to the same time in 2007, the prices for extra virgin olive oils are 1% lower in Spain, down 15% in Greece and down 15% in Italy. . . . The world economic situation, with the USA officially in recession and most of the major olive oil consuming countries in Europe also in recession, will affect retail sales which can be expected to fall, putting further downward pressure on prices.[10]

You can see from this expert's opinion that because there was a recession across the US and Europe at the time, the price of olive oil would have naturally fallen. This makes sense when one considers that if the prices for staples rise dramatically, there will be less demand for expensive foods like olive oil and wine. Prices of commodities like olive oil would remain relatively untouched, and therefore olive oil would be "unharmed." As far as wine is concerned, almost all sources I found reported unremarkably that wine prices were relatively stable. Though production fell a few percentage points, demand fell further because of the recession in 2008.

So I believe in 2008 we saw a preview of the economic conditions during the Third Signpost. Petroleum and fertilizer prices shot up, and so did the prices of staple foods. But wine and olive oil prices remained stable or fell.

SUMMARY

We saw in the Third Signpost how the four-nation Sunni Confederacy would retake the lands conquered by Iran and conquer Iran itself. It would also put an end to the Iranian regime that started in 1979. Most likely the Confederacy would attempt to reestablish order and restore any reductions in the oil supply. Unfortunately, during this time there may be a food crisis like never seen before, far beyond the prelude we saw in 2008. Finally, this Confederacy will break into four new nations that will provide the stage for the final Signpost, the Fourth Signpost.

CHAPTER 12

THE FOURTH SIGNPOST: THE COALESCING OF AN EMPIRE

IF THE INTERPRETATIONS OF THESE VISIONS IN DANIEL AND Revelation are correct, our voyage of discovery has led us here to the fourth and final Signpost. In the First Signpost we saw the leader of Iraq who was bent on conquest, and his country that was forced to become a democracy. We saw Iran begin a war across the Middle East in the Second Signpost. We saw the four-nation Sunni Confederacy take back what Iran had conquered and rule across much of the Middle East in the Third Signpost. In the Fourth Signpost we witness the final series of events before the Antichrist takes his reborn Islamic Realm and the world into the seven-year Tribulation. We will now see the Antichrist arise in one of the four new nations created at the end of the Third Signpost. He will go on to conquer three of the four new nations, and then the fourth one will bow to him. Then the rest of Islam will declare him the Mahdi—the Christians' Antichrist.

During the time of the Antichrist's rise and his reign, according to prophecy, there will be considerable death and destruction. Do not despair though, for the Lord of Hosts will put an end to his reign and his kingdom at the end of the Tribulation.

THE THREE VISIONS APPLIED TO
THE FOURTH SIGNPOST

To help remind us which parts of the three visions are involved here in the Fourth Signpost, the appropriate portion of figure 8-6 is repeated in figure 12-1. As shown in figure 12-1, this Signpost is made up of the last of the four beasts of Daniel, the horns of the goat, and the rider on the green horse.

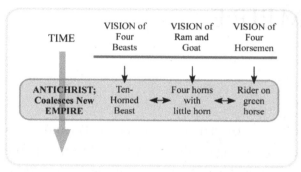

Figure 12-1. The Fourth Signpost: the ten-horned beast, the four horns, and the fourth horseman

We will now review the various aspects of these three visions and collect them into a scenario for the Fourth Signpost, summarized in table 12-1.

The fourth and last beast of the four beasts in Daniel 7 represents Islam as we saw in chapter 5 of this book. Of this beast, Daniel 7:7–8 reveals:

> After that, in my vision at night I looked, and there before me was a fourth beast—terrifying and frightening and very powerful. It had large iron teeth; it crushed and devoured its victims and trampled underfoot whatever was left. It was different from all the former beasts, and it had ten horns. While I was thinking about the horns, there before me was another horn, a little one, which came up among them; and three of the first horns were uprooted before it. This horn had eyes like the eyes of a man and a mouth that spoke boastfully.

First, Daniel 7:7 describes the fourth beast. We saw earlier in chapter 5 that this beast represents Islam. What must be noted first in this chapter is that this beast's ten horns represent the ten nations that will exist at the time the Antichrist emerges and reigns.

Second, Daniel 7:8 says that there "was another horn, a little one, which came up among them." We also see that the horn had eyes and a mouth and spoke boastfully. This little horn is the Antichrist. The word in the original text for "boastfully" is *rabrab* (Strong's #7260, pronounced rab-rab') and it means in this verse "great things." We actually don't know if they are just boasts. The little horn might be speaking great promises or speaking of great goals. Another possibility is that he is declaring himself to be the Mahdi while he rises.

Third, the little horn came up among the ten horns that were already there. Daniel 7:8 also says of the little horn when it comes up that "three of the first horns were uprooted before it." The word in the text for "uprooted" is *aqar* (Strong's #6131, pronounced aw-kar') and it means to be plucked up by the roots. Three of the horns, therefore, are plucked up by the roots.

The second vision, of the ram and goat, has a scenario also with its own version of the little horn. Daniel 8:8 speaks of the four horns that sprouted from the one single horn of the goat. Then, in turn, Daniel 8:9–11 goes on to say about the little horn that it sprouts from one of the four horns:

> Out of one of them came another horn, which started small but grew in power to the south and to the east and toward the Beautiful Land. It grew until it reached the host of the heavens, and it threw some of the starry host down to the earth and trampled on them. It set itself up to be as great as the Prince of the host; it took away the daily sacrifice from him, and the place of his sanctuary was brought low.

The first thing to note is that a little horn started to grow out of one of the four horns of the goat and it starts small. The second thing to note is that it "grew in power to the south and to the east and toward the Beautiful Land." The Beautiful Land, of course, is the land of Israel. Third, the little horn, the Antichrist, will "set itself up to be as great as the Prince of the host." In other words, he will prepare himself to claim to be as great as Jesus Christ who is God.

In addition, the angel in the vision tells Daniel more about this little horn.

> In the latter part of their reign, when rebels have become completely wicked, a stern-faced king, a master of intrigue, will arise. He will become very strong, but not by his own power. He will cause astounding devastation and will succeed in whatever he does. He will destroy the mighty men and the holy people. (Dan. 8:23–24)

Daniel 8:24 says the Antichrist will "become very strong" and he "will cause astounding devastation." This he will do as he arises to power just prior to the Tribulation.

Then there is the third vision, the vision of the four horsemen. Here in the Fourth Signpost we come to the fourth and last rider.

> I looked, and there before me was a pale horse! Its rider was named Death, and Hades was following close behind him. They were given power over a fourth of the earth to kill by sword, famine and plague, and by the wild beasts of the earth. (Rev. 6:8)

There are only two details to capture here. The first is the color of this fourth horse. The second is the rider is Death.

We now arrange the captured details of each of these three visions into the major events of the Fourth Signpost, as shown below in table 12-1. The four events in the first column of table 12-1 are the events of the Fourth Signpost. The events are in chronological order. For the remainder of this chapter we will explore these four events in the same order as shown in the table.

Table 12-1. Vision details form four major events within Fourth Signpost

FOURTH SIGNPOST EVENTS TIME LINE	VISION OF TEN-HORNED BEAST (DANIEL 7:7–8, 23–25)	VISION OF LITTLE HORN GROWING (DANIEL 8:9–12)	VISION OF RIDER (REVELATION 6:8)
A) Antichrist Emerges in Turkish Sector	• Little horn emerges among ten horns	• Little horn emerges from one of Goat's four horns	—
B) Antichrist Takes Turkish Sector, Egyptian and Arabian Sectors	• Uproots three of the ten horns as it emerges	• Little horn grows south, east, toward Israel • Causes astounding devastation	• Green horse • Rider named Death
C) Seven Nations Join Antichrist	• Little horn rules with ten nations	—	—
D) His Rule Begins	• Oppressed saints • Crushed and devoured its victims • Horn spoke boastfully	• Sets self up as Prince of the host	

ANTICHRIST EMERGES IN TURKISH SECTOR

This first event of the Fourth Signpost begins immediately following the last event of the Third Signpost. At this point, we may see a glimpse for the first time of the person who is to be the Antichrist.

We are told by Daniel 7:7 that the beast of Islam has ten horns, and we are told by Daniel 8:8 that the goat has four horns. This is just prior to the appearance in both visions of a little horn—the Antichrist. What do the ten horns and the four horns represent?

In the vision of the four beasts, Scripture reveals that the fourth beast has ten horns. The ten horns represent ten kings ruling ten nations that have sprouted out of Islam, which is represented by the fourth beast. These will be the same ten kings represented by the ten toes of the statue in Daniel 2. Recall that we discussed this toward the end of chapter 1. Since these ten nations come out of Islam, they could be anywhere over a quarter of the earth since the Islamic Realm is quite large.

Figure 7-1 in chapter 7 illustrated the quarter of the earth that is the Islamic Realm. The realm of Islam extends from Morocco in the west to Pakistan in the east, and from Kazakhstan in central Asia south to Sudan and Somalia in Africa.

Of the ten horns, Daniel 7:8 then says, "another horn, a little one . . . came up among them." Daniel 7:24, the interpretation of Daniel 7:8, says that the ten horns are ten kings and "after them another king will arise, different from the earlier ones." This is the Antichrist, who will emerge among ten Islamic nations. As this chapter unfolds we will identify likely candidates for all ten nations.

Parallel to the fourth beast with ten horns is the vision of the goat and its four horns. The four horns of the goat are referring to the four new nations that arise from the territory of the Confederacy headed by the "king of Yavan." This happens at the end of the Third Signpost. The Confederacy will cover much of the Middle East, which is but a part of the Islamic Realm. The area of the Confederacy and the four new nations that replace it are shown in figure 11-3 in the last chapter.

The four nations that arise from the Confederacy are in fact four of the ten nations based in Islam. In other words, the nations represented by the four horns of the goat in Daniel 8 are included as part of the ten horns of the fourth beast in Daniel 7. Because four of the nations will be new and are part of the ten nations of Islam, some of the ten nations do not exist today.

FOURTH SIGNPOST EVENTS TIME LINE	VISION OF TEN-HORNED BEAST (DANIEL 7:7–8, 23–25)	VISION OF LITTLE HORN GROWING (DANIEL 8:9–12)	VISION OF RIDER (REVELATION 6:8)
A) Antichrist Emerges in Turkish Sector	• Little horn emerges among ten horns	• Little horn emerges from one of Goat's four horns	–

Of the four horns, Daniel 8:9 says, "Out of one of them came another horn, which started small but grew in power." Daniel 8:23 adds the interpretation saying of the little horn that it represents, "a stern-faced king, a master of intrigue, will arise." This little horn is also the Antichrist, who will emerge from one of the four new nations.

In summary, the vision of the four beasts reveals that the Antichrist will emerge among the ten nations of Islam. The four new nations arising from the territory of the Sunni Confederacy are counted among the ten Islamic nations. In parallel, the vision of the ram and goat reveals that the Antichrist will emerge from one of the four new nations. We know what the four nations are—what I call New Turkey, New Egypt, New Arabia, and New Iran. But first we will identify from which of the four new nations the Antichrist will emerge. I believe the Bible gives three clues.

FIRST CLUE

The first clue is related to the discussion in chapter 2 where we sought the identity of the people in Roman uniform who destroyed the temple. Daniel 9:27 tells us that the people who destroyed the temple will also be the people from whom the Antichrist will come. We saw in chapter 2 that those people were, among others, Syrians, Egyptians, and Arabians from their respective Roman provinces. Looking at the map in figure 11-3 in the preceding chapter we can see that this would mean that the Antichrist is either from New Turkey or New Egypt.

SECOND CLUE

The second clue requires that we look to an additional prophetic passage in Ezekiel 38. Ezekiel 38 tells of a great war, an invasion of the Holy Land by a host of nations, led by a great leader. A popular picture of prophecy over the last several decades has been that this was going to be some intermediate war before the end of the Tribulation led by someone other than the Antichrist. I believe this passage says something different: that the leader is the Antichrist himself. The nations that are allied with the Antichrist are listed in Ezekiel, and are consistent with our interpretation of the visions of the four beasts and of the ram and the goat. I also believe this isn't some intermediate war, but the last war of the age, the Battle of Armageddon. Why? Toward the end of Ezekiel 38:18 the prophet refers specifically to that day.

> This is what will happen in that day: When Gog attacks the land of Israel, my hot anger will be aroused, declares the Sovereign LORD.

It is the day when, in Ezekiel 38:20–22,

> [A]ll the people on the face of the earth will tremble at my presence. The mountains will be overturned, the cliffs will crumble and every wall will fall to the ground. I will summon a sword against Gog on all my mountains, declares the Sovereign LORD. Every man's sword will be against his brother. I will execute judgment upon him with plague and bloodshed; I will pour down torrents of rain, hailstones and burning sulfur on him and on his troops and on the many nations with him.

Mountains overturned, torrents of hailstones, and all people trembling are descriptions, in other places in the Bible, of the Second Coming of Christ. The passage even mentions the trembling "at my presence." Ezekiel 38 is a description of the Antichrist leading the armies of his ten nations. They will surround Israel in an attempt to utterly destroy it. This will be attempted on the eve of Christ's return.

Going back to the beginning of Ezekiel 38, we will now look at the leader of this army so we may see where he originates. First, Ezekiel 38:1–4 says,

> The word of the LORD came to me: "Son of man, set your face against Gog, of the land of Magog, the chief prince of Meshech and Tubal; prophesy against him and say: 'This is what the Sovereign LORD says: I am against you, O Gog, chief prince of Meshech and Tubal. I will turn you around, put hooks in your jaws and bring you out with your whole army—your horses, your horsemen fully armed, and a great horde with large and small shields, all of them brandishing their swords.' "

Gog is a name given to this great leader. Gog could be the name of a demonic entity, or perhaps the name of the Antichrist, but could also be a title. No one knows for sure. But this Gog is leader "of the land of Magog" and is "the chief prince of Meshech and Tubal." These names belong to some of the sons of Japheth from Genesis 10. In the preceding chapter of this book we saw another son, Yavan. The people of Magog, Meshech, and Tubal are believed to have settled in what is now Turkey. Tubal is in the northeast part of the country, and Meshech in the eastern part.[1] Magog is believed to have settled along the shores of the Black Sea—both on the north and northeast sides where Ukraine is now, as well as on the south side—in northern Turkey.[2]

Gog, the Antichrist, comes from the land containing Magog, Meshech, and Tubal, which is in northern and eastern Turkey. This second clue narrows the field of two candidate nations identified in the first clue, to one—New Turkey. As shown in figure 11-3, New Turkey not only contains the lands of Magog, Meshech, and Tubal, but also the old Roman province of Syria. In retrospect back to chapter 2, this would mean that the specific soldiers directly responsible for the destruction of the Jewish temple who started the fire were Syrians.

The man who is the Antichrist will be mixed up somewhere within the politics and power struggles of New Turkey which would have risen as one of the four nations out of the Sunni Confederacy. We have no idea what the conditions may be like in those countries at that time. There may be a dozen or more petty warlords fighting among themselves. Or there may be various political leaders shuffling around and all vying for power. But only one will be the man who is to be the Antichrist. I imagine if one leader takes over that Turkish nation, another may then do so, and another. We may not know who the Antichrist really is until, having taken over New Turkey, he reaches out to conquer the other new nations and succeeds, adding the other nations in the area to his own.

THIRD CLUE

The third and final clue is saved for the very next section. The vision of the ram and goat gives us that clue. It will not only confirm for us that New Turkey will be the nation from which the Antichrist emerges, but it will also tell us which three nations are the three horns of the ten that are uprooted.

ANTICHRIST TAKES TURKISH SECTOR, EGYPTIAN AND ARABIAN SECTORS

FOURTH SIGNPOST EVENTS TIME LINE	VISION OF TEN-HORNED BEAST (DANIEL 7:7–8, 23–25)	VISION OF LITTLE HORN GROWING (DANIEL 8:9–12)	VISION OF RIDER (REVELATION 6:8)
B) Antichrist Takes Turkish Sector, Egyptian and Arabian Sectors	• Uproots three of the ten horns as it emerges	• Little horn grows south, east, toward Israel • Causes astounding devastation	• Green horse • Rider named Death

Daniel 7:8 reveals that when the Antichrist appears three of the ten horns on the fourth beast are plucked up by the roots. Horns may represent nations, but they also represent power. He will take over power in three

of the ten nations. But which ones? We just saw two clues that tell us that the Antichrist will come out of what will be New Turkey. The third clue gives the same answer, but also answers the question of which three nations' leaders are uprooted.

The vision of the ram and goat tells us the answer in Daniel 8:9, which says that the little horn, the Antichrist, "started small but grew in power to the south and to the east and toward the Beautiful Land." Looking at figure 12-2, it is easy to see which nations are to the south and east. He will conquer the newly formed nations of New Egypt and New Arabia, the nations labeled with the numerals 2 and 3 in the figure. His power will also expand toward Israel. As you can also see in figure 12-2, the three nations that will all become part of the Antichrist's growing empire will geographically surround Israel.

Figure 12-2. The Three Horns that the Little Horn Uproots

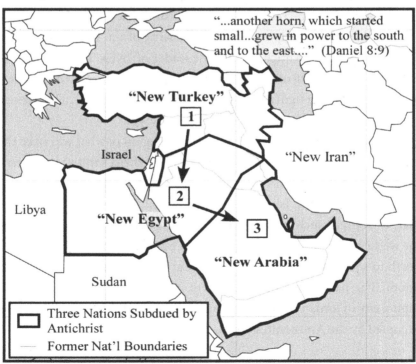

An additional passage from Scripture sheds a little more light on the emergence of the Antichrist. Daniel 11 is a prophetic chapter describing the events between a King of the North and a King of the South. There is general agreement among many interpreters of prophecy that it was fulfilled in the days of the Greek kingdoms of Syria and Egypt back in the second and third centuries BC. However, in Daniel 11:40 the narrative suddenly changes to the last days when it says, "at the time of the end." Of the emerging Antichrist, who is the King of the North, Daniel 11:40–42 reads,

> He will invade many countries and sweep through them like a flood. He will also invade the Beautiful Land. Many countries will fall, but Edom, Moab and the leaders of Ammon will be delivered from his hand. He will extend his power over many countries; Egypt will not escape.

We have some incredible detail here. In the scenario that we have put together in this chapter, I believe the King of the North (relative to Israel) is the rising Antichrist and the leader of "New Turkey." He will fight against the King of the South, which could be either of the two new southern nations in figure 12-2—New Arabia or New Egypt. The passage specifically says the Antichrist will conquer Egypt.

For some reason, the Bible says that the region of what was once the country of Jordan will be spared from the Antichrist's initial conquests. I believe it is because in the days when Iran charges out westward (in the Second Signpost), Israel will defend herself. It would be at this time that, to counter such a terrible onslaught, Israel would need to occupy the western half of the nation of Jordan. The western half of Jordan from north to south is comprised of the ancient lands of Ammon, Moab, and Edom. The passage says the leaders of Ammon will be delivered. The capital city of Jordan is Amman, which is commonly known to have been occupied by the Ammonites thousands of years ago.

Daniel 8:41 also says the Antichrist will invade the "Beautiful Land," Israel. However, this may simply be a pass through to invade Egypt. The real invasion of Israel, spoken of in Ezekiel 38, will come at the end of the Tribulation as I mentioned before.

Once the Antichrist has fulfilled Daniel 8:9 and moved "to the south and to the east," he will have added the new Egyptian and Arabian nations to his Turkish nation as shown in figure 12-2. He will now have under his control three of the four new nations that rose from the Confederacy.

In summary then, the Antichrist will emerge from New Turkey. That nation, New Egypt, and New Arabia are the three nations to be subdued, the three horns to be uprooted.

The third vision included in this event of the Fourth Signpost is the vision of the fourth horseman.

Of the fourth rider, Revelation 6:8 simply says he rides a "pale" horse and its rider was named "Death." The word for "pale" in the text is *chloros* (Strong's #5515, pronounced khlo-ros'). It means "green." Just before Jesus multiplied the bread and fishes, He told the people to sit down on the green grass. The word for green used there is *chloros*. Popular theology says that the green of Revelation 6:8 is a sickly, deathly green because Death is the rider. I believe this is why many Bible translations say "pale green" or "pale." In other words, the translators are forcing a translation due to their presumptions.

In chapter 7 we discussed briefly the colors of the horses and how they match the colors used in Islam.

This Fourth and last Signpost is the one in which the Antichrist himself appears and assembles his Islamic Empire. Of the Four Signposts, this is the climactic one, the last one, and probably the greatest in terms of misery. Of the four colors (white, red, black, and green), green is considered symbolic of, and central to, Islam. It was Muhammad's favorite color. The only one who may wear a green turban is the caliph, who will be the Antichrist. It is the color of Islam's heaven. If a copy of the Qur'an has a colored cover, the color is typically green. The green of Islam is a rich, deep green. Look at the flag of Saudi Arabia if you want to see an example of Islamic green. Based on the fact that the four colors of the horses match those of Islam, I believe this horse, whose color is *chloros*, is as deep, rich, and leafy a green as any grass the Lord Jesus told the people on which to sit.

The rider of this Islamic green horse invokes death, for the rider is Death. These horsemen have been indicators of the conditions that will exist in their respective Signposts. The major theme in the Fourth Signpost is death, as unpleasant as that is. With the lively, rich green of Islam comes death.

Alongside the theme of death during this time, the vision of the ram and goat says of the little horn in Daniel 8:24, "He will cause astounding devastation and will succeed in whatever he does. He will destroy the mighty men and the holy people."

We saw in Daniel 11:41 that the Antichrist will sweep through many countries. Here Daniel 8:24 says he will cause astounding destruction. Add to that the people during the Third Signpost who could barely get enough to eat. It all adds up to what will probably be a heavy toll on human life.

Though, of course, the human tragedy played out here is horrendous, let me remind you that in Revelation 6:8 the four horsemen "were given power over a fourth of the earth to kill by sword, famine and plague." In chapter 7 we saw that the quarter in which they will have authority is the Islamic quarter. The "astounding destruction" that the Antichrist brings about should be confined to the Islamic quarter.

To summarize here, the Antichrist's conquests of New Turkey, New Egypt, and New Arabia will have exacted a terrible toll in human life. The Antichrist will have, at this point, his three subdued kings, his three uprooted horns.

SEVEN NATIONS JOIN ANTICHRIST

FOURTH SIGNPOST EVENTS TIME LINE	VISION OF TEN-HORNED BEAST (DANIEL 7:7–8, 23–25)	VISION OF LITTLE HORN GROWING (DANIEL 8:9–12)	VISION OF RIDER (REVELATION 6:8)
C) Seven Nations Join Antichrist	• Little horn rules with ten nations	—	—

At this point, with three nations conquered, the Antichrist will attain the allegiance of the remaining seven nations, for a total of ten. We saw earlier that Ezekiel 38:1–4 speaks of the Antichrist coming out of his home country (in New Turkey) with his whole army. To identify the remaining seven nations of the ten who will be allied to, and rule, with the Antichrist, we continue on in the passage in Ezekiel 38.

Ezekiel 38:5–6 goes on to mention the groups of people that will be with this leader:

Persia, Cush and Put will be with them, all with shields and helmets, also Gomer with all its troops, and Beth Togarmah from the far north with all its troops—the many nations with you.

We see five people groups mentioned. These additional five peoples are "with" the leader; they are allies. Let us identify the nations associated with these five peoples, because the remaining seven nations of the Antichrist that we want to identify are associated with these peoples. As we go through the identity of these nations, we can follow the discussion on the map in figure 12-3. The map shows the Islamic Realm from Morocco to Pakistan, with the three nations that the Antichrist will subdue, and the additional seven candidate nations that will ally with him.

The first nation mentioned in the passage is Persia. Today we think of this as being Iran. But, more accurately, it will be the new nation, New Iran, that will replace Iran as one of the four new nations arising from the lands of the Confederacy at the end of the Third Signpost. I think it is interesting that Persia is listed as the first of the allied nations. For when the Antichrist unites all the lands in the Middle East except New Iran itself, the people of "New Iran" swear allegiance to him as the Mahdi— our Antichrist. The fourth nation will most likely be New Iran.

Remember from chapter 10 in the Second Signpost that Iran's population is mostly Twelver Shia Muslims. The people of that nation will probably believe that the Mahdi has just emerged. The Iranians would have been watching all the chaos still going on from the time that the leaders of Iran started a war in the Middle East back in the Second Signpost. They will most likely see a mighty and charismatic man reuniting the lands of Islam in the Middle East.

In an ironic twist of fate, former President Ahmadinejad's dream of his nation being the trigger to bring about the coming of the Mahdi will have come true. Once the new Persian nation bows to him, the remainder of the Islamic Realm will fall into submission like dominoes. Of the remaining six nations, Ezekiel 38:5–6 says they will ally with him, and Revelation 17:12 reveals that they will rule with him.

The next group mentioned in Ezekiel 38:5–6 is Cush. Cush has been ascribed to Ethiopia in times past, but it is not Ethiopia. It is actually the upper Nile River area located in the modern nation of Sudan.[3] Only a single major tributary of the Nile winds up into the mountains of Ethiopia. Also, Sudan is a Muslim country, while Ethiopia is predominantly Christian, which lends credence to the idea that it is Sudan and not Ethiopia. Sudan is shown in figure 12-3 as the fifth nation of the ten.

Then after Cush is Put, which contained the ancestors of the North Africans west of Egypt. This would include Morocco, Tunisia, Libya, and Algeria. figure 12-3 assumes the nations there will still exist. Libya and Algeria are shown as two nations from Put. We do not know exactly which of the four nations of Put will be included, but my guesses are Libya and Algeria, as the sixth and seventh nations.

As confirmation that Sudan and Libya ally with the Antichrist,

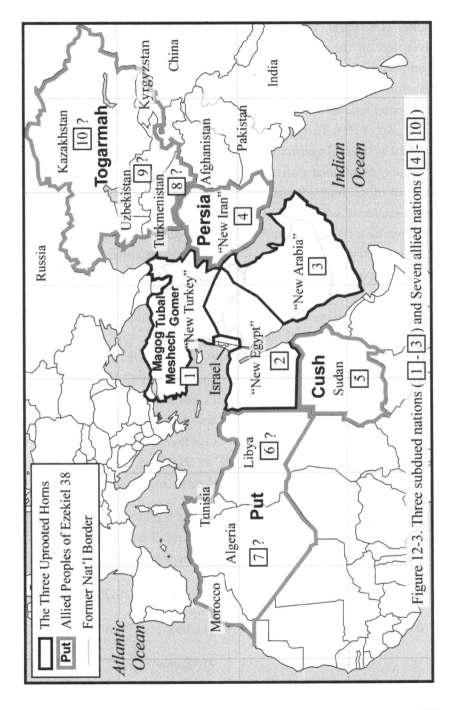

Figure 12-3. Three subdued nations (1 - 3) and Seven allied nations (4 - 10)

Daniel 11:43 says, "He will gain control of the treasures of gold and silver and all the riches of Egypt, with the Libyans and Nubians in submission." The Libyans are descendents of Put, and the Nubians are descendents of Cush.

Gomer follows in Ezekiel 38:5–6. Gomer is in northern Turkey, so it is just part of New Turkey.

Last is "Beth Togarmah," or the "House of Togarmah." This is the only name mentioned with its house. This suggests to me that the descendents of more than one son of Togarmah will be involved. Togarmah had descendents who founded the Hittite Kingdom in southeast Turkey.[4] Armenia also claims descendency from Togarmah. However, I believe the more relevant fact is that Togarmah was also the ancestor of the Turkic peoples of Central Asia. I believe it is among the Muslim and Turkic nations of this region that we will find the remainder of our ten nations. Kazakhstan, Uzbekistan, and Turkmenistan are all Turkic and Muslim. These nations are shown in figure 12-3.

I list the nations below, both those that are part of the Antichrist's empire directly, and those that will submit and ally with him.

As a side note, a major region of the Islamic Realm, Southeast Asia, has been ignored. I do not believe the nations of Indonesia and Malaysia are part of the ten nations simply because there is no mention of ancestors corresponding to them in Ezekiel 38. However, they are part of the quarter of the earth that is the Islamic Realm that we saw in chapter 7.

ANTICHRIST'S EMPIRE	ANTICHRIST'S ALLIES	
1) New Turkey	4) New Iran	8) Turkmenistan
2) New Egypt	5) Sudan	9) Kazakhstan
3) New Arabia	6) Libya	10) Uzbekistan
	7) Algeria	

THE ANTICHRIST'S RULE BEGINS

FOURTH SIGNPOST EVENTS TIME LINE	VISION OF TEN-HORNED BEAST (DANIEL 7:7–8, 23–25)	VISION OF LITTLE HORN GROWING (DANIEL 8:9–12)	VISION OF RIDER (REVELATION 6:8)
D) His Rule Begins	• Oppressed saints • Crushed and devoured its victims • Horn spoke boastfully	• Sets self up as Prince of the host	

When the Antichrist has his three nations as the core of his empire, and the other seven in submission, then he will be free to rule as prophecies in the Bible describe. These are all the prophecies that talk about the Beast, the lawless one, and his reign during the seven years of the Tribulation.

At the time that the Antichrist has assembled his new empire within the Islamic Realm, Revelation 13:3 will be fulfilled. It says, "One of the heads of the beast seemed to have had a fatal wound, but the fatal wound had been healed. The whole world was astonished and followed the beast." In chapter 5 we saw that the beast with seven heads is a combination of the four beasts in Daniel 7. The wounded head is the Islamic Realm, having been occupied by the European powers from the 1830s to the 1960s, and having lost the caliphate in 1924. But now the head will have been healed with the Antichrist restoring the caliphate as the Mahdi, and ruling over a reunited Islamic Empire. Indeed the whole world will be astonished.

We don't know from prophecy how much time there will be after he assimilates his realm and before the Tribulation begins. Just know that when you see these nations being assembled into an empire the time is very short. The seven-year Tribulation will be at the world's doorstep. It is at this point that this book's narration of the Four Signposts comes to a close. We have arrived at the final seven-year period that these Signposts are telling us is coming.

According to prophecy, Israel will still be there through all of these Signposts. We know this because the Antichrist will be dealing with Israel directly during those last seven years.

Of the times of the Tribulation, Daniel 7:8 says the Antichrist will speak boastfully. Daniel 7:23–25 says he will devour the earth and oppress the saints, and they will be handed over to him for three and a half years. Daniel 8:11 says he sets himself up as the "Prince of the host," in other words, as Jesus Christ. Daniel 9:27 says that the Antichrist will deal harshly with Israel.

But he will meet his end quickly, being removed at the end of the Tribulation by the real King of kings and Lord of lords, Jesus Christ. Daniel 8:25 says, "Yet he will be destroyed, but not by human power."

The return of Christ is what we look for and is what we yearn for. It is the Blessed Hope.

FINAL WORD

I did not intend for this book to go into any great detail about the rule of the Antichrist during the Tribulation. Many books and articles have already been written regarding those seven years. The purpose of this book is to show that the Bible and all of world history points to an Islamic Antichrist, and that the Bible gives us four specific events to watch for prior to the final seven years known as the Tribulation.

God has given us Signposts to watch for the coming of the lawless one so His church can be ready. God has not been silent in His Word about the years leading up to the Antichrist. Instead, He has provided a rich narrative that gives us enough to tell us where we are in the seasons that He has set.

I believe God has given us all of the biblical prophecies discussed in this book to warn us, strengthen us, and encourage us during this coming dark time so we may know how close we are to the season of His return. There will be terrible times coming that will precede, and aren't even a part of, the Tribulation. These events will change our world for the worse in ways that we cannot even anticipate. As these events occur brothers and sisters could lose faith.

But no longer are the events unfolding in the Middle East just a jumble of things with no meaning. Realizing the Bible is not silent about events prior to the Tribulation opens our eyes and allows us to sort out what is happening and to better prepare. As we see terrible event after terrible event occur, we will know in a real and concrete way, the return of Christ is getting closer and closer.

God's Word is telling us that when a leader in Iraq appeared and tried to conquer other nations, he wasn't the Antichrist. When Iranian forces run out across the Middle East, many will be fearful of what is happening and may wonder, "Is this the start of the end?" or "Is the Antichrist appearing now?"

God's Word tells us that these things are merely precursors. When Turkey and some other nations band together and fight back, taking over the Middle East including Iran, people may wonder then, "Is the leader of Turkey the Antichrist?"

God's Word is saying, "No."

The time of the Antichrist and the ultimate persecution to come will not have yet arrived at that point, though it will be much closer.

When the newly united Middle East all of a sudden falls apart into four nations and there is war between them, some may wonder if this is the time for the emergence of the Antichrist. It is here that God's Word is telling us that he is now at the threshold.

When he begins uniting the nations in the Middle East, this is the time to be ready. This is the time to make sure one is ready in prayer, in Christ, to brace for the times of the Tribulation.

The biblical significance of all these events is no longer hidden; no longer are they just a random string of terrible events leaving people confused. His saints will know what is happening. They will be able to point to all of these events and know that Bible prophecies in the end times are necessarily being fulfilled. They won't wonder where certain events are going. They will know what to watch for. They will know they must prepare for a number of years instead of just waiting for the Rapture. They will witness to the lost and the fencesitters that these signs are real and concrete indicators of the approaching Christ. They will see firsthand the unfolding of God's plans and be comforted knowing He is in control, and that our Savior Jesus Christ is indeed at the door. The saints can be just as sure that Christ is returning soon as the very Signposts they are witnessing right before their eyes. Hallelujah!

A History of the Commentary of Daniel 2:40

THE PURPOSE OF THIS APPENDIX IS TO PROVIDE A MORE COM-
plete history of the commentaries of Daniel 2:40 than that given in
the introduction to this book. The details given here are meant to provide the rationale for the statements made in the introduction pertaining
to these same commentaries.

The reader is also reminded that the purpose of this history is not to
argue that Rome is not the fulfillment of Daniel 2:40, though this history
does contribute to the argument for such a position. Rather, the argument against Rome fulfilling Daniel 2:40 is reserved for chapter 1 where
that false notion is more thoroughly treated and refuted. The main purpose of this history is to show how the commentaries supporting this
erroneous position regarding Daniel 2:40 got started, and evolved, and to
show how these same commentaries actually contributed to the sealing
of Daniel even for people living in the end times.

The Verse, Daniel 2:40

Daniel 2:40 says, "Finally, there will be a fourth kingdom, strong as iron—
for iron breaks and smashes everything—and as iron breaks things to
pieces, so it will crush and break all the others."

This verse is part of the text in Daniel 2 that gives us the interpretation of the dream of the metal statue. Daniel 2:40 tells us that the empire represented by the iron legs must crush and break into pieces "all the others," that is, all the preceding empires in the statue which were Babylon, Persia, and Greece—the gold head, silver chest, and bronze belly and thighs, respectively. Suffice it to say for now that, at the very least, the empire that does the crushing must completely conquer the empire that is to be crushed. Conquest would include occupation of the enemy capital city; capture, exile, or death of the ruling dynasty of the conquered empire; and conquest of most of the enemy empire's land area and population.

It is the identity of the iron leg empire that is in question. Depending on which empire it is, it completely changes the picture of end-time prophecy. Is it Rome or some other empire?

What runs counter to all the arguments of the popular view of a Roman Antichrist is the hard fact of ancient and medieval world history that Rome *never* conquered Persia. They were archenemies who were at war with each other on and off for six centuries, with neither empire able to conquer the other. Rome would conquer a few outlying province of Persia, and Persia of Rome, but that is as far as it went.

It Started With A Supposition . . .

Probably the first Christian scholar to write a commentary on Daniel 2:40 was Hippolytus, a bishop of Rome just after AD 200. He wrote "the legs of iron . . . expressed the Romans, who hold the sovereignty at present."[1] There are three reasons that can be proposed here for his position. First, he believed that Rome was going to be the only world power for the remainder of world history. He had written in another work that he believed and presumed that Christ would return in AD 500.[2] He also wrote that Rome would last until that time, and be the world power for a total of 500 years (from AD 1 to AD 500).[3] So, in his opinion there was going to be no other power. Secondly, Hippolytus lived in the city of Rome and saw persecution day to day, and how Christianity was being pressured.

Third, some Roman historians faithfully recorded either the false claims of Emperor Trajan who tried to conquer Persia, or wrote how those in government gave him more credit than his achievements were due. One historian who was a contemporary of Hippolytus, Cassius Dio, wrote that Trajan was given the title of "Parthicus" ("victor over Parthia," which was Persia) and the senate granted him "the privilege of celebrating as many triumphs as he should desire."[4] In fact, Trajan only conquered two outlying regions of Persia—Armenia and Mesopotamia. Trajan may have been victorious in a couple of battles, but conquest was something else. It would be the same as a Persian general being a victor over Syria and Egypt and claiming he had conquered Rome. At this time Rome had been at war with the Persians but had not conquered them. Therefore, this first commentary was a *supposition* based on Hippolytus' own presumptions about the end times, and the false reports surrounding an egotistical emperor.

. . . That Became Assumption . . .

The next commentator in this history is the great church father Jerome, who created the first widely used Latin translation of the Bible known as the Vulgate. Jerome wrote a commentary on Daniel dated AD 408. He expressed his opinion regarding which empire was represented by the iron legs when he wrote, "Now the fourth empire, which *clearly* refers to the Romans, is the iron empire which breaks in pieces and overcomes all others" (emphasis added).[5]

There are a few reasons Jerome might have expressed his supposition so boldly as to say it "clearly" was the Romans. He lived in the Eastern Roman Empire, in Antioch and near Jerusalem. He saw how Rome crushed Judea three hundred years before, and how Rome subdued everything it conquered. This might have given him an impression of the power of Rome. Jerome also had the "benefit" of histories written in the third and fourth centuries. Eutropius, the historian, wrote that Trajan "conquered and kept . . . Ctesiphon" and "obtained the mastery over . . . an extensive region of Persia."[6] Both statements are false: he was not able to keep the Persian city of Ctesiphon, and his conquests took away only the outlying provinces of Persia, much as Egypt was an outlying province of Rome. The written histories of Trajan's conquests would have presented a false idea to Jerome and reinforced what was also available earlier to Hippolytus.

We do have a clue as to his assumptions on this matter, due to an interesting but very tragic development. This development would have been a divergence of real-world events from prophetic interpretation in his time. Two years after Jerome wrote his commentary on Daniel, Alaric the Visigoth leader sacked Rome. Jerome was aware of this for in a letter he writes "a dreadful rumour came from the West . . . as I dictate, sobs choke my utterance . . . the City which had taken the *whole* world was itself taken" (emphasis added).[7] In writing "the whole world was itself taken" he made the *assumption* that the iron leg empire was Rome and it had *already* taken Persia. This position would have been bolstered by the fact that Rome was already in decline and its best days were behind it. The belief that Rome had already taken Persia could have been based on Hippolytus' position as well as the exaggerated histories regarding Trajan. One thing we do know is that Jerome never saw Islam and its complete conquest of Persia.

Going forward over eleven centuries we arrive at the time of the great theologian John Calvin, at the time of the Reformation. During those interim centuries between Jerome and Calvin, Rome and Persia were at a standoff for over half that time until Islam came along and conquered Persia thoroughly. Over the remaining centuries up to Calvin's time, Islam changed Persia's religion and culture and alphabet and laws. Islam thoroughly conquered and crushed Persia.

In the 1560s, John Calvin, probably one of the most influential theologians of the last five hundred years, stated which empire fulfilled Daniel 2:40 when he wrote, "Here the Fourth Empire is described, which agrees only with the Roman, for we know that the four successors of Alexander were at length subdued."[8]

Calvin gives us the benefit of providing an argument for his position of Daniel 2:40 referring to the Romans. Alexander's Greek and therefore bronze empire of the statue broke into four successor empires. He wrote that Rome subdued all four successors of Alexander, which is true. The four empires were Macedonia, Thracia (also known as Thrace), Egypt, and Syria. He wrote "Macedonia was reduced to a province" and "the kings of Syria and Asia suffered in the same way; and, lastly, Egypt was seized upon by Augustus."[9] This seems to cover the conquest of the four successors of Alexander. The problem with his argument is he covers only the bronze part of the statue as being crushed and subdued by the Romans.

Prior to Rome arriving, the "Syrian" successor of Alexander came in the form of the Seleucid Empire that stretched from Syria east through Persia and into Afghanistan. However, the only part of that empire Rome conquered was Syria itself. The remainder of the empire—perhaps 90 percent of its land area and people—was conquered by the Persian (Parthian) Empire. The Persian Empire reasserted itself to hold these areas and was a thorn in the side of Rome for six centuries.

Calvin then moved on in his argument by stating, "When, therefore, the three monarchies were absorbed by the Romans, the language of the Prophet suits them well enough; for, as the sword diminishes, and destroys, and ruins all things, thus those three monarchies were bruised and broken up by the Roman empire."[10]

The three monarchies Calvin was referring to are the three empires in the statue prior to the iron: the gold/ Babylon, silver/ Persia, and bronze/ Greece. Thus, Persia, the silver monarchy, is one of the "three monarchies" that he mentions from Daniel 2:40. What Calvin did here was to take the conquest of Syria, which was one of the Greek and bronze successors of Alexander's empire, and call it the conquest of Persia, the silver. Though Calvin provided rationale for his position, the logic is faulty and so he didn't address the problem of Persia directly. He counted the conquest of Syria as the conquest of Persia. It seems to me that perhaps Calvin bent history and the meaning of the verse to fit his own *assumption*.

By AD 1600 then, this assumption of Rome fulfilling Daniel 2:40 had two champions with powerful and influential voices: Jerome and Calvin.

In 1712, a century and a half after Calvin, Matthew Henry, a Presbyterian minister who wrote the exhaustive Bible commentary that bears his name, commented on Daniel 2:40. He wrote, "The Roman kingdom was strong as iron (*v.* 40), witness the prevalency of that kingdom against all that contended with it for many ages. That kingdom *broke in pieces* the Grecian empire and afterwards quite destroyed the nation of the Jews."[11]

Notice Henry did not say anything about how Rome had conquered Persia or broke it in pieces. He mentions the Jews and Greece by name, but assigns Persia by omission to those against whom Rome had "prevalency." History, of course, shows Rome did not prevail against Persia. Therefore, Henry's statement is not completely true. He made an assumption likely based on the position of earlier commentators, and the issue of Persia was again ignored. Henry only made a statement about the situation with Persia while giving no rationale. At this point the assumption was still growing in strength.

Forty years after Henry, John Gill, the great Baptist and Calvinist theologian in the 1750s, commented on Daniel 2:40 and continued the assumption. He wrote of Rome, "*forasmuch as iron breaketh in pieces and subdueth all things*; so this kingdom has subdued and conquered all others; not the Jews only, but the Persians, Egyptians, Syrians, Africans."[12] Yes, the Romans conquered the Jews and the Egyptians and the Syrians. But, those people are not included in the text of Daniel 2:40, and so are irrelevant and do not need to be mentioned. "All the others" in

Daniel 2:40 refers to the other empires mentioned in Daniel 2: Babylon, Greece, and Persia. Again, the Persians were not conquered by Rome. The Persians do not belong in Gill's list.

Gill's position is also confirmed when he says, "as iron that breaketh, or 'even as iron breaketh *all these*', shall it break in pieces, and bruise; *all nations and kingdoms*" (emphasis added).[13] Here Gill incorrectly takes the term "all these" where "all these" refers to the "three monarchies" (as Calvin described them) of the statue, and equates the phrase to "*all* nations and kingdoms" to support his position, which is incorrect. We see here another bending of the meaning of Daniel 2:40 to fit the assumption. The assumption known as Rome was now strong enough to say outright—albeit incorrectly—that "Rome subdued and conquered the Persians."

. . . That Grew Into "Common Knowledge" . . .

With the arrival of the nineteenth century, the assumption had become *common knowledge*, and we see proof of this with the next commentary. At this point two influential voices (Jerome and Calvin) supported Rome in addition to two popular eighteenth century commentaries (Henry and Gill) following after them. The number of "votes" for Rome was growing.

One century after Gill, Albert Barnes, the Presbyterian theologian and pastor born in Rome, New York, in the 1860s addressed Daniel 2:40 with Rome being the iron leg empire. He wrote, "It is *scarcely necessary* to observe that this description is applicable to the Roman power. In nothing was it more remarkable than its 'strength;' for that irresistible power before which all other nations were perfectly weak" (emphasis added).[14] When Barnes wrote, "it is scarcely necessary to observe" that Rome fulfills Daniel 2:40, he expressed an assumption as if it had become common knowledge. Indeed, it had.

Edward Gibbon, the famed historian who in the 1770s authored *The*

Decline and Fall of the Roman Empire, took the role of theologian when he wrote of Rome, "The arms of the republic, sometimes vanquished in battle, always victorious in war, advanced with rapid steps to the Euphrates, the Danube, the Rhine, and the ocean; and the *images of* gold, *or* silver, *or brass,* that might serve to represent the nations and their kings, were successively broken by the *iron* monarchy of Rome" (emphasis added).[15] Gibbon was a professed Christian, and so perhaps including this reference to Daniel is not surprising. However, there it is in a respected historical reference that "iron" Rome conquered and broke the "image" that was the "silver" Persia. Gibbon had included the assumption about Daniel 2:40 referring to Rome. Now the assumption was common knowledge for it had found its way into a respected and formal history of Rome. Gibbon wrote this soon after Henry's and Gill's commentaries were available, so it is possible that Henry and Gill affected Gibbon.

So it was that Barnes took that same aforementioned quote from Gibbon's work regarding the silver kingdom to support his own position, but ignored what Gibbon wrote in a later chapter suitably titled "Troubles in Persia."[16] In that chapter Gibbon wrote,

> The conflict of Rome and Persia was prolonged from the death of Craesus [Crassus] to the reign of Heraclius. An experience of seven hundred years might convince the rival nations of the impossibility of maintaining their conquests beyond the fatal limits of the Tigris and Euphrates. [17]

Crassus was the first Roman general to cross the Euphrates with the goal of conquering Persia and was soundly defeated in 53 BC. Heraclius was the last Roman emperor to fight Persia and was victorious, having won a long war in AD 628. What did he conquer? He took back Syria from the Persians. So Gibbon wrote here that Rome did not conquer Persia, but earlier in the same volume wrote that iron Rome "broke" the "silver" that was Persia. We see here that Gibbon unwittingly contradicts himself in his book. Gibbon could have ended the whole notion of Rome being the iron empire. He knew Rome did not conquer Persia, but let the earlier commentaries influence him.

In addition to Barnes including only one side of the contradiction in Gibbon's work, Barnes also added to his commentary of Daniel 2:40, "The Roman, in addition to what it possessed in the West, actually occupied in the East substantially the same territory as the Babylonian, the Medo-Persian, and the Macedonian."[18] This statement, however, is boldly untrue, for Rome never conquered Persia itself, but only its outlying provinces like Syria and Mesopotamia. Rome never substantially occupied Persia. If Rome had, its eastern border would have had to extend all the way to Pakistan, which it clearly did not. Perhaps having the wind of a respected historical reference at your back allowed for bold and exaggerating, but untrue, statements to be made with confidence.

It is interesting to see that where something is "common knowledge," only certain facts are used and not delved into too deeply. I cannot completely fault Barnes here. Gibbon's writing supported Barnes' assumption about Rome. Gibbon being a historian and not a theologian crossed a boundary and made the assumption part of the history books. Barnes merely reinforced this notion in the commentaries. Not only were certain facts ignored to argue an assumption, but at this point, the available facts themselves had become muddied.

(Note: Just for the sake of touching major bases, and due to its immense popularity, I mention here the Scofield reference work in case the reader is wondering about Scofield's position on the subject. There is nothing to say here though since Scofield's Bible, which came along in 1917, was silent on the subject of Daniel 2:40.)

. . . That Finally Became Canon

Finally, "common knowledge" became part of *canon* in the twentieth century. The Lockman Foundation, an interdenominational, nonprofit ministry, has published and made available various translations of the Bible. One of them, the Amplified Bible, was published in 1962. Daniel 2:40 is translated as, "And the fourth kingdom [Rome] shall be strong as iron, since iron breaks to pieces and subdues all things; and like iron which crushes, it shall break and crush all these" (AMP). Do you see that? The word *Rome* in brackets is inserted into the scriptural text to mean that which is bracketed is what was actually meant. Please don't misunderstand me. My intention is not to discredit any mainstream Christian translation of the Bible, including the Amplified. They are all capable of giving us a saving knowledge of Jesus Christ and Him crucified. However, for the translators to add "[Rome]" to the text of Daniel 2:40 when that verse is simply not saying that, shows how the assumption that was "common knowledge" became canon in everything but name. So the last step was taken and "Rome" was added to the biblical text.

Confirming this new canon, Hal Lindsey, the famous prophecy expert of the last four decades and staunch supporter of the Roman Antichrist theory, quoted this same Amplified Bible translation of Daniel 2:40 in his landmark book *The Late Great Planet Earth* in 1970. He wrote, "And the fourth kingdom [Rome] shall be as strong as iron, since iron breaks to pieces and subdues all things."[19] Lindsey quoted the translation that best served his purpose, as it is the prerogative of every author to quote the sources that best support his or her opinion. It was convenient that the translators of the Amplified Bible made "Rome" canon by inserting it in the Scriptural text. This made Lindsey's argument that much more persuasive. His book *The Late Great Planet Earth* went on to provide a platform for the theology of today that supports this popular notion about Rome.

CONCLUSION

In summary, therefore, across the span of eighteen centuries the first supposition became assumption, assumption became common knowledge, and finally common knowledge became canon. This went on during those many centuries, while all the while Daniel was sealed until the end times. Indeed, the early false histories, supposition, assumptions, and misunderstandings all built on each other and conspired to seal the words of Daniel. As long as men were going to keep actively propagating this notion about Rome, the seal on Daniel was going to become more binding. The multicentury history of these commentaries stands as a witness and testimony to the fact that parts of Daniel are indeed sealed. If there was a word stamped on these seals that keeps the reader from reading "Islam" in Daniel as the main player in the end times, it might be "Rome."

Bible References Quoted or Mentioned

Genesis 10:5; 16:11–12; 25:12-18

Exodus 1:14–22; 20:2–3

Judges 6:26–32

Ruth 1:20

1 Kings 11:33; 18:16–46

2 Kings 2:23–24; 17:1–23; 23:13; Ch. 24–25

2 Chronicles 24:7; 33:3

Esther 3:5–15; Ch. 8–9

Psalm 103:12

Proverbs 28:15

Isaiah 9:1; 11:1; 14:13–14

Jeremiah 5:6, 23:27; 51:24–25

Ezekiel 38:1–6, 18, 20–22

Daniel 2:31–45; 7: 2–14, 17, 19, 23–25; 8: 2–12, 17, 19–21, 23–25, 41; 9:4, 26–27; 11:2–35, 41–43

Hosea 2:17; 13:7

Amos 3:8

Micah 5:2

Zephaniah 1:2–4

Matthew 2:23; 24:7–8, 32

Luke 2:25–33; 14:32; 21:20

John 1:1; 7:41–42; 8:24

1 Corinthians 14:3; 15:17

2 Thessalonians 2:3

1 Peter 5:8

1 John 2:22–23; 4:2–3

Revelation 3:3; 6:1–8; 12:3-5; 13:1–2; 17:9–12; 20:4

NOTES

INTRODUCTION

1. Hippolytus, "Treatise on Christ and Antichrist", par. 28, in Alexander Roberts, and James Donaldson, *The Fathers of the Third Century: Hippolytus, Cyprian, Caius, Novatian, Appendix*, vol. 5 of *Ante-Nicene Fathers: The Writings of the Fathers Down to A.D. 325* (1886; reprint, Peabody, MA: Hendrickson Publishers, Inc., 1994), http://www.ccel.org/ccel /schaff/anf05.txt.

2. Hippolytus, "The interpretation by Hippolytus, (bishop) of Rome, of the visions of Daniel and Nebuchadnezzar, taken in conjunction," par. 4–6, in Roberts and Donaldson, *The Fathers of the Third Century*, http://www.ccel .org/ccel/schaff/anf05.txt.

3. Jerome, *Jerome's Commentary on Daniel*, trans. Gleason Leonard Archer, Jr., (Grand Rapids, MI: Baker Book House, 1958), chap. 2, verse 40, http://www .tertullian.org/fathers/jerome_daniel_02_text.htm.

4. Jerome, "Letter CXXVII. To Principia," par. 12, in Philip Schaff and Henry Wace, *Jerome: Letters and Select Works*, vol. 6 of *Nicene and Post-Nicene Fathers, Second Series*, (1893; reprint, Peabody, MA: Hendrickson Publishers, Inc., 1994), http://www.ccel.org/ccel/schaff/npnf206.txt.

5. John Calvin, vol. 1 of *Commentaries on the Book of the Prophet Daniel* (1561; reprint, Edinburgh, UK: The Calvin Translation Society, 1852), Daniel 2:40–43, http://www.ccel.org/ccel/calvin/calcom24.txt.

6. Matthew Henry, *Isaiah to Malachi*, vol. 4 of *Commentary on the Whole Bible*, unabridged, (1708–10; reprint, Peabody, MA: Hendrickson Publishers Marketing, LLC, 1991), 809.

7. John Gill, *Jeremiah to Malachi*, vol. 4 of *Exposition of the Old and New Testaments* (1748–63), http://www.sacred-texts.com/bib/cmt/gill/dan002.htm.
8. Edward Gibbon, *History of the Decline and Fall of the Roman Empire* (1782; reprint, Boston, MA: Aldine Book Publishing Co., 1845), vol. 3, chap. 38, part 6, par. 1, http://www.ccel.org/ccel/gibbon/decline.v.xlviii.html.
9. Albert Barnes, *Daniel*, vol. 7 of *Notes on the Old and New Testaments* (1873; reprint, Grand Rapids, MI: Baker Book House Company, 1996), Daniel 2:40, http://www.sacred-texts.com/bib/cmt/barnes/dan002.htm.
10. Ibid.
11. Gibbon, *History of the Decline and Fall of the Roman Empire*, vol. 4, chap. 46, part 1, par. 1, http://www.ccel.org/ccel/gibbon/decline.vi.xxxiii.html.
12. Hal Lindsey, *The Late Great Planet Earth* (Grand Rapids, MI: Zondervan Publishing House, 1970), 90.

CHAPTER 1

1. Theodor Mommsen, *The Provinces of the Roman Empire, Volume II* (New York, NY: Barnes & Noble Books, 1996), 68.
2. Stephen Dando-Collins, *Legions of Rome: The Definitive History of Every Imperial Roman Legion* (London, UK: Quercus, 2010), 417–418.
3. Mommsen, *The Provinces of the Roman Empire*, 71.
4. Will Durant, *Caesar and Christ, Volume 3 of The Story of Civilization* (New York, NY: Simon and Schuster, 1944), 530.
5. Will Durant, *The Age of Faith, Volume 4 of The Story of Civilization* (New York, NY: Simon and Schuster, 1950), 139, 142.
6. Mommsen, *The Provinces of the Roman Empire*, 85.
7. Durant, *The Age of Faith*, 19.
8. Ibid., 151.
9. Ibid., 189.
10. Ibid., 190.
11. Ibid.
12. Ibid.
13. Ibid., 152;
14. Tamim Ansary, *Destiny Disrupted: A History of the World Through Islamic Eyes* (New York, NY: Public Affairs, 2009), 46.
15. Will Durant, *The Life of Greece, Volume 2 of The Story of Civilization* (New York, NY: Simon and Schuster, 1939, 1966), 572.
16. Ansary, *Destiny Disrupted*, 24.
17. John Clark Ridpath, *Ridpath's History of the World, Volume IV, Book XII, The Mohammedan Ascendency* (Cincinnati, Ohio: The Jones Brothers Publishing Company, 1907), 462.

18. Ibid., 463

19. Durant, *The Age of Faith*, 188.

20. Qur'an 8:12, 8:39–41; Sahih al-Bukhari 4:52:280

21. Albert Hourani, *A History of the Arab Peoples* (Cambridge, MA: Harvard University Press, 1991), 46.

22. Ibid., 47.

23. Ibid.

24. Durant, *The Age of Faith*, 188.

25. Hourani, *A History of the Arab Peoples*, 23–24

26. Ansari, *Destiny Disrupted*, 47.

27. Ibid., 78.

28. Durant, *The Age of Faith*, 212.

29. Sahih al-Bukhari 9:84:57.

30. Hourani, *A History of the Arab Peoples*, 47.

31. Ibid., 96.

32. Durant, *The Age of Faith*, 289.

33. Ansari, *Destiny Disrupted*, 77.

34. Ibid., 82.

35. Durant, *The Age of Faith*, 190.

36. Pact of the League of Arab States, March 22, 1945; http://avalon.law.yale.edu /20th_century/arableag.asp.

37. Wafa Sultan, *A God Who Hates* (New York, NY: St. Martin's Press, 2009), 205.

38. Durant, *The Age of Faith*, 219.

CHAPTER 2

1. Stephen Dando-Collins, *Legions of Rome: The Definitive History of Every Imperial Roman Legion* (London, UK: Quercus, 2010), 21.

2. Ibid.

3. Stephen Dando-Collins, *Caesar's Legion* (Hoboken, NJ: John Wiley & Sons Inc, 2002), 199.

4. Flavius Josephus, *Josephus: The Complete Works, The War of the Jews*, trans. William Whiston, 1737, book 5, chap. 2, sec. 3, plain text version retrieved from Christian Classics Ethereal Library, http://www.ccel.org /ccel/josephus/complete.txt

5. Dando-Collins, *Legions of Rome*, 351.

6. Ibid., 136.

7. Ibid., 165–166.

8. Ibid., 172.

9. Dando-Collins, *Caesar's Legion*, 6–7.

10. Dando-Collins, *Legions of Rome*, 152–160.

11. Dando-Collins, *Caesar's Legion*, 7.
12. Ibid., 179.
13. Ibid., 196, 198.
14. Ibid., 198.
15. Ibid., 199.
16. Ibid., 211, 214.
17. Ibid., 263–264.
18. Adrian Goldsworthy, *The Complete Roman Army* (London, UK: Thames & Hudson, 2003), 80.
19. Dando-Collins, *Caesar's Legion*, 21.
20. Josephus, *Josephus: The Complete Works*, trans. Whiston, book 5, chap. 13, sec. 5, plain text version retrieved from Christian Classics Ethereal Library, http://www.ccel.org/ccel/josephus/complete.txt.
21. Goldsworthy, *The Complete Roman Army*, 80.
22. Josephus, *Josephus: The Complete Works*, trans. Whiston, book 6, chap. 4, sec. 5, plain text version retrieved from Christian Classics Ethereal Library, http://www.ccel.org/ccel/josephus/complete.txt.
23. Ibid., book 6, chap. 4, sec. 6.
24. Ibid., book 7, chap. 1, sec. 2.

CHAPTER 3

1. Theodor Noldeke, "Arabs (Ancient)," in John Hastings, *Encyclopaedia of Religion and Ethics*, Volume 1 (New York, NY: Charles Scribner's Sons, 1908), 664.
2. Ibid., 663.
3. Ibid.
4. Ibid., 664.
5. Ibid.
6. Albert Hourani, *A History of the Arab Peoples* (Harvard University Press, Cambridge, MA, 1991), 19.
7. Wafa Sultan, *A God Who Hates* (New York, NY: St. Martin's Press, 2009), 61.
8. Muhsin Khan trans., *Sahih al-Bukhari*, book 9, vol. 84, no. 57, Center for Muslim-Jewish Engagement, University of Southern California, www.cmje.org/religious-texts/hadith/.

CHAPTER 4

1. Hal Lindsey, *The Late Great Planet Earth* (Grand Rapids, MI: Zondervan Publishing House, 1970), 145.
2. David Jeremiah, *What In The World Is Going On? 10 Prophetic Clues You Cannot Afford to Ignore* (Nashville, TN: Thomas Nelson, 2008), 100.

CHAPTER 5

1. Wafa Sultan, *A God Who Hates* (New York, NY: St. Martin's Press, 2009), 205.
2. Edwin Jacques, *The Albanians: An Ethnic History from Prehistoric Times to the Present* (London, UK: McFarland & Company, Inc. 1995), 38–39.
3. Will Durant, *The Life of Greece, Volume 2 of The Story of Civilization* (New York, NY: Simon and Schuster, 1939, 1966), 127–128.
4. Jacques, *The Albanians*, 38–39.
5. John D. Grainger, *Seleukos Nikator: Constructing a Hellenistic Kingdom* (New York, NY: Routledge, 1990), 2.
6. Ibid.
7. George Cawkwell, *Philip of Macedon* (London, UK: Faber and Faber Ltd, 1978), 20.
8. Ian Worthington, *Philip II of Macedonia* (New Haven, CT: Yale University Press, 2008), 6–7.
9. Grainger, *Seleukos Nikator*, 2.
10. Ibid.
11. N. G. L. Hammond, *A History of Macedonia,* Volume I (Oxford, UK: Oxford University Press, 1972), 103.
12. Ibid., 111.
13. Ibid.
14. Ibid., 115.
15. Jacques, *The Albanians*, 38.
16. Pollo Stefanaq, *The History of Albania: From its Origins to the Present Day,* trans. Carol Wiseman and Ginnie Hole (London, UK: Routledge & Kegan Paul Ltd. 1981), 30–32.
17. Ibid., 213.
18. Ibid., 230.
19. Christopher Deliso, *The Coming Balkan Caliphate* (Westport, CT: Praeger Security International, 2007), 38.
20. Ibid., 56.
21. Ibid., 112.
22. Will Durant, *Caesar and Christ, Volume 3 of The Story of Civilization* (New York, NY: Simon and Schuster, 1944), 548.
23. D. M. Low, *The Decline and Fall of the Roman Empire by Edward Gibbon: An Abridgement* (1830, reprint, New York, NY: Harcourt, Brace & Company, 1960), 523.
24. Ibid., xii.
25. Will Durant, *The Age of Faith, Volume 4 of The Story of Civilization* (New York, NY: Simon and Schuster, 1950), 4.
26. Ibid., 5
27. Ibid., 389.
28. Ibid.

CHAPTER 6

1. "Country Profiles," Library of Congress Federal Research Division, 2005–2008, http://lcweb2.loc.gov/frd/cs/profiles.html; "Country Studies" Library of Congress Federal Research Division, 1990–2010, http://lcweb2.loc.gov/frd/cs/; "Country Profile: Turkey" Library of Congress Federal Research Division, 2008, http://lcweb2.loc.gov/frd/cs/profiles/Turkey.pdf, p. 25

2. "Country Profile: Turkey" Library of Congress Federal Research Division, 2008, http://lcweb2.loc.gov/frd/cs/profiles/Turkey.pdf, p. 25

CHAPTER 7

1. Pew Research Center, *Mapping the Muslim Population: A Report on the Size and Distribution of the World's Muslim Population* (Washington D.C.: Pew Forum on Religion & Public Life, October 2009), 31–36.

2. Ibid.

3. Ibid.

4. Ibid.

5. *The World Factbook 2009* (Washington D.C.: Central Intelligence Agency, 2009).

6. Pew Research Center, *Mapping the Muslim Population*, 4.

CHAPTER 9

1. Thomas M. Leonard, *Encyclopedia of the Developing World,* Volume 2 (New York, NY: Routledge, Taylor & Francis Group, 2006), 793.

2. Scott Pelley, "Interview of FBI Agent George Piro, Saddam's Confessions" (*60 Minutes*, CBS, 2008).

3. Ibid.

4. Ibid.

5. Ibid.

6. "Saddam Hussein Talks to the FBI: Twenty Interviews and Five Conversations with 'High Value Detainee # 1'" in *2004, National Security Archive Electronic Briefing Book No. 279*, "#24 Casual Conversation, June 11, 2004" (Washington D.C.: The National Security Archive, 2009), http://www.gwu.edu/~nsarchiv/NSAEBB/NSAEBB279/24.pdf, p. 1.

7. Ibid., 1–2.

8. Alex Spillius, "Saddam Hussein 'lied about WMDs to protect Iraq from Iran'" *Telegraph,* July 3, 2009, http://www.telegraph.co.uk/news/worldnews/middleeast/iraq/5727868/Saddam-Hussein-lied-about-WMDs-to-protect-Iraq-from-Iran.html.

9. Marine General Anthony Zinni, retired head of US Central Command from 1997 to 2000, speaking at the Middle East Institute, Washington DC,

"A General Speaks on War With Iraq," Center for Defense Information, October 10, 2002, http://www.cdi.org/terrorism/zinni-iraq-conditions -pr.cfm.

10. Joseph Logan, "Last U.S. troops leave Iraq, ending war," Reuters, December 18, 2011, http://www.reuters.com/ article/2011/12/18/us-iraq-withdrawal -idUSTRE7BH03320 111218.

CHAPTER 10

1. Ali Alfoneh, *Iran Unveiled: How the Revolutionary Guards Is Turning Theocracy into Military Dictatorship* (Washington D.C.: AEI Press, 2013), 17.
2. Ibid.
3. Ibid., 49.
4. Ibid., 50.
5. Ibid., 221.
6. Ibid.
7. Ibid., 27.
8. Ibid., 165, 171.
9. Ibid.
10. Ibid., 175.
11. Ibid., 176.
12. Ibid., 191.
13. Ali Alfoneh, "All The Guards Men: Iran's Silent Revolution," *World Affairs*, September–October 2010, http://www.worldaffairsjournal.org/article/all -guards-men-irans-silent-revolution.
14. Jason Gewirtz, "Revolutionary Guard Has Tight Grip on Iran's Economy," CNBC, December 8, 2010, http://www.cnbc.com/id/40570657.
15. Farnaz Fassihi, "Protests in Iran Diminish Amid Security Crackdown," *Wall Street Journal*, June 23, 2009, http://online.wsj.com/article/SB124566035538436595.html.
16. "Khamenei, Iran Choose Statesman Rouhani," *Al Monitor*, June 15, 2013, http://www.al-monitor.com/pulse/originals/2013/06/iranians-choose-hassan -rouhani.html.
17. Ali Alfoneh, "Ahmadinejad versus Khamenei: IRGC Wins, Civilians Lose," Middle Eastern Outlook, no. 3, May 2011, American Enterprise Institute (AEI) for Public Policy Research, http://www.aei.org/files/2011/05/25/MEO-2011-03-g.pdf.
18. Ibid.
19. Alfoneh, *Iran Unveiled*, 246.
20. Steven O'Hern, *Iran's Revolutionary Guard: The Threat That Grows While America Sleeps* (Washington D.C.: Potomac Books, 2012), 131.
21. Ali Alfoneh, "Khamene'i's Balancing Act," *Middle East Quarterly*, winter 2011, vol. 18, no. 1, http://www.meforum.org/2847/khamenei-balancing-act.

22. Emanuele Ottolenghi, *The Pasdaran: Inside Iran's Islamic Revolutionary Guard Corps* (Washington D.C.: FDD Press, 2011), 39.

23. Jean Calmard, "Ayatollah," *The Oxford Encyclopedia of the Islamic World*, accessed October 23, 2015, http://www.oxfordislamicstudies.com/article/opr /t236/e0088.

24. Alfoneh, *Iran Unveiled*, 17.

25. Kasra Naji, *Ahmadinejad: The Secret History of Iran's Radical Leader* (Berkeley, CA: University of California Press, 2008), 92.

26. Charles Krauthammer, "Today Tehran, Tomorrow the World," *Time*, March 26, 2006, http://www.time.com/time/magazine/article/0,9171,1176995,00 .html.

27. Naji, *Ahmadinejad*, 69.

28. Mark Davidson, "Ahmadinejad's Speeches to the U.N.: Talks of the Second Signpost," Four Signposts, October 8, 2012, http://foursignposts.com/2012/10 /08/ahmadinejads-speeches-to-the-u-n-talks-of-the-second-signpost/.

29. Naji, *Ahmadinejad*, 93.

30. Ibid., 92.

31. Ibid., 69.

32. Ibid., 92.

33. Farnaz Fassihi, "Protests in Iran Diminish Amid Security Crackdown," *Wall Street Journal*, June 23, 2009, http://online.wsj.com/article/ SB124566035538436595.html.

34. Mohebat Ahdiyyih, "Ahmadinejad and the Mahdi," *Middle East Quarterly*, Fall 2008, vol. 15, no. 4, pp. 27–36, http://www.meforum.org/1985/ ahmadinejad -and-the-mahdi.

35. Alfoneh, *Iran Unveiled*, 151.

36. Ibid., 160.

37. Ibid., 159.

38. Ehsan Ahrari, "Tehran Sharpens Its Sword," Asia Times Online, August 23, 2006), http://www.atimes.com/atimes/Middle_East/ HH23Ak01.html.

39. Ibid.

40. "Country Profiles" Library of Congress Federal Research Division, 2005–2008, http://lcweb2.loc.gov/frd/cs/profiles.html.

41. "Country Studies" Library of Congress Federal Research Division, 1990–2010, http://lcweb2.loc.gov/frd/cs/.

42. "Country Profile: Iran" Library of Congress Federal Research Division, 2008 http://lcweb2.loc.gov/frd/cs/profiles/Iran.pdf, p. 18.

43. Hossein Aryan, "Iran's Basij Force—The Mainstay Of Domestic Security," Radio Free Europe/ Radio Liberty, December 7, 2008, http://www.rferl.org /content/Irans_Basij_Force_Mainstay_Of_Domestic_Security/1357081.html.

44. Mordechai Kedar, "Iran Has Defeated the US in Iraq," Center for the Study

of the Middle East and Islam (Bar Ilan University, Ramat-Gan, Israel), November 2, 2012, http://mordechaikedarinenglish.blogspot.co.il/.

45. Mordechai Kedar, "The 'Sushi' is Heating Up," Center for the Study of the Middle East and Islam (Bar Ilan University, Ramat-Gan, Israel), June 13, 2013, http://mordechaikedarinenglish.blogspot.co.il/.

46. Kedar, "Iran Has Defeated the US in Iraq."

47. Mordechai Kedar, "The Collapsing Crescent" Center for the Study of the Middle East and Islam (Bar Ilan University, Ramat-Gan, Israel), May 2, 2013, http://mordechaikedarinenglish.blogspot.co.il/.

48. Mordechai Kedar, "The Truth—and the Enmity—Behind the Slogans," Center for the Study of the Middle East and Islam (Bar Ilan University, Ramat-Gan, Israel), December 13, 2012, http://mordechaikedarinenglish .blogspot. co.il/.

49. Alfoneh, *Iran Unveiled*, 232.

50. "Iran Missile Arsenal," IranIntelligence.com (American-Israeli Cooperative Enterprise, Washington D.C.), http://www.iranintelligence.com/arsenal, accessed September 28, 2015.

51. "Iran Nuclear Program, By the Numbers," IranIntelligence.com (American-Israeli Cooperative Enterprise, Washington D.C.), http://www.iranintelligence .com/arsenal, accessed September 28, 2015.

52. Ibid.

53. Tim Arango, "U.S. Marks End to 9-Year War, Leaving an Uncertain Iraq," *New York Times* December 15, 2011, http://www.nytimes.com/ 2011/12/16 /world/middleeast/end-for-us-begins-period-of-uncertaintyforiraqis.html ?pagewanted=all&_r=0.

54. "Country Analysis Briefs," U.S. Energy Information Administration (EIA, Washington D.C.), http://www.eia.gov/countries/, accessed September 28, 2015.

55. Michael Mackenzie, "Fed Passes China in Treasury Holdings," *Financial Times*, February 2, 2011, http://www.ft.com/intl/cms/s/0/ 120372fc-2e48-11e0 -8733-00144feabdc0.html#axzz2Xq7ozJFG.

56. Joshua Zumbrin and Jeff Kearns, "Fed Maintains $85 Billion Pace of Monthly Asset Purchases," Bloomberg, March 20, 2913, http://www.bloomberg.com /news/2013-03-20/fed-keeps-85-billion-pace-of-bond-buying-as-job-market -improves.html.

57. Steve Denning, "Big Banks and Derivatives: Why Another Financial Crisis Is Inevitable," Forbes, January 8, 2013, http://www.forbes.com/sites/stevedenning /2013/01/08/five-years-after-the-financial-meltdown-the-water-is-still-full-of -big-sharks/.

58. Nassim Nicholas Taleb, *The Black Swan: The Impact of the Highly Improbable* (New York: Random House, 2010), xxi–xxii.

59. Mordechai Kedar, "Rouhani and Iranian Deceit," trans. Sally Zahav, Center for the Study of the Middle East and Islam (Bar Ilan University, Ramat-Gan, Israel), June 20, 2013, http://mordechaikedarinenglish. blogspot.co.il/.

CHAPTER 11

1. Susan Gusten, "Mandate for a New Turkish Era," *New York Times*, June 15, 2011, http://www.nytimes.com/2011/06/16/world/europe/16iht-M16 -TURKEY-POLICY.html?pagewanted=all&_r=0.
2. "Era of military coups over in Turkey: Erdogan," *Tehran Times*, October 1, 2012, http://tehrantimes.com/world/101966-era-of-military-coups-over-in -turkey-erdogan.
3. Ibid.
4. Stefan Steinberg, "Financial Speculators Reap Profits from Global Hunger," Centre for Research on Globalisation (CRG) (Montreal, Canada), April 24, 2008, http://globalresearch.ca/index.php?context=va&aid=8794.
5. Ibid.
6. Derek Headey, "Reflections on the Global Food Crisis," International Food Policy Research Institute (Washington, DC), 2010, http://www.ifpri.org/sites /default/files/publications/ifpridp00958.pdf, p. 11.
7. Editorial, "The World Food Crisis," *New York Times*, April 10, 2008, http:// www.nytimes.com/2008/04/10/opinion/10thu1.html.
8. "Olive Oil Prices to Remain Stable," *Times of India*, June 25, 2008, http:// articles.timesofindia.indiatimes.com/2008-06-25/india-business /27769171_1_olive-oil-oil-prices-indian-olive-association-president.
9. Simon Field is the managing director of Salsi Pty Ltd., a food production company in Australia; he was executive director of the Australian Institute of Agricultural Science from 1989 to 1996, editor of the *Journal of Agricultural Science* and a member of the board of the faculty of agriculture, forestry, and horticulture of the University of Melbourne.
10. Simon Field, "Market Outlook for Olive Oil," *Olive Business*, November 2008, http://olivebusiness.blogspot.com/2008/12/market-outlook-for-olive -oil-november.html.

CHAPTER 12

1. Lyman Coleman, *An Historical Textbook and Atlas of Biblical Geography* (Philadelphia, PA: Claxton, Remsen & Haffelfinger, 1874), Map II—The World As Known to the Hebrews According to the Mosaic Account.
2. Ibid.

3. Ibid.
4. Ibid.

APPENDIX A

1. Hippolytus, "Treatise on Christ and antichrist", par. 28, in Alexander Roberts and James Donaldson, *The Fathers of the Third Century: Hippolytus, Cyprian, Caius, Novatian*, Appendix, vol. 5 of *Ante-Nicene Fathers: The Writings of the Fathers Down to A.D. 325* (1886, reprint, Peabody, MA: Hendrickson Publishers, Inc., 1994), http://www.ccel.org/ccel/schaff/anf05.txt.

2. Hippolytus, "The interpretation by Hippolytus, (bishop) of Rome, of the visions of Daniel and Nebuchadnezzar, taken in conjunction", par. 4–6, in Roberts and Donaldson, *The Fathers of the Third Century*, http://www.ccel.org/ccel/schaff/anf05.txt.

3. Ibid., par. 7.

4. Cassius Dio, vol. 8 of *A Book of Roman History*, trans. Earnest Cary (Cambridge, MA: Harvard University Press, 1925), book 68, par. 18, 28, http://penelope.uchicago.edu/Thayer/E/Roman/Texts/Cassius_Dio/68*.html.

5. Jerome, *Jerome's Commentary on Daniel*, trans. Gleason Leonard Archer, Jr., (Grand Rapids, MI: Baker Book House, 1958), chap. 2, verse 40, retrieved from http://www.tertullian.org/fathers/jerome_daniel_02_text.htm.

6. Eutropius, *Abridgement of Roman History*, trans. John Watson (London: Henry G. Bohn, 1853), book 8, par. 3, http://www.forumromanum.org/literature/eutropius/trans8.html#2.

7. Jerome, "Letter CXXVII. To Principia," par. 12, in Philip Schaff, Henry and Wace, *Jerome: Letters and Select Works*, Volume 6 of *Nicene and Post-Nicene Fathers, Second Series*, (1893; reprint, Peabody, MA: Hendrickson Publishers, Inc., 1994), http://www.ccel.org/ccel/schaff/npnf206.txt.

8. John Calvin, vol. 1 of *Commentaries on the Book of the Prophet Daniel* (1561, reprint, Edinburgh, UK: The Calvin Translation Society, 1852), Daniel 2:40–43, http://www.ccel.org/ccel/calvin/calcom24.txt.

9. Ibid.

10. Ibid.

11. Matthew Henry, *Isaiah to Malachi*, Vol. 4 of *Commentary on the Whole Bible*, unabridged (1708–10, reprint, Peabody, MA: Hendrickson Publishers Marketing, LLC, 1991), 809.

12. John Gill, *Jeremiah to Malachi*, vol. 4 of *Exposition of the Old and New Testaments* (1748–63), http://www.sacred-texts.com/bib/cmt/gill/dan002.htm.

13. Ibid.

14. Albert Barnes, *Daniel*, vol. 7 of *Notes on the Old and New Testaments* (1873, reprint, Grand Rapids, MI: Baker Book House Company, 1996), Daniel 2:40,

retrieved from http://www.sacred-texts.com/bib/cmt/barnes/dan002.htm, chap. 46, "Troubles in Persia."

15. Edward Gibbon, *History of the Decline and Fall of the Roman Empire* (1782, reprint, Boston, MA: Aldine Book Publishing Co, 1845), vol. 3, chap. 38, part 6, par. 1, http://www.ccel.org/ccel/gibbon/decline.v.xlviii.html.

16. Barnes, *Daniel*, Daniel 2:40.

17. Gibbon, *History of the Decline and Fall of the Roman Empire*, vol. 4, chap. 46, part 1, par. 1, http://www.ccel.org/ccel/gibbon/decline.vi.xxxiii.html.

18. Barnes, *Daniel*, Daniel 2:40.

19. Hal Lindsey, *The Late Great Planet Earth* (Grand Rapids, MI: Zondervan Publishing House, 1970), 90.

GLOSSARY OF ISLAMIC TERMS

ALLAH—Islam's deity; also, the Arabic name of God.

CALIPH—Literally, *successor.* The successor to Muhammad and the ruler of all of Islam.

CALIPHATE—The office of the caliph.

HADITH—Literally, *speech.* The second holy book of Islam; a series of books that contain recorded sayings and traditions of Muhammad.

IMAM—Literally, *leader.* To Sunnis it is a religious leader of a community, but to Shias it is one of the twelve successors of Muhammad.

ISLAM—Literally, *submission*; the religion founded by Muhammad.

JIHAD—Literally, *struggle*; the struggle both against self to follow God, and the struggle against non-Muslims, to further Islam.

JIZYA—The tax that all non-Muslim males in a Muslim-controlled area are to pay, simply because they are not Muslim.

KAABAH—Literally, *cube.* The cube-shaped structure at the center of Mecca, to which all Muslims pray five times a day.

KUFFAR—Non-Muslim. Also *infidel.*

MAHDI—Literally, *guide.* The leader of Islam who is to appear before the end of the age. To Shias he is the twelfth Imam.

MECCA—The first holy city of Islam.

MUHAMMAD—(Also spelled "Mohammad.") The founder and Prophet of Islam. Died in AD 632.

MUSLIM—Literally, *one who surrenders*. A follower of Allah and Muhammad.

QUR'AN—(Also spelled "Koran.") Literally, *recitation*. The first holy book of Islam. To a Muslim it contains the very words of Allah.

SHIA—The large minority sect of Islam that believes Imam Ali and his family are the leaders of Islam.

SIRA—The third holy book of Islam. It is a series of books that contain biographies of Muhammad.

SUNNI—The majority sect of Islam.

TWELVER—The majority sect within Shia Islam that believes there will be exactly twelve imams; also a believer within that sect.

UMMA—Literally, *nation*. The worldwide community of all Muslims.

BIBLIOGRAPHY

Alfoneh, Ali. *Iran Unveiled: How the Revolutionary Guards Is Turning Theocracy into Military Dictatorship.* Washington, DC: AEI Press, 2013.

Ali, Maulana Muhammad. *The Holy Qur'an: Arabic Text with English Translation and Commentary.* Dublin, OH: Ahmadiyya Anjuman Isha'at Islam Lahore Inc., 2002.

Ansary, Tamim, *Destiny Disrupted: A History of the World Through Islamic Eyes.* New York, NY: Public Affairs, 2009.

Cawkwell, George, *Philip of Macedon.* London, UK: Faber and Faber Ltd, 1978.

Central Intelligence Agency, *The World Factbook 2009.* Washington, DC: CIA, 2009.

Coleman, Lyman, *An Historical Textbook and Atlas of Biblical Geography.* Philadelphia, PA: Claxton, Remsen & Haffelfinger, 1874.

Dando-Collins, Stephen, *Caesar's Legion: The Epic Saga of Julius Caesar's Elite Tenth Legion and the Armies of Rome.* Hoboken, NJ: John Wiley & Sons Inc., 2002.

———, *Legions of Rome: The Definitive History of Every Imperial Roman Legion.* London, UK: Quercus, 2010.

Deliso, Christopher, *The Coming Balkan Caliphate.* Westport, CT: Praeger Security International, 2007.

Durant, Will, *Caesar and Christ,* vol. 3 of *The Story of Civilization.* New York, NY: Simon and Schuster, 1944.

———, *The Age of Faith,* vol. 4 of *The Story of Civilization.* New York, NY: Simon and Schuster, 1950.

———, *The Life of Greece,* vol. 2 of *The Story of Civilization.* New York, NY: Simon and Schuster, 1939, 1966.

Fletcher, Richard, *The Cross and the Crescent.* New York, NY: Penguin Group, 2003.

Gabriel, Brigitte, *They Must Be Stopped.* New York, NY: St. Martin's Griffin, 2009.

Goldsworthy, Adrian, *The Complete Roman Army.* London, UK: Thames & Hudson, 2003.

Grainger, John D., *Seleukos Nikator: constructing a Hellenistic Kingdom.* New York, NY: Routledge, 1990.

Green, Jay P., *The Interlinear Bible: Hebrew-Greek-English,* second edition. Peabody, MA: Hendrickson Publishers, 1986.

Hammond, N.G.L., *A History of Macedonia, Volume I.* Oxford, UK: Oxford University Press, 1972.

Hastings, John, *Encyclopaedia of Religion and Ethics, Volume 1, A-Art.* New York, NY: Charles Scribner's Sons, 1908.

Hourani, Albert, *A History of the Arab Peoples*. Cambridge, MA: Harvard University Press, 1991.

Jacques, Edwin, *The Albanians: An Ethnic History from Prehistoric Times to the Present*. London, UK: McFarland & Company, Inc., 1995.

Jeremiah, David, *What In The World Is Going On? 10 Prophetic Clues You Cannot Afford to Ignore*. Nashville, TN: Thomas Nelson, 2008.

Josephus, Flavius, *Josephus: The Complete Works*. Translated by William Whiston, 1737.

Leonard, Thomas M., *Encyclopedia of the Developing World, Volume 2*. New York, NY: Routledge, Taylor & Francis Group, 2006.

Lindsey, Hal, *The Late Great Planet Earth*. Grand Rapids, MI: Zondervan Publishing House, 1970.

Low, D. M., *The Decline and Fall of the Roman Empire by Edward Gibbon: An Abridgement*. New York, NY: Harcourt, Brace & Company, 1960.

McReynolds, Paul R., *Word Study Greek-English New Testament*. Wheaton, IL: Tyndale House Publishers, Inc., 1998.

Mommsen, Theodor, *The Provinces of the Roman Empire*. New York, NY: Barnes & Noble Books, 1996.

Muthuswamy, Moorthy S., *Defeating Political Islam: The New Cold War*. Amherst, NY: Prometheus Books, 2009.

Naji, Kasra, *Ahmadinejad: The Secret History of Iran's Radical Leader*. Berkeley, CA: University of California Press, 2008.

O'Hern, Steven, *Iran's Revolutionary Guard: The Threat That Grows While America Sleeps*. Washington, DC: Potomac Books, 2012.

Pew Research Center, *Mapping the Muslim Population: A Report on the Size and Distribution of the World's Muslim Population*. Washington, DC: Pew Forum on Religion & Public Life, October 2009.

Richardson, Joel, *The Islamic Antichrist: The Shocking Truth about the Real Nature of the Beast*. Los Angeles: WND Books, 2009.

Ridpath, John Clark, *Ridpath's History of the World, Volume IV, Book XII, The Mohammedan Ascendency*. Cincinnati, Ohio: The Jones Brothers Publishing Company, 1907.

Spencer, Robert, *The Complete Infidel's Guide to the Quran*. Washington, DC: Regnery Publishing, Inc., 2009.

Stefanaq, Pollo, *The History of Albania: From Its Origins to the Present Day*. Translated by Carol Wiseman and Ginnie Hole. London, UK: Routledge & Kegan Paul Ltd., 1981.

Strong, James, *Strong's Exhaustive Concordance of the Bible*. Lake Wylie, SC: Christian Heritage Publishing Company, 1988.

Sultan, Wafa, *A God Who Hates*. New York, NY: St. Martin's Press, 2009.

Taleb, Nassim Nicholas, *The Black Swan: The Impact of the Highly Improbable*. New York, N.Y.: Random House, Inc., 2010.

Worthington, Ian, *Philip II of Macedonia*. New Haven, CT: Yale University Press, 2008.

Index

ABOUT THE AUTHOR

MARK DAVIDSON (A PEN NAME) IS A FOLLOWER OF JESUS CHRIST. He is a graduate-degreed Aerospace Engineer having worked thirty years in the defense and space industries. He and his wife live in Colorado.

Being a life-long student of the Bible, eschatology, world history, and geopolitics, he has connected the dots yielding a new interpretation of Daniel which is being proven by current events.

The author may be contacted at:
mark.davidson.1234@gmail.com

For more information please visit:
www.foursignposts.com

www.ingramcontent.com/pod-product-compliance
Ingram Content Group UK Ltd.
Pitfield, Milton Keynes, MK11 3LW, UK
UKHW020806120325
456141UK00004B/262